Pearls of the Prairie
Life in Small Dakota Towns

Pearls of the Prairie
Life in Small Dakota Towns

by Robert G. Cunningham

Northern Lights, ND Press
Bismarck, North Dakota
2002

Published in 2002 by Northern Lights, ND Press

1001 Arthur Drive
Bismarck, North Dakota
58501-2444
northernlightspress.com
editor@northernlightspress.com

Printed in Canada

10 9 8 7 6 5 4 3 2 1

First Printing

International Standard Book Number: 0-9717181-3-X
      Pearls of the Prairie:
      Life in Small Dakota Towns
      by Robert G. Cunningham

Library of Congress Control Number: 2002112496

The paper in this book meets the requirements of
ANSI/NISO Z39.48-1992 (Permanence of Paper).

All illustrations in this book are from the collection of the author.

The Northern Lights, ND Press is on the web at
northernlightspress.com

Dedication
for Marilyn and Myrtle

*T*able of Contents

Acknowledgments & Observations

*M*Y MOTHER, MYRTLE LARSON CUNNINGHAM, was my inspiration for taking on the task of chronicling the early portion of our family history and adding a few stories and events. For years and years, prior to her death in 1998, she urged me to write about some of the amusing, and some not so amusing, episodes in our lives and about the many small towns we were constantly moving to. I'm sorry I didn't get started earlier, so she could have had the pleasure of reading about them.

Although I call it a book, it is not a book in the usual sense. It is, rather, a compilation of the trials and tribulations of family, friends and acquaintances. My memory of some events may be faulty and therefore not recorded precisely the way they happened. I acknowledge with gratitude the help I received from my sister-in-law, Juleen Cunningham and that of my daughter, Judy. A special thanks to Everett Albers of Northern Lights, ND Press for his incredible skills and indomitable spirit.

During the years I was growing up, and later as an employee of the railroad, I had the opportunity to live and work in dozens of small North Dakota towns. They were indeed "Pearls of the Prairie." The railroad played a significant role in sustaining the vitality of these small towns.

I have found that people differ greatly in the way they view things. What appears amusing to one person might be viewed quite differently by another. I tried to maintain a non-controversial perspective. I hope I haven't offended anyone. If I did, it was not my intention and I apologize. Some names have been changed to protect the innocent from any embarrassment.

RGC. September 2002

Preface

Grandfather Cunningham, Grand Rapids & The LaMoure County Farms

*M*Y GRANDFATHER, A. W. (WEBB) CUNNINGHAM, came to Dakota Territory from Homer, Michigan. He arrived in Jamestown by train in the year 1881 with his wife and young son, Durward, and bought a homestead relinquishment seven miles northwest of that city where he farmed for the next twelve years. The crops were good, and he prospered. Born there were three daughters — Lina, Eva, and Mame — and two sons, Arthur, and my father, George. Arthur died shortly after birth.

While looking for additional land to buy, my grandfather met E. P. Wells, land agent for the Northern Pacific Railroad. Mr. Wells had taken up land near the budding city of Grand Rapids in LaMoure County, a place that became known as the Cold Spring Farm. There was not yet a railroad into Grand Rapids, so Mr. Wells

Above —
Alexander (Webb)
Cunningham
05-23-1853 -
03-19-1919

arranged to have five loads of lumber to be rafted from Jamestown via the James River to where the buildings comprising the Cold Spring Farm were erected. There were several barns, an icehouse, chicken house, a few other buildings and a large house, which is described later in a brief history sent me years ago by my Aunt Mame. The first furrow was plowed here in 1880. After being convinced by Wells to rent the Cold Spring, consisting of more than 2,000 acres, my grandfather moved his family there in 1893.

It was a welcome move for my Grandmother Jennie, who was in very poor health. In addition to being unwell physically, she had suffered from extreme loneliness during those first years on the Dakota prairie. The Cold Spring Farm was less than a mile from town, close enough for her to be near other families.

From that time on, Grand Rapids was considered to be the "hometown" of the Cunningham family. It was here that my grandfather chose to settle down and raise his children to adulthood. It is where my brother Philip, my sister Genevieve, and I were born. Two younger brothers came along later — David was born in Oakes, and Doug (Terry) in LaMoure.

Above —
Rachel (Jennie)
Jane Perry
07-22-1852 -
08-24-1897
First wife of A. W.
Cunningham

The town of Grand Rapids actually began after Captain Homer T. Elliot filed the first landowner paper in LaMoure County in March of 1880 and constructed the first buildings between Jamestown and Huron, Dakota Territory. He built an overnight stagecoach stop for the Jamestown & Columbia Stage Line. Later, when the railroad reached Ellendale, another stage line began with Grand Rapids as the overnight stop between Ellendale and Jamestown. The stage-stop was located a short distance south of present day Grand Rapids.

"The Cold Spring Farm,"
1895
Aunt Lina in back,
Aunt Eva, Aunt Mame,
my father, George,
and Grandfather A.W.

I might mention that the only vestige of an original building left on the Cold Spring Farm is a small portion of the icehouse. All the barns blew down or collapsed in the '30s and '40s. The farmers simply did not have the funds to repair, replace, or decently maintain their buildings due to the Great Depression of the '30s. The house, which served as a landmark for more than a century, was finally torn down in the middle 1990s.

Land Agent, E. P. Wells, became a very good friend of my grandfather, eventually selling him most of the land comprising the Cold Spring Farm. Those acres encompassed much of the valley surrounding Grand Rapids. In August of 1897 Grandma Jennie passed away. A year later my grandfather married Anna Kinney, a young woman that had been staying with relatives in the area, and continued to farm the Cold

The Cold Spring
Farm circa 1895
There were many
other buildings not
visible in this picture.
The James River is
in the foreground.

Spring. After farming there for twenty-three years, and partly due to his failing health, he decided to split his land into small farms and sell them to local people, some of them former employees. He then bought 360 acres one-half mile east of Grand Rapids, which he named "Elmwood Farm." A complete set of buildings was erected there along the banks of the James River. Though the acreage was small compared to the Cold Spring, it was the same rich, black, highly productive river-bottom land. With the proceeds from his land sales, Grandfather easily paid off his debts and lived out his remaining years in relative comfort on Elmwood Farm.

⟹⬥⟸

What made Elmwood Farm so beautiful was its picturesque setting, nestled as it was below the high hills to the east and the James River to the west, lazily wending its way south just yards from the house. This was where I was to spend some of the most enjoyable and enriching years of my life. The original house still stands, surrounded by trees, stalwart and undaunted by time. After being renovated, it is more beautiful and majestic today than at any time in memory.

⟹⬥⟸

This picture of Elmwood Farm was taken about 1914.

A.W. Cunningham played a significant role in the development of the valley surrounding Grand Rapids. He was well known and respected throughout the county. He was elected to represent the people of his district for three successive terms in the North Dakota Legislature. His picture still hangs in one of the hallway galleries.

It is generally believed Grand Rapids got its name from the rapids and stepping stones located about one-half mile south of Elmwood Farm. They could usually be seen in late summer or whenever the river reached a low point. During the drought years of the Great Depression, the James River was reduced to a mere trickle, and the stepping stones became visible the year round. Then one could easily cross the river hopping from stone to stone without getting wet. During periods of rainy weather, water rushed over and around the larger stones, creating a rapids. A short distance from the stepping stones was a shallow point with a gravel bottom where the river could be forded. In winter, straw was spread over the ice to give our horses sure footing as we crossed from one side to the other. At this point along the James River, we owned land on either side, and the ford saved us many miles of travel, both winter and summer.

When I was four years old, I accompanied my mother and a few of her friends to pick berries along the riverbank. We began to ford the river in our Essex automobile when it sputtered to a halt midway across. Sitting in the car — surrounded by water — convinced me we were all about to drown. I was terrified. Of course, as soon as the motor dried off, we made it the rest of the way without difficulty. In earlier days, fording the river was as commonplace as crossing a bridge is today.

The James River can become very dangerous, depending on the snowfall in winter and rainfall in spring. Since the day our family left the farm in 1946, the James has flooded several times, leaving untold devastation in its wake. Federal assistance was unheard of back then; everyone managed the best they could. When the floods came, it was a common sight to see entire buildings floating down the main channel. Thousands of acres of land would be covered with water, resulting in lost livestock and flooded farmyards. Floods were just one more of the many hazards facing the early settlers. Despite many flood controls, there remains a danger each spring.

The river could be one's enemy, but more often it was a friend. It offered a constant supply of water for our livestock, even in winter. Our farm was without electricity, and we lacked the resources to pump water other than by hand. So, when the river froze over, either Dad or I had to find a suitable location to chop a watering hole through the ice. Our livestock became so accustomed to this ritual, even in stormy weather it did not present a major problem.

Skating parties were held each winter, provided there wasn't too much snow. After building a huge bonfire, many neighbors came by for an evening of fun; the high riverbanks provided a natural shelter from the wind. After skating a few hours, logs would be rolled near the fire to sit on while we told stories and had lunch.

Grand Rapids, North Dakota, about 1912

Grand Rapids celebrated its 100th anniversary in the year 1980. The picture above was probably taken on the Fourth of July or some other holiday. The buildings pictured above were built sometime after 1880. The general store to the left had living quarters and storage rooms on the upper floor. My father owned this store for several years in the middle '20s, first as a partner with my uncle, and later by himself.

The original brick store building was destroyed in a windstorm in the late '40s and replaced with a wood structure which now houses a restaurant. Across the street to the right is the former Yeoman Hall. It served for much of its lifetime as a community building where dances, card parties, basketball games, and other functions were held. It is now a machine repair shop. To the right of the Yeoman Hall is the pool hall. It is still in business today and looks much the same as it did in the 1912 photograph.

Grand Rapids probably would have died years ago had it not been for the LaMoure County Memorial Park, one mile north. The park played a significant role in the lives of the citizens of LaMoure County and was largely responsible for the survival of the little town of Grand Rapids. It was here that the Old Settlers' picnic was held each summer. Ball games, swimming, scouting, school functions, and political gatherings were a few of the events held each summer. A large auditorium was built in the early '20s and is well preserved today, in spite of several damaging floods. Many governors, including that great orator, Governor Langer, spoke here on special occasions. In recent years it has been used extensively as a summer theater. Many young people from far and wide have participated in the production of musicals and plays each summer. Next to the park is one of North Dakota's most beautiful golf courses. When my grandfather lived on the Cold Spring Farm, the Memorial Park was part of his pasture. It was known as the "Cunningham Grove."

Chapter I

The Letters

*T*O HELP THE READER GAIN A LITTLE INSIGHT into the thinking of the early pioneers of Dakota Territory, I begin this book by transcribing a collection of letters written by my grandparents and others. Those brave pioneering people that came to this territory, my grandparents included, arrived with great expectations — the men, that is, not necessarily the women. For the most part, wives obediently accompanied their husbands to this hostile land where they encountered drought, prairie fires, unfriendly Indians, blizzards, and a host of other hazards. Due to the scarcity of doctors, many children, as well as adults, lost their lives to a host of ailments and diseases which would have been curable had medical care been available.

Generally, the pioneer's dream of free land and a better life was fulfilled, but it took backbreaking work and enormous sacrifice. It is evident by her letters that my grandmother was desperate to have some member of her family — her younger brother, George, in particular—

to come live with her, The incredible loneliness and desolation of the Dakota prairie was frightening to many of the women coming here from the populated areas back east. Grandma Jennie was very close to her family, and leaving them and a relatively secure lifestyle was extremely difficult. Her plight arouses deep emotion for those of us with but the least bit of imagination. And that feeling must be directed toward all the early settlers, many of whom suffered untold hardship and despair.

Letters from my grandparents to Grandma Jennie's brother, George, in Michigan

The following three letters were written in 1883-84 by my grandparents when they lived on a small piece of land in a remote area northwest of Jamestown. They were addressed to Grandma Jennie's brother, George Perry, in Michigan, and returned to our family many years later. My grandfather wrote letter 1, and my grandmother wrote letters 2 and 3.

The letters in this chapter are transcribed exactly as written, with minor exceptions.

Letter from Grandfather A. W. (Webb) Cunningham to his brother-in-law, George Perry

Jamestown, ND
July 14, 1883

Dear George [Perry]

Your letter of the 8th was duly received. Was very glad to hear from you. It found me well. Harvest will commence in two weeks. Wages will be from 2.50 to 3.00 a day. You can get all the work you can do here until snow flies and get good wages. There will be a very large crop here this year. You could work for some man taking care of stock. You could get from 10 to 15 dollars a month. Or if you wanted to clerk in a store I could get you a place in a dry goods & grocery store. If you can't get anything to do you can stay with me & it won't cost you a cent, only what fun I can get out of you. Be sure & come. I am sure you will like it here. I will help you hunt a farm. I will leave the rest for Jennie to finish. I could tell you more in a minute than I can write in a week.

Webb

A letter from Grandma Jennie to her brother, George Perry

Jamestown, July 14, 1883

My Dear Brother George,

I hasten to answer your good long letter which I was glad to get. Webb has just got done plowing for this year. He has got one hundred acres plowed. I wish it was all in wheat this year for wheat is going to be such a nice crop I hear. We have got 25 acres of barley which they think will go 50 per acre. We have had lots of rain this season. It is cool and the wind is blowing today.

Webb will soon go to haying and see he has written you what he thinks the wages will be in harvest. I would like to have you come but I shall not look for you. Webb is going to look for more land after harvest and if you were here you could go with him. Wheat they think will go 30 per acre this season. I see green apples in market. Cabbage beds, turnips and cucumbers. Can you beat that? Our little cow gives about 20 quarts a day of milk. She is just as fat as she can be. I make from 8 lbs to 10 lbs a week of butter.

Where do you board and what do you give a week for board? Where is Harvey? We expect to have a school meeting at our house next week and then we will know where our schoolhouse will be.

I am glad to hear that Mamre is better and hope she will keep on doctoring until she gets well. Then Seth got homesick you think. Did he say anything about going east after harvest?

I read Durward your letter. He thinks you are surely coming and he tells the places he is going to take you. He says he is not a baby any more. He wears pants all of the time and has a revolver. He got the four and ten which he shoots with. I had some antelope that was killed here which I think goes far ahead of deer meat.

Write me another good long letter soon.

From your loving sister,
Jennie

———

A second letter from Grandma Jennie to her brother George Perry

Jamestown, Feb. 8th 1884

Dear Brother George,

I received your ever welcome letter in due season. Should have answered sooner but have been sick a bed for one week but am feeling better now. All the rest are well. Webb weighs 180 lbs. and Durward is fat for him. Lina is not quite as fleshy as she was. She has not got a tooth yet nor does not creep nor walk yet. I would like to get her picture taken and send it to you if I ever get any money. Mamre sent her baby's picture. I cannot see who he looks like. He looks as large as Lina.

You did well in answering so soon and writing such a long letter. I just give you a long mark for it.

It is quite a nice day but lots of snow on the ground. It has been very cold. Jim [brother to A.W.] got a box from home. They sent mince pie and oranges and so on. He seems very contented. Barbara says she would write you if Jim would let her. Jim says he would sell out to you the interest in Barbara cheap if you want her. Durward has lost his dog Tim. He used to hitch him on his sled. He ran away with his sled and broke it all to pieces. Webb went to town last week and Tim went off and did not come back. I presume you have seen account in the paper of the Jamestown fire. It burned the Dacota House and all that side. It makes it look bad.

The teacher at Eldridge was here last Sunday and wants to teach our school. She will board here commencing April the first. Is Seth teaching this winter? I expect all the young people over from Eldridge this week. They said they were coming when it got to be moonlight nights and that is this week.

It will soon be time for the people to come back and I shall be glad of it. It has been so very lonesome this winter. I wish you and Park would come this spring home. I would like to see you all. Did you get the two kids those pins and did they like them?

I have not heard from Pa in a long time. I wonder how long Disiree will stay.

Webb killed one of his pigs.

I want Mamre to come here this summer. I think it would do her good to get away from home. I hope she can come. I will bring my letter to a close. Hoping to hear from you soon.

With love to all from your loving sister,

Jennie

———

GRANDMA JENNIE HAD BEEN IN ILL HEALTH for several years prior to her death on August 24, 1897, at the young age of forty-five. She suffered from what was called "dropsy," later to become known as "edema." Edema (the retention of excess fluid in the tissues) is a symptom of a disorder or disease rather than a disease itself. She most likely was suffering from congestive heart failure or the onset of kidney disease, or perhaps both. In any case, her son, Durward, then twenty years of age, took her by train to Fargo the last week in June of 1897. There she took a room in a boarding house and was treated by an osteopath. Durward stayed with her for about a week and wrote the following letter to his father, A.W. (Webb) Cunningham, shortly after their arrival.

Rachel (Jennie)
Jane Perry
Cunningham

Letter from Durward to his father, A. W. Cunningham

Fargo, June 25 1987

Dear Father,

We arrived safely in Fargo yesterday about 4 o'clock. Mother stood the ride real well. She saw the Dr. this morning and took the first treatment, which was a grand success. After it, she stepped into the carriage alone, that is, without any help. The Dr. seemed to hit every spot that is afflicted without telling him.

When we asked if he could cure her he said that he never told any person what he could do but told what he had done, and he said he had cured many worse cases. He says she will have to stay two months.

We are well pleased with the first treatment. He treats her two times a week. He says that is as much as she can stand now. Her worst place is in the spine between the shoulders. Mother did not tell him any of the afflicted. He first placed his hand at the back of her neck, followed the spinal column down and all over different parts of the body. Then he placed it between her shoulders again and said there is the worst place. She has a splendid place to stay. They are very nice people that will take good care of her. Mr. Hanson has a nice horse and carriage and he says he will take her for a ride any time she wishes to go. We had the horse this morning and rode all over the city.

What size pants do you wear and what color. I think you said light, but am not sure. Everything seems to work together for good of them that love the Lord.

Good Bye,
Durward

P.S.
Mother feels better today than she has felt for a long time. She just told me this, this minute. When she comes home this time, she will be cured without a doubt.

MY GRANDMOTHER WROTE THE FOLLOWING LETTER to her family during her illness. It is so ironic that her anguish continued and that she was destined to suffer even beyond that of a homesteader's wife.

Letter from Grandma Jennie
to her husband, A.W. (Webb) Cunningham

Fargo, June 30, 1897

My Dear Webb and loved ones,

How delighted I was to get your letter. Today I had began to cry. Had sent the boy to the [post] *office thinking you had not put the No. of the street and house on the envelope when the mailman came with it. I am feeling better today. The Dr. was here yesterday to give me a treatment. He said if I did feel bad it was like stirring up a mud puddle. When I got settled I would feel better. Oh such a improvement in my water. It does not smell like it did or make my bowels move only once a day. But my mouth tastes so much better and I am not near so lame. The Dr. said the change of life was troubling me. Said I could go home on a visit in a month if I wished. I do long to see my loved ones. It seems as that I had been gone two months now.*

I can not comb my hair yet, but dress myself but shoes and stockings. I am quite weak but sleep good. All but last night, did not sleep good. Sleep down stairs all alone.

I hope Mrs. Robertson will come. She could board near me- the next house. The lady is very good to me and buys fruit for me to eat. I had cherries and blackberries. She leaves a bell for me to ring in the night if I need anything. She wants $5.00 a week for my board. I get the best of care. I told the Dr. I was in a hurry to get well and if he could not treat me oftener. He said I could not stand any more, would not get well any sooner, but would help me as fast as he could.

If Mrs. Robertson hasn't gone yet, let Mame [youngest daughter] *come with them, the lady will not charge for her board. She likes children so much. She would be company for me and sleep down stairs with me. Do let her come if there is a chance with anyone. You could send a telegram to Mr. Hanson and they would meet her. I see so many little boys that make me think of my own baby* [Jennic refers to my father, George Cunningham, who was five years old].

I am so tired I will close. Hoping you will write me every day. With love to all. Goodbye.

Ever yours,
Jennie

Letter written, literally from her death bed, by Grandma Jennie to her husband A. W. Cunningham

Fargo, N. Dak.
July 7, 1897

My Dear Webb,

It rains all the time here. I did not sleep good last night. I have asthma so I could not lie down but it has cleared up now and I feel better. The Dr. was here yesterday. Says in a week I will be able to walk up town.

I suppose Durward is home now and has told you all of the news and about me going down to Sheiks. I just cried the last night. I sit on the veranda all alone. The lady was out to ride. How I did wish I was home to be with my dear Webb.

I guess you did not write me Sunday for I have not got any letter yet. Is Mrs. Robertson coming down here?

I owe the Dr. $10 then my month pay will be up. I have been as saving as I could.

I have not got any under clothes yet. I got a dress and stockings that is all and paid a week's board, and let Durward have $5. Said he would send it back.

Send me the Jamestown and the Chronicle if there is any news.

I remain as ever, your loving wife,
Jennie C

⟹◆⟸

*T*HIS WAS THE LAST LETTER WRITTEN BY MY GRAND-MOTHER. Her health continued to deteriorate and she died just five weeks later on August 24, 1897. She never gave up hope, however, that she would someday be able to return to her family on the Cold Spring Farm. My grandfather was with her at the time of her death.

⟹◆⟸

Six weeks after Grandma's death, Grandpa Cunningham wrote the following letter to his brother-in-law, Park Perry, Grandma Jennie's elder brother.

Grand Rapids, N. Dak.
October 4, 1897

Dear Brother,

Your kind and welcome letter received a long time ago and though at that time thought I would answer right away, but have had my hands full. This is Sunday evening. Durward and Lina have gone to Epworth League and the three little ones [Eva, Mame, and George] *are standing at the desk by my side. Yes Park. I wrote you two letters at Gladstone* [Wisconsin] *and wired you at the time she died. I wrote Jo at the same time but he was away at the time. Lina received a letter from Maud. They are all well. I received a letter from Geo. He said he did not know where any of you boys' addresses were. Said Father's* [stepfather's] *health was very poor. Said he spent the most of his time in bed and he could not walk in and out of the house alone. It won't be long before he will cross the river.*

Now I am very lonesome tonight without my dear wife. Six weeks ago tonight I was with her in Fargo. It seems as if it were six years instead of six weeks. Yes Park, I have lost a true and loving wife. I do not believe any man ever had any better wife than I had and the longer we lived together, the more we loved one another. Our love was a growth from the time we first met in Homer, Wisc., 22 years ago last 4th of July.

It seems as if I could not give her up. It seems as if she must come back to me and I believe she is with me every day. I can feel her influence but cannot see her. I wish so much that she might appear to me.

Are you going to stay there and did you get pay for your goods that burnt in Arthur?

I wish you would write me all your plans. The crop is turning out very poorly. Have from 4 to 10 bushels per acre. Durward will be 21 years old this month, 28th of October. Park, is Aunt Ann dead? We see by the Jackson paper that she died last winter but the folks never wrote anything about it so do not know whether it was true or not. Do you ever hear from [illegible] *and what is he doing? Has he got the rest of his children with him? Well, it is getting late and the little ones are getting sleepy and I must put them to bed. I read to them every night out of the Bible and recite the Lord's Prayer.*

Well, goodnight, and may God bless you and your family.
Love to all. I remain, as ever, your brother,
A. W. Cunningham

*Grandpa
Cunningham and
second wife, Anna*

*Anna Kinney was a
dressmaker who
came to North
Dakota from
Wisconsin to visit
relatives.*

I **HAVE WRITTEN EARLIER** about the friendship that developed between my grandfather and Land Agent, E.P. Wells. During the years he was paying off the mortgage on land he bought from Wells, my grandfather and Wells wrote each other regularly, mixing business with pleasure. The depth of their friendship is born out by the tenor of the letters that Wells wrote. In reading the first letter, one must consider the enormous debt incurred — $13,700 back then was equivalent to a fortune in today's dollars. The first letter is dated October 3, 1914; the second letter, October 11, 1917. At the time the second letter was written, Grandpa Cunningham was seriously ill. He passed away less than a year later on March 19, 1918. My father was serving in the Army over in France at the time and did not learn of Grandpa's death until months later.

The following letters, reproduced from the originals, were written much later, after most "homesteaders" were well established. Nevertheless, they provide an interesting insight into the early days in North Dakota.

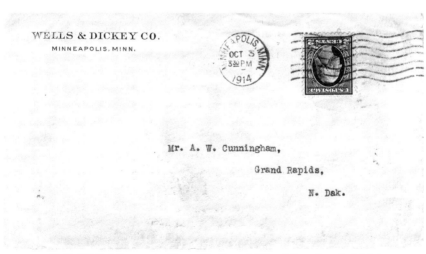

E.P. Wells' Letter to Grandfather A.W. of October 3, 1914
is reproduced on the following two pages.

ESTABLISHED 1878

WELLS & DICKEY CO.
MINNEAPOLIS, MINN.

BOND DEPARTMENT

October 3, 1914.

Mr. A. W. Cunningham,
Grand Rapids,
North Dakota.

My dear Web:

I have yours of October 1st, covering remittance, $600, which has been applied
as follows:

Interest to Oct. 2nd
on your note originally
made for $13,700 and on
which there was a balance
due as of Oct. 8, 1913 of
$4,000 . . . .$ 236.00

Interest on your other
note, on which a balance
of $4844.58 was due 268.45

Endorsed on the principal
of the second note 95.55

This leaves the amount of your obliga-
tions now

$4,000.00 on the first note and
4,749.03 on the second note.

No apology is due from you for the
meagreness of your remittance. On your own account, much more than mine, I am very sorry that
the misfortune to your crop would not permit you
to make a larger remittance. It is certainly a
discouraging proposition to see one's earnings

ESTABLISHED 1878

WELLS & DICKEY CO.

MINNEAPOLIS, MINN.

BOND DEPARTMENT

Mr. A. W. Cunningham - Page 2.

almost within his grasp and then lose them
through misfortune. You have had so many experiences that I am sure you are somewhat
hardened to them and that they will not seriously affect your enjoyment of life nor your
final and complete prosperity. I have no friend
anywhere whose progress and success in life I
watch with deeper interest and solicitude, and
I hope that the next year will give you a return
sufficient to compensate you for the year's service and for your disappointment this year. Everything appears to indicate that there will be an
unusual demand for next year's food products and
correspondingly good prices.

       With the warmest of regards for your
family,

             Yours sincerely,

EPW/VM

ESTABLISHED 1878

WELLS - DICKEY CO.

MINNEAPOLIS, MINN.

October 11, 1917.

Mr. A. W. Cunningham,
Grand Rapids,
North Dakota.

My dear Mr. C.

I have yours of October 10th as stated.
I have endorsed on your note interest to the 14th
of this month, $395.18, and have endorsed on the
principal $304.82, leaving a balance due on the
note of $2,988.55.

I am mighty pleased to know that you
are engaged in the Liberty Bond selling campaign
and wish you could be privileged to attend some of
the meetings and hear some of the speeches that we
are getting these days. They certainly are stem-
winders and raise one's hair. I hope that a few
weeks later in November you will be equally interested in the Y.M.C.A. war relief work. I would
have given $10 willingly to have had you present
night before last to hear Mr. Eddy, who has been
conducting the Y.M.C.A. war relief work for three
or four years in Russia, Italy, Belgium, France
and England, tell us of his experiences. It has
convinced me that really the best work that we
can perform in connection with this war is to furnish money with freedom and sustain the hands of
the Y.M.C.A. I believe that it means the salvation of our young men and the bringing them home
to us pure, honest and worthy of respect, as I do
not think they could hope to be returned to us
but for the work being done by the Y.M.C.A.

Yours sincerely,

EPW:FF

Letter from my father, George Webster Cunningham, to his stepmother while he was in the Armed Forces during World War I

France
May 21, 1918

Dear Mother and All:

Just learned of Father's death yesterday. Happened to see one of the John Good boys and he told me of it, but did not know the date, thought tho that it was sometime in April. I can't seem to realize that he is gone and yet I was not so surprised knowing the condition he was in. Somehow I had a feeling that something was wrong. I could not keep it off my mind. I haven't had any mail yet but am expecting to get some any day now. I have been in the trenches and am none the worse for wear as I can see. I have not received any pay since leaving the states but I also expect to get that soon. Be sure and let me know how many letters you have received from me. I haven't written quite as often as I might have perhaps, but until a couple of months ago have just been here and there, not with any regular company, or organization, and that's the reason that I haven't received any mail. And it has been hard just to keep on writing and not getting any mail.

My one wish has been that I could get back and see Father once more but it couldn't be, so must content myself with thinking that it is all for the best and I hope that my last letter reached him so that he knows I was thinking of him. You must be very careful of yourself now and not overdo in any way. There are so many things I'd like to know and long for the time to come when I can get some mail. I wrote once to Captain Gray to have my mail sent but it must be that he did not receive my letter and I am going to write again today. Somehow everything looks different to me since that news reached me. I just can't make it seem possible. I can't picture home without my dad there and he was always so much of home to all of us. I can't write any more now, but will try and write again soon.

With love and best wishes to all,
Your son,
George

Corporal G. W. Cunningham
Co. A, 161st Infantry Brigade
American Expeditionary Forces

A.W. CUNNINGHAM'S ELDEST SON, DURWARD, DIED in Canada in 1912 at age thirty-five. He left his wife, Mary, and three young children — Laura, Wilfrid, and Mildred. Some years after his death, Mary and her children moved — first to Seattle, then to Los Angeles, California — to begin a new life. Unfortunately, it was at the beginning of the Great Depression, and they had a very difficult time making a living. Wilfrid married Stella Prestrud in 1927 or 28 in Seattle. They later moved to Los Angeles where he found work. His wife, Stella, wrote the following two letters addressed to my father, George Cunningham, in 1932, four years into the Depression.

Letter from Stella Prestrud Cunningham to George Cunningham

Los Angeles, Calif.
Mar. 14, 1932

Dear Mr. Cunningham:

You will perhaps be as surprised to get this letter as I am in writing it. Wilfrid received a letter from you a year after we were married and he never did answer it. I ran across it the other day so will take the task unto myself.

All the Cunninghams' are fine. Mildred is married to Ralph W. Duty, a Navy man and now she lives in West Virginia. They have a daughter, Mary Ann, who is about three years old. Laura and Jack Evart live here in Los Angeles. Their daughter, Rita, is six and a very talented young girl. Mrs. [Mary] *Cunningham, the mother, lives with Laura.*

Wilfrid and I moved here from Seattle last year. Wilfrid works in a grocery store, which is his line of work. We have a son four years old last Dec. 20th. We named him George Durward, after you and his dad.

Times are very hard here. So many people out of work. Jack [Evart] *has been idle for so long, which makes Laura worry so. Mrs. Cunningham* [Mary] *is thankful for her pension of $30 per month* [a Spanish-American war widow's pension].

The weather here is fine, so warm and nice. All the flowers are in bloom and the beaches are always crowded with bathers. I guess it's rather cool back there now. I have relatives all over N. Dak. Mostly in Minot, Eastedge, and Fargo. My folks once lived there.

Will cut this letter short and hope we hear from you folks in the near future. Hope you are all well as this leaves us.

Love, from Mrs. Wilfrid Cunningham and families.

⇒◆⇐

Second Letter from Stella Prestrud Cunningham
to George Cunningham

7001 S. Arlington Ave.
Los Angeles, Calif.
June 24, 1932

Dear Mr. Cunningham:

Your letter came last Monday. I had given up hopes of hearing from you almost.

We are witnessing real California weather here now and I don't mind the heat at all.

Wilfrid got a new job at a larger grocery store so we moved out here to be near his work. He is a mighty fine groceryman but has to work such long hours. It wouldn't be so bad if he got paid accordingly.

It was so nice of you to tell all about all the relations. You are lucky to be making as much as you do.

Mary Cunningham works evenings at a place, answering telephone, for her board and room. She likes it fine. Her pension goes plenty toward eats for Laura and Jack, who certainly are having their share of bad luck. Jack hasn't made a living since I came down here. Work is so scarce. They have been hit by this depression for the past three years but before that they were making quite good. We are all "hard up" down here I guess. It isn't much of a place for work of any kind.

I haven't heard from the Perrys' [Grandma Jennie's relatives] *since I came down here. We have a friend in Seattle who runs a boat to the San Juan Islands and we used to take trips to Friday Harbor to visit the Perrys'. They are all fine. Mrs. Perry was ill and came down here for a while but is back home now. Mable came with her. They are such a nice family I think.*

My name before I was married was Stella Prestrud. My folks live now at Kalispell, Montana. I have a sister living at Ft. Ransom and plenty of relatives whom I've not met yet living there. I have an Uncle, Mr. T. I. Nelson, living near Paynesville, Minn., where your head offices are [North American Creamery Co.]. *Some of the names of some of my relatives in N.Dak. are Emerson, Prestrud, Baarstad and Anderson. Real Norwegians eh? Neither Jack Evart nor Mary C. own homes.*

With love to yourself and family from us all. Please write.

Mrs. W. D. [Wilfrid] *Cunningham*

⇒◈⇐

SEVERAL YEARS PRIOR TO HER DEATH IN 1979, my aunt, Mame Stinchfield, was asked to write down what she remembered about life on the prairies of Dakota Territory, later to be the state of North Dakota. Aunt Mame was born in 1889 on a farm northwest of Jamestown, the fifth child of A.W. and Jennie Cunningham. What follows was written in her words and transcribed exactly:

Aunt Mame's Story

The marriage of my parents, Alexander Webster Cunningham and Rachel Jane [Jennie] Perry, took place in Michigan on November 24, 1875. The location of this wedding I never learned. They first lived with my father's parents, the Alexander Cunninghams [Sr.] in Homer, Michigan. Grandfather evidently enlarged his home and my parents lived in that part of the house. My dad helped with his father's farming. My brother, Durward, was born here on October 28, 1878.

From what my sister Lina told me, I know that grapes were raised here and perhaps apples. Lina also said the Grandmother Cunningham was a very particular person, putting paper in the spouts of tea and coffee pots to keep the dust out. Also when they were plastering, the floor had to be mopped before it was completed every night. My grandfather was a great reader having read the Bible twice. In later years he lost his eyesight.

My dad's parents seemed to have been well-fixed as I know they loaned money to my father and every year Grandma wrote and said, "Son, your interest is due."

When Durward was three or four years old, my dad left Michigan and the family consisting of my mother, Dad and Durward, went to make a home on a farm near Jamestown. At this time North Dakota hadn't yet become a state. My father didn't homestead but bought what was called a relinquishment on a homestead and a tree claim.

The move to North Dakota was made because my dad's health was poor. He was having trouble with rheumatism and his doctor advised a dryer climate. As his oldest brother, Isaiah, lived at Jamestown, perhaps this decided his choice.

Arthur, Lina, Eva, George and I were all born near Jamestown. I have no record of Arthur's birth date, but he died when an infant and suffered much before his death. Lina was born in 1883, Eva in 1887, Mame [Marion] in 1889, and George in 1892. Eva was born with a congenital heart ailment and didn't walk until two years of age. So many years I ran up stairs and down waiting on her. We were very close and nearly always dressed alike.

Those early years at Jamestown were hard on my parents, as my mother wasn't at all well, spending most of one winter in bed. My sister Lina said it seemed as though she spent most of her time washing dishes, leaving much of the inside work and outside work for my dad with what help she could give. Lina and Durward went to school in the country and there was one teacher that took Eva and I and taught us. Not because she had to but because we were too young for school as we were only three and four years of age. We learned to make grapes out of clay and things of that sort. I was made to take a nap at which I rebelled but took anyway.

One home we lived in was destroyed by fire. We never saved a thing but a table that I have and my mother's sewing machine. On another occasion, our barn burned and my brother's pony was badly burned. My mother had wanted Durward to sleep in the barn that night as we had some extra people staying and were crowded for room. He said he didn't want to as he felt something awful was going to happen that night and it did. He always seemed to have an "extra" sense about these things.

When I was three years old, we left Jamestown and moved to Grand Rapids, North Dakota. We rented a place from Wells Dickey & Company called the Cold Spring Farm. It was located about a mile north of Grand Rapids on the James River. My dad did well on this farm. He rented it for twenty-three years. He raised cattle, sheep, hogs, chickens, and horses besides putting in many acres of farm land. There was a large pasture that had five miles of riverbank so water was never a problem. Along that river plums, chokecherries, and wild grapes grew. The latter were hard to get as so many times they hung out over the river.

There was a large basement barn with a windmill on top, a sheep barn, and cattle and horse barns. The house was large with four bedrooms upstairs and one down. Also a living room, dining room, pantry and kitchen. It was really two houses put together as we had another upstairs with two small sleeping rooms where the hired men slept. There was also a large dining room which was used in the summer. This was sometimes called the milk room.

My mother was away from home a lot as she went to Michigan to find help for her illness, which continued to worsen. As long as I can remember we had a hired girl to help with the inside work and hired men to help outside.

The picnics held in our grove, which is now the Soldiers and Sailors Memorial Park, were a fun time for us children. My dad had a concession stand there and sold homemade ice cream, lemonade, candy and peanuts. The band came from LaMoure and people came from miles around for the Pioneer Old Settlers Picnics, Fourth of July, and other celebrations. We children watched the rigs go by from our front porch. We couldn't go until after dinner as a rule, but people usually brought their lunch and many families ate together at the picnic grounds.

My mother's health continued to fail and the year I was seven years old, she spent considerable time in Fargo taking treatments from an osteopath. I went up by train care of a Mr. Shields to stay in Fargo with my mother to wait on her as it was hard for her to put on her stockings and so forth. This I did in fear as she had a large mole that hung by a slender thread underneath her knee. I was afraid it would drop off. We came home early in August but my mother returned later and died on the 24th day of August 1897. The funeral service was held in our home and the interment in the LaMoure Cemetery.

The year after my mother's death it seemed to me we had so many different people in our home. That first winter my dad seemed to take care of us alone for a while. I can remember he braided my hair so tight and so often. On Sunday night for our evening meal we had mush and milk, which I disliked very much.

My cousin, Arthur Danforth, came and stayed and helped with cooking making what he called his India Rubber Pies. Later, Aunt Alice Perry came from Michigan bringing her son Danny with her. He was about my sister Eva's and my age, and he went to school with us. Lina came home from boarding school and came down with the measles and later we all got them. Aunt Alice returned to Michigan and my dad hired a housekeeper from Minneapolis. That fall on the 4th of November, my dad married Anna Kinney, a young woman who was a dressmaker and had come to North Dakota to visit her brother Charley Kinney.

My dad went on his wedding trip to Wisconsin to Fox Lake where his bride's people lived. We had hired help and Lina was home so we managed to get along until my dad's return. In the meantime, one of the hired men said, "You'll have to do so and so after Bridget gets home," as he referred to our stepmother. I often think our new mother had her hands full with three growing children and a grownup daughter and son besides managing a very big household.

Dad made butter for sale at this time. There wasn't any such thing as a [cream] separator. We had a milk house containing a tank where cold water from the well, which was pumped by the windmill, kept the tank full to a certain level. Anything over this level ran out a hole and down the hill into the river. The tank was for keeping the milk cold. The milk was strained into five-gallon cans with wide lids and gauges on the sides to show where the cream came. After standing a certain length of time, it was skimmed off by hand. After the cream was churned, it was packed in one-, two- and three-pound boxes and sold. Later we did have a separator.

In the winter the butchering was done, sometimes doing ten hogs at a time. The side meat was put into a brine called salt pork. Some was smoked for bacon as were the hams and shoulders. The rest was frozen in an outbuilding. We also butchered a beef in the winter.

My brother, Durward, was in the Spanish American War, so he wasn't home long. My sister Lina married not long after my dad's second marriage. It was a great event in our lives when a little baby name Lenore came to live with us in 1899. My brother, George, Eva and I really liked her and as we were all older, she had things pretty much her own way.

I attended country school one and one-half miles away from home through the eighth grade. After that I attended St. John's Academy in Jamestown. Eva had started school there but was unable to attend after six months because of her health. I graduated in 1909. During this period my father was elected to the legislature for two terms. He often stopped to visit me on his trips to Bismarck. We often went to the theater or had dinner for an evening out.

After twenty-three years in the same place, my father bought land he used to rent and built a large house, barn, garage, and a well house. This was on the banks of the James River. It was a lovely place and is still there with a few changes. My father died there on March 19, 1918, and is buried in the Catholic Cemetery near LaMoure. I was married at the Cold Spring Farm near Grand Rapids, and my sister Eva was married in the LaMoure Catholic Church. Durward was married a few years after he came back from the Army to Mary McIntosh.

Mame Cunningham Stinchfield

Chapter II

The Cunninghams of Grand Rapids

GRAND RAPIDS WAS ALREADY SHOWING SIGNS OF DECLINE by the time I was born in October of 1924. It went relentlessly downhill after the county seat was moved to LaMoure.

My father returned home after WW I and managed the farm during which time he courted my mother, Myrtle Larson. They were married on November 3, 1920. Shortly after the wedding, A.W.'s second wife, Anna, and her daughter, my Aunt Lenore, moved to Jamestown, and some time later to Valley City. Grandpa Cunningham had left a sizable estate, but in just a few short years, due mostly to ill-advised investments, all the money left in the estate was lost. The hard feelings generated by these events were deep and long lasting, especially among

Grandpa's children from his first wife. My father and Aunt Mame were the exception. The rest had little to do with our family thereafter.

While it had been expected there would be enough income from the farm to support Aunt Lenore and Grandma Cunningham, as well as my parents, that wasn't the case. Crops were only marginal for the three years following the war resulting in my father deciding to seek a different line of work. He advised Grandma to rent the farm to her brother-in-law, Jim Cloke, which she did.

Shortly afterward, Dad and Mom's brother, Uncle Ed Larson, formed a partnership and bought the only general store in Grand Rapids. My parents moved from the farm to a small house in town where things went comparatively well for the next two years. Then a disagreement arose over management of the business, and the partnership was dissolved. Though the breakup wasn't entirely amicable, they managed to stay on friendly terms.

Uncle Edward was both personable and generous. He married and moved to Oakes where he began a hardware and gas business. He subsequently became a millionaire and retired quite young. As a teenager, people from his hometown of Dickey thought I bore a strong resemblance to my Uncle and often called me Ed.

There were but a few years separating Uncle Edward and my mother, so they shared many experiences growing up together, and as a result they were very close. It was great fun listening to them relate the more hilarious stories of their youth.

Ed's first wife died of cancer in 1948, not many years after they were married. His second wife suffered a similar fate. After selling his business and retiring to Florida, he married for a third time. Our family visited Ed at his home in Sarasota shortly before his death. Despite the fact he had suffered a stroke, we had an enjoyable time. There were tears of sorrow, however, when we bid each other farewell, with the knowledge that it was likely our last time together. He died just a few months later.

≫•◦•≪

My brother, Philip, was born on the farm. Genevieve and I were born in Grand Rapids. There was no running water or even a well at our house, making life miserable for my mother. Water had to be transported in ten-gallon cans from the store. My father worked from daybreak to dark, leaving the responsibility of raising the family almost entirely to my mother.

My memory of our home in Grand Rapids is quite vivid from the time I was three years old. For example, I recall sleeping on the porch on a hot summer night, fending off swarms of mosquitoes. There was the evening my father came home after dark and rapped on our bedroom window, scaring us half to death. I remember the orange glow from our giant coal-burning parlor stove with its tiny isinglass windows. In spite of vast technological advances in home heating, nothing can compare to the warmth and feeling of security that radiated from our old parlor stove on a cold winter morning.

Mr. & Mrs. Hans Hennings lived next door in a small, cottage-style home with a big red barn out back. Hans was a retired cattle-buyer and horse-trader. He was a jolly old man with a wide girth, which tended to accentuate his short stature. Mrs. Hennings was a small woman with gnarled hands and a weather-beaten face. She was badly stooped from years of hard work. Philip and I were frequent visitors at the their house and were always rewarded with something good to eat. Mr. and Mrs. Hennings had raised a large family, all of whom had married and moved away. She missed her children and always smiled broadly when we came calling.

The school where Philip entered first grade back in 1929 still stands, but has been vacant for decades. I was completely lost when he left each day and wanted desperately to attend school myself. Without telling anyone, he let me accompany him one afternoon. When I turned up missing, the townspeople organized a giant search party. Everyone was visibly relieved when school was dismissed, and I came walking home.

The store was an exciting place. It was a typical general store where one could buy nearly anything, including dry goods, groceries, meat, shoes, harness, and a host of other items. A favorite place to play was in the storeroom on the upper floor. Many seasonal items, including Christmas toys, were stored there during the summer months. We once found a large toy dump truck with a working steering wheel. Philip decided we should have it for our own. But in spite of an awesome paint job, it mysteriously disappeared from our bedroom soon after my father saw it.

My mother was an accomplished piano player, able to play both by note and by ear. She had the unique ability to play a tune after hearing it once. Due to this rare gift, she was in constant demand by local bands. For several years she played at barn dances, very popular back then. Alvin Kratz owned one of the largest barns in the area, just a mile from town. He held a dance every week during the summer. One Saturday night Dad loaded Gen, Philip, and me into the car and took us out to hear the band. We didn't own a piano then, so none of us had heard my mother play; it was a memorable experience.

Some years later, my mother began teaching piano to augment the family income. If I remember correctly, she was paid twenty-five cents a lesson.

In addition to selling at the store, there was a good deal of buying, including chickens, turkeys, eggs, cream and animal hides. The North American Creamery Co. of Oakes picked up these commodities weekly. Years later, we took great pleasure in listening to the many humorous stories about the store. On one occasion, a farmer had brought in several plucked turkeys and stacked them on the floor of the weighing room. When my father went back he was shocked to find four turkeys walking around in a daze without so much as one feather on their bodies. Another time, he accused a farm wife of selling him hatching eggs, ones a hen had been setting on. When she denied it, he broke one open on the counter and out popped a baby chicken. That was the major reason for candling eggs.

There was a small post office at the back of the store. It was common back then, and is the case today in small communities. Dad was the official postmaster, but other employees were allowed to sell stamps and sort mail as well. While playing in the store one afternoon I got into the postal funds and spirited away a handful of coins. At the end of the day Dad thought he'd been robbed. Fortunately, after a short search, the missing money was found inside a pair of shoes.

A year earlier, my father brought home a two-month old German-Shepherd pup we named Sandy. Sandy played an important role in my life. He was a wonderful dog and devoted friend. When he grew older, Dad fitted him with a harness, hitched him to our wagon, and coaxed him into pulling us around the yard. Sandy didn't enjoy that activity so we seldom made him do it. He was highly intelligent and a little overprotective. For example, he wouldn't tolerate anyone touching us, unless he knew who they were. Even then he eyed them with suspicion. That was a laudable trait except it got him into trouble at times. In most cases, all he had to do to discourage anyone from getting too close was show his teeth and growl a little.

———

In 1928 Dad was offered a position with the North American Creamery Co. in Oakes. Grand Rapids continued to decline, adding weight to his decision to leave. There were several buyers interested in the store, so he accepted the job and we began making plans to relocate. This was a major event for all of us, but especially for Dad, who had lived in or near Grand Rapids his entire life, except for the years he had spent in the army.

Moving to Oakes, a distance of about fifty miles, was a massive undertaking back then. It was therefore providential indeed when North American offered to furnish us with a truck and driver. In the meantime, we made several trips in the car, loading our little Essex automobile to overflowing each time.

It was a big adventure for me; something I'd never experienced before. The whole family was excited. Oakes was a giant metropolis compared to Grand Rapids, with block after block of businesses along Main Street. All east-west streets, except one, were named after trees. It was a well-planned city with wide avenues and an abundance of sidewalks. Even Sandy seemed to sense a dramatic change in our lives was about to take place. Dad and Mom didn't seem at all sorry about leaving the store business.

———

Grand Rapids to Oakes

Chapter III

On to Oakes

N THE DAYS AHEAD, my mother's life would experience the greatest change, due mostly to the availability of sewer and water and a bathroom. Oakes was a growing community, however, and suitable housing was not readily available. So my father temporarily rented a three-bedroom apartment. Actually, it was the back part of a large house. We lived in one end and our landlord in the other. The owner and landlord, Mr. Rancor, was a short, wizened up little Frenchman who spent most of his time hovering about the place like a ghost, usually dressed in a bathrobe and slippers. He was a suspicious man who continually spied on us. Fortunately, we didn't plan on living there long, only until a better place could be found. We had moved the middle of June and Dad wanted to be settled in our own house before school started that fall.

One Saturday, my parents took along my sister while they searched for a suitable house, leaving Philip and me home alone. Time weighed heavily on our hands. We had little to keep us occupied since most of our possessions had yet to be unpacked. Philip racked his brain and finally decided it would be great fun to wash clothes in our new washer. We filled the machine with warm water, adding plenty of soap. Philip made the first mistake by climbing upon an apple box with wet hands to plug in the cord. He got a nasty shock that knocked him to the floor. "I'm killed! I'm killed!" he screamed. But after discovering he wasn't really dead, he got up from the floor and we continued our project. The fun part, I decided, would be running the clothes through the ringer. A little lever on top started the rollers and everything was going great until I accidentally got my hand caught. In no time my arm was swallowed up to the elbow, resulting in some horrible screams emanating from my voice box. Philip had enough presence of mind to yank out the cord stopping the machine, but that didn't help my arm any. In a panic, he hollered for Rancor, who must have been just outside the door, for he appeared at once. Rancor didn't have a clue about what to do, unless one counts jumping up and down, waving one's arms about.

I was busy with my free hand pulling on everything in sight, finally stumbling unto the release lever. When the folks got home, old Rancor put the whole episode on a scale several points above the San Francisco earthquake. He was visibly relieved when two weeks after the washing machine incident we moved to a house across town.

We still hadn't recovered all our belongings from Grand Rapids, so one final trip with the car was required. Dad was reluctant to leave Sandy alone at the house, so we took him along. When we were finally loaded and ready to return home, Sandy was no where to be found. We searched and searched. We drove down every street in town. We hollered and we yelled, all without success. He had vanished without a trace. I was devastated when we finally had to leave without him.

Dad assured us we would return some day soon and find him. Secretly, I rather suspect he was hoping he had seen the last of Sandy. In subsequent years, I came to think of that whole episode as a conspiracy to get rid of a big problem.

Two weeks passed without my constant companion and protector; I had seldom gone anywhere without him. When things weren't going well, I'd sit on the floor with my arm around his neck, comforted by the constant thumping of his tail. I was heartbroken.

Another week went by. Then one morning I looked out the window — and by the gods, there he was, wagging his tail like crazy. It was a miracle. He was but a skeleton of his former self, mangy and barely recognizable. Dad's eyes opened wide in disbelief. With all our love and devotion he quickly recovered. How he had managed to find his way to our house in Oakes is one of those incredible mysteries.

Some time later we planned to visit Uncle Connie and Aunt Amanda in Marion, a distance of about sixty miles. We didn't want Sandy running loose, so Dad put him in the basement. When we returned that evening, there he was, standing by the garage wagging his tail. Dad's first words were, "How in the world did that dog get out of the basement?" I ran to the back of the house where I found a big, round hole that had been chewed through the basement door. We were all amused except Dad — he didn't think it was funny.

The Brennan family from across the street was of Irish descent. Despite being poor, they were generous neighbors. How such a large family managed to sustain itself during those depressed times was a credit to human ingenuity. We spent a lot of time with the Brennan kids. One day out in their yard, I carried my air rifle under my arm looking for a suitable target. Why Dad ever entrusted me with a gun is yet another mystery. Genevieve didn't believe it was real so I talked her into bending over while I offered a demonstration. I cocked the gun and pulled the trigger. There was a "pop" but no response from Gen, so I moved in a little closer, thinking her coat was blunting the effect. I fired again. Yowie!! She leaped about three feet straight up. Her legs were already in motion when she hit the ground, screaming at the top of her lungs. There was a good-sized welt on her butt, somewhat smaller than one I received later that evening. My hunting days ended abruptly.

That fall of 1929 Philip and I were enrolled at St. Charles Catholic School. Philip in the second grade and I in the first, despite the fact I hadn't quite reached my fifth birthday. That may have been a mistake. I was still but four years old and school was difficult for me.

The nuns were very strict, but I liked them, except for Sister Wilhemina, who just happened to be my teacher. The older children had a little nickname for her, "Meana Wilhemina." She lived up to her name and then some.

It was during the third week of school that Sister Wilhemina came marching down to my desk one afternoon, just before dismissal and said, "Robert, you will remain seated at your desk, I want to talk to you." I could detect a bit of anger in the tone of her voice, so it definitely wasn't going to be a reward for being extra good. Her words were then, and are still today, indelibly etched upon my brain. I was so frightened I felt weak and nauseous, like I needed to go to the toilet. I tried to recall what had transpired during the day — if I had done something to antagonize her — but I couldn't come up with a single thing. My brain was going numb.

After my classmates had left the room, Sister Wilhemina went to the blackboard and picked up the long pointer she referred to as the "black master." After surreptitiously concealing it behind her back, thinking I hadn't seen her put it there, she marched up to my desk. Then in her most authoritative voice she almost shouted, "Robert, before you leave this room, you are going to learn the ABC's!" With that said, she whipped the black master from behind her back, like she was "Attila the Hun," and, in an almost invisible arc, brought it crashing down upon my desk. I reared back and let out a scream, convinced she meant to harm my body. Ten minutes later, however, I exhibited one of the most amazing feats of memorization in history. I was able to recite the ABC's forward and backward. I knew it was either that or die. My knees felt weak all the way home.

The nuns, for the most part, were very easy going and treated us kindly. The school held a "play-day" that spring, but most of us in the first grade were too small to compete in any races. Sister Agnes allowed a friend and me to run a couple of races after which we each received a piece of candy and a St. Christopher medal. It made me feel good and I never forgot her kindness.

The county fair was scheduled for the end of September along Main Street. I had heard there was going to be a free movie at the theater called *The Adventures of Tom Sawyer*. All the kids in school were talking about it, and though I'd never been to a movie, I had heard about them. The students at St. Charles, of course, were not allowed to skip classes for such frivolous things, so I hadn't thought much about it until my friend, Jimmy Monkors, suggested we sneak away from school and see the show.

Each school day began with Mass at 8:30 A.M. Afterward we were marched single file to the school, one block away. On the first day of the fair, however, Jimmy and I made a little detour after Mass and headed toward Main Street. There were movies all day. The first showing hadn't begun yet when we entered the theater so we quickly made our way to a front row seat. That movie was so scary, I almost preferred the perilous Sister Wilhemina. We sat on pins and needles through the end of the scene where Indian Joe chases Tom and Becky in the cave.

It was shortly thereafter that I began getting really scared, with serious doubts about the wisdom of having skipped school. The "black master" loomed ever larger in my mind, prompting me to whisper my misgivings to Jimmy, and suggesting we both return to school at once. We rushed back and made our way to our respective desks as quietly and unobtrusively as possible. To my absolute amazement, Sister Wilhemina never bothered to look up from the book she was reading. To this day I'm not sure if she just didn't see us, or if she thought we were returning from the restroom.

⊰─◆─⊱

Looking back, all things considered, Dad's job with North American was a good one. I never knew precisely what he did, except that he worked in an office on the upper floor of the plant. It was a huge building with as many as fifty employees. North American was a wholesale outlet for candy, peanuts, gum, pop, and beer. In addition to that, they made many different varieties of ice cream, delivering to stores over a wide area. Whenever Dad took us to the plant we got free candy. Naturally, we were always anxious to go along.

That fall, on October 7th, a blessed event took place at our house, my mother gave birth to a child. It is curious how totally unaware I was of my mother's pregnancy. I'm not certain of the hour, but early that evening my brother, David, was born in an upstairs bedroom. After the doctor left we were allowed to go up and see our new brother. I wasn't at all impressed with that tiny, red-faced, squawking baby, but he grew up to be Mom's favorite.

We remained in Oakes until the fall of 1930. Then Dad accepted a job managing the North American Cream Station in LaMoure, a city of about 700 people. It was somewhat smaller than Oakes, yet was a good-sized town, not far from Grand Rapids and Elmwood Farm. This new job paid quite well, comparatively speaking, and included living quarters on the upper floor, an important consideration with four children to support. Jobs were extremely scarce during the Great Depression, so we were fortunate indeed. Also, the drought was taking a toll on farmers, driving many off the land into other lines of work.

Grandma Cunningham still owned Elmwood Farm, but like many other landowners, she was unable to pay the taxes. There was little income from farming during those years, causing great hardship. After several years of unpaid taxes, land foreclosures became commonplace.

Two weeks before we were to leave for LaMoure, Mom's sister, Amanda, and her husband drove all the way from Marion to spend the day. We hadn't seen them for months and were looking forward to their visit. Uncle Connie was cashier at the bank in Marion. He was a quiet, highly intelligent man who preferred the outdoors to working in the bank. Aunt Amanda was a vivacious lady. Her infectious laugh and glowing personality radiated a warmth that made everyone around her feel good.

After one of Mom's delicious dinners, everyone retired to the living room to visit. Not having seen our Aunt and Uncle for a long while there was much to talk about. Sometime into the conversation there came a knock at the front door. We were all a little startled since that door was seldom used. Dad had gone somewhere so Philip was delegated to see who it was. When he opened the door, in burst the strangest looking creature we had ever seen. An ugly old lady leaning on a cane stood before us. She was quite stooped, wearing a long coat, and had a scarf tied about her neck. She wore a hat decorated with long, brilliantly colored feathers that waved about as she moved her head. In addition to her outlandish clothing, her face was heavily painted with rouge.

She immediately hobbled over to the couch where she squeezed in between Connie and Amanda. That seemed like a lot of nerve. Then, in a high-pitched raspy voice, she demanded to be fed, all the while waving her cane about. Worse yet, she insisted on moving into our house, perhaps in my bedroom. If that wasn't bad enough, Aunt Amanda was placing herself in jeopardy by writhing about in uncontrolled fits of laughter, tears streaming down her cheeks. Even Uncle Connie, who seldom laughed aloud, began to chuckle with a broad grin on his face. Philip and I stood well back, staring transfixed at this sinister-looking old witch. I was concerned that any minute Aunt Amanda might be clubbed over the head if she didn't quit that laughing. No one knew where Dad had gone, we'd searched everywhere.

It was Philip who finally tumbled to the identity of this crazy old woman. After daring to creep a little nearer for a better look, he jumped up and down exclaiming, "It's Dad! It's Dad!"

Off came the disguise, revealing we had indeed been taken in. I stared in utter amazement, trying to fathom how he had fooled me so completely by transforming himself into that evil-looking witch. It took Aunt Amanda several minutes to compose herself. Of course, the grownups had been in on the joke from the beginning. It also explained Dad's sudden disappearance.

We were sorry when the day was over and our company had to leave. Connie and Amanda were parents of two grown daughters, Helen and Virginia, but both had remained home that day. Before moving to Marion, the Ardusers had lived in the small town of Adrian, where Uncle Connie began his career in banking, and where my cousins Helen and Virginia were born. An interesting story involving Helen, the younger of the two, had its beginning in the little town of Adrian.

The James River and Oakes Branch of the Northern Pacific Railroad had one round-trip mixed train each day. It included both a passenger coach and freight cars and ran through Adrian on its way to Oakes. Helen and Virginia often boarded the train around midday and rode as far as Dickey, the next town, to visit my mother's parents, Grandpa and Grandma Larson. For the return trip, Grandma always sent along a jar of her homemade pickles. Invariably, the pickles got left on the train, and would have to be retrieved the following day. The conductor was a good-hearted young man and always made sure his two young passengers got their pickles.

Many years later, during World War II, Lt. Col. Helen Arduser was traveling on a train out of Chicago when she recognized none other than the conductor she had known as a child. She rushed up to him and asked if he remembered her. When he seemed puzzled, she quickly explained, "I'm the girl that always left the pickles on the train!" The look on his face melted into a wide grin as he gave her a giant hug. They spent the next half-hour recalling the days, so long ago, on the James River and Oakes Branch, when his two young passengers rode the train to Dickey.

————⊰◆⊱————

The next week we began packing in preparation for the move to LaMoure. I don't know about Mom, but Dad was definitely looking forward to being closer to the farm. As is usually the case, we had all made good friends in Oakes and it was hard to say good-by.

————⊰◆⊱————

Chapter IV

Learning to Love LaMoure

THE NORTH AMERICAN CREAMERY CO. once again furnished a truck and driver for our move. Dad had known Lee McCann, the truck driver, ever since he had owned the store at Grand Rapids. Lee was a giant of a man, strong as a bull, and he had a heart of gold. Unfortunately, he had inherited the "Curse of the Irish." He loved taking a nip or two now and again. That bad habit was nearly his undoing, as we will learn later.

Dad rode in the truck with Lee and the rest of us, including Sandy, crowded into the Essex. Sandy loved to ride and spent the entire trip alternately looking out the window and licking our faces. We anxiously followed the truck to our new home.

The upper floor living quarters was in dire need of repair, so Dad temporarily rented a house near the cream station. It was a three-bedroom bungalow-type home on the corner of the block. The Pugh family and their six-year old granddaughter, Delores, were our neighbors to the south. Delores had been cursed with a hair-lip, which caused her untold misery and embarrassment. Most disconcerting was her inability to speak coherently. She didn't attend school because of it and was extremely self-conscious around strangers. I had never seen a hair lip before so it was several weeks before I had the courage to look directly at her face. Everyone in our family felt sorry for Delores, and we went out of our way to be nice to her. Dad befriended her early on and she soon enjoyed coming over to play with us.

The Bitz family lived just across the street with their two mean daughters, Audrey and Tootie. In addition to making fun of Delores, they were constantly getting into trouble. For that reason they weren't welcome in our yard, especially after Audrey had pulled out Dad's peach tree and stomped on it, just to be mean. He had painstakingly transplanted it into a pail after finding it growing in the garden.

School began the day after we got moved. The curriculum and teaching standards at St. Charles were unacceptable to the LaMoure school system, with the result Philip and myself were both set back a grade. Later, my teacher wanted to advance me to the second grade, but my parents decided against it. In retrospect, I believe that was a mistake. It was terribly boring going over the nearly identical material again, and my study habits suffered as a result.

LaMoure had an excellent school system, always hiring the best teachers available. Since we were constantly moving I wasn't able to take advantage of that fact. I remember well my first day at school in LaMoure. The floors mirrored what I'm sure were several fresh coats of varnish. And the smell of new books filled the air. Superintendent Wakefield stood like a statue near the water fountain in the common hallway, scrutinizing every student. His arms were held akimbo and he wore a stern, intimidating look on his face, or so it seemed to me at the time.

—◆—

1935
Philip-Robert-David-Genevieve

The Cunningham Children at LaMoure

Genevieve and Mom

David

It was difficult making new friends, and I felt uncomfortable for the first two weeks. I relied on Sandy for companionship during this time. It didn't take him long to figure out where I went each day. He walked me to school and never failed to meet me at the end of the day. He'd wag his tail like crazy the minute he had me spotted. No one dared poke fun or otherwise harass me unless they wanted to be frightened half to death. Sandy had the biggest incisors ever seen by man, and when he decided to scare someone he simply curled his lip back and gave everyone a good look.

One Halloween night, we kids walked along Main Street soaping windows. One of the first places we stopped was the barbershop, which remained open evenings. Foster Gordon, the barber, came bounding out the door to scare us. Sandy let out a roar and leaped up at him. In all my life I'd never before seen a man move so fast. He wore the look of fear on his face for a week afterward.

Every summer, shortly after school was dismissed, Philip and I were required to attend Bible School for two weeks. We both hated going so soon after public school was out. There were two nuns teaching the classes. One taught the first through fourth grades, and the other, fifth through eighth. There were between twenty and twenty-five children in each class. Midway between our house and the church was a large patch of weeds three- or four-feet high. For two successive days we skipped classes and hid in those terrible weeds. It was so hot and disagreeable Sandy couldn't bear to stay more than a few minutes. He did come back to check on us a few times though, no doubt to see if we were still alive. Most of our time was spent bobbing up and down, watching for the kids to be dismissed. It was positively demoralizing having to watch them play ball during recess. We had our lunch with us, including water, but that ran out early in the afternoon. By four o'clock we were cooked.

While eating our noon lunch the following day we decided bible school wasn't so bad after all. Somewhat subdued, we returned to the church.

The nuns cautioned us about missing classes since we were making our First Holy Communion and would be facing Father Cahil for an oral examination at the end of each week. Philip and I had a little make up work to do. Two brothers, Jim and Willie, were experiencing more difficulty than usual memorizing the longer prayers. When it became their turn to stand and recite The Apostles Creed, they both suffered a mental block — a condition shared by others as well, myself included.

At the end of the first week, as promised, Father Cahil assembled us at the front of the church for a quiz. On a small table to his immediate right was a neat row of long tapered candles. I recall thinking it a little unusual and wondered what they were for. I soon found out. When it was Willie's turn to recite a prayer he stood in complete silence, with a forefinger against his temple. Wham! Right on top of his head. Father had let him have it with a candle. When it was time for his brother Jim to get up, he was so frightened he refused to stand. I wasn't much better, and by the time the session ended there were broken candles all over the floor. It did seem to have the desired effect, however, since our learning ability showed marked improvement the next week.

Father Cahil had an Irish Setter he called Gabriel that he occasionally brought with him to Bible Classes. Most of the time Gabriel remained in the sacristy, but each Friday he was allowed into the church proper. It was Father Cahil's contention that Gabriel knew his prayers better than any of us. To demonstrate that fact he snapped his fingers and said, "Gabriel, go say your prayers." Gabriel trotted up to the communion rail, put his paws together, and howled. Willie and Jim were impressed with that performance.

Philip, Richard Witt, the Mangin boys and I were all altar boys, but not all at the same time. Four of us were designated to be at the church, with our cassocks on at least fifteen minutes before Mass. We didn't pay much attention to that, since Father Cahil was never on time. The parish house was in the town of Verona, ten miles east, where he usually said the first Mass, then drove like a maniac to LaMoure. With nothing better to do until he arrived, we usually stood on the back step watching for a cloud of dust from the east. Later than usual one Sunday, we saw him coming incredibly fast. Seconds later he careened off the road at such a high rate of speed we had to run for our lives. There was a terrible crash and splintering of wood. That was the end of the back steps. Fortunately, we had managed to escape in time.

⇒◆⇐

By early summer of 1933 we were finally able to move into the living quarters above the cream station. There was but one bedroom and that was reserved for my parents and sister, Genevieve. David had a small bed in the living room, Philip and I slept in the boiler room downstairs. The boiler room was uncomfortably warm day and night during the winter, but in summer the fire was allowed to die out after the station closed for the day. Because steam was required the year round, it was always hot in the boiler room during the daytime, especially in summer.

Philip and I slept on the floor while Dad built bunk beds at the far end of the room, away from the boiler. When they were finally completed there arose the question of which of us was to have the privilege of sleeping on top. Philip, being the eldest, demanded that right for himself, and that was that. It was a decision he was soon to regret. It was so hot near the ceiling he nearly suffocated. He slept without blankets and kept a jar of water by his side each night. I was forever grateful it wasn't I up there. The next fall, Dad moved the bunk beds into the egg room where it was noticeably cooler. David moved in with us, taking over Philip's upper bunk, and I had a small cot on the other side of the room. Philip managed to scare David every night with his wild stories, some times leaving him in tears.

From the time Philip was old enough to talk he was a great storyteller. He had an entire repertoire we called the "Hank Stories." They were funny, and we loved listening to them. Philip had a vivid imagination and the ability to make up a story as he went. As an inducement, we were required to rub his back. Unfortunately, by the time we finished rubbing he was often fast asleep, or pretended so. No matter how hard we shook him, he refused to wake up.

While we were still living in Oakes, he came home from school one day claiming to have seen a little man walking along the telephone wire. I believed him but the folks were more than a little skeptical. Once he had made up a story, however, there was no changing his mind.

A year later, Dad convinced his boss at North American to build a bedroom onto the south side of the cream station, it was just too inconvenient having us sleep in the egg room. Except for the fact it wasn't heated, the new room was a major improvement. But, in the dead of winter, it became a little chilly by bedtime. On the coldest nights we took great pride in our ability to remove every stitch of clothing in one operation, so that when morning came we could slide back into them precisely as we had removed them the night before, and in record time. For entertainment on nights the temperature reached below zero, Philip and I sometimes held a little contest. We removed our pajamas and stepped out onto the porch completely naked, just to see which of us could stand it the longest. We generally called it a tie after freezing for four or five minutes. It was surprising how warm the room felt afterward.

There was a game we played every night during the winter called "Pump, pump, pullaway, run or I'll pull you away." Playing began right after the evening meal and would continue until the 9:00 P.M. whistle. All the kids in the neighborhood would be on hand and the noise would become deafening. It made no difference how miserable the weather, the game went on without letup.

The city always provided a good-sized skating rink with a warming house. There was an old pot-bellied stove near the center of the room, which sometimes got red-hot. When it reached that point, we took turns spitting on it, marveling at how our saliva sizzled. The caretaker didn't take kindly to spitters, sometimes throwing us outdoors. The hot stove was dangerous for those clomping around on skates; one misstep could lead to disaster.

Shoe-skates were too expensive for most kids, including me. It was obvious to me, though, that those who had them were better skaters than the rest. Due to their high cost, I knew it was a long shot when I asked for a pair. But as my birthday neared, Dad decided he would make me pair of skates. I was skeptical to say the least. I watched while he removed the clamps and riveted the skate portion to a pair of old boots. When he finished, I went to the rink and was amazed at how well they worked. It was a wonderful birthday gift, one I've never forgotten.

Bill and Agnes Kranz were good friends of our parents. They had but one child – a boy named Billy. He was big for his age and a spoiled brat to boot, whom we were expected to include in our activities. So when Philip decided we were going to build a raft, Billy was invited over. Philip was head carpenter, and Billy was second in command. I was in charge of supplies. In just a few days we had a raft so large it would have taken a forty-mule team to move it, and the river was nearly a mile away. I could see the concern building on Dad's face as the raft took on larger and larger proportions. It was beginning to resemble an ark. And we had reached a point where we were running out of building material.

Quite suddenly, we were struck with the realization that this raft was never going to see the James River, or any other river. For the next few days we were content to just stare at this ugly mosaic of discarded planks, sticks, and boards, wishing it would disappear. Our wishes came true the very next morning. Like magic, when we looked out, there was nothing left but a pile of smoldering rubble. Philip and I had a sneaking suspicion that the person responsible for the demise of our raft was someone well known to us.

———

There were two cream stations in LaMoure in addition to a large Creamery. Selling cream, eggs, and poultry was a basic source of income for farmers during the Great Depression. Cream stations were one of the few enterprises found to be successful during those years. Ours was a busy place, especially Saturday evening. Each time a customer drove up, one of us rushed out for their cream, a special service appreciated by the farmers. As a result, we had the best business in town. A more personal service Dad provided was weighing the women on the station scale. They depended on us to determine any gain or loss. Dad made an elaborate ritual of this, maintaining accurate records for each woman. There was a lot of embarrassed giggling at weigh-in time.

Everyone had a job to do on Saturday night. Dad and Philip did the testing while I steamed and dried the empty cans. In addition to that, I candled eggs. If we were exceptionally busy, Mom was called upon to help out. Most of our customers went to the grocery store, returning later for their checks. We remained open Saturday until 10:00 or 11:00 at night. The truck would show up about closing time to load cream, eggs, poultry, and empty pop cases. By midnight we were all tired. Looking back, despite all the hardship caused by the Depression, it was surprising how happy people seemed to be.

Lee McCann arrived with the truck each Tuesday to deliver pop, ice cream, empty cream cans, and poultry crates. On one of these trips I happened to be outdoors when he drove through the alley. As he backed toward the station door he didn't notice a car directly behind him, resulting in a small collision. I waved and shouted to let him know he had banged into the village barber's car. When he nearly fell climbing out of the truck it was obvious to me he'd been nipping at the bottle. He staggered toward the barber's car, jerked the door open, and began pounding on poor Mr. Gordon. That's when I ran for Dad. It took several minutes to calm Lee down; he was hard to reason with when he'd been drinking. Dad managed to patch things up without a lawsuit, but North American got stuck for the damage to Mr. Gordon's car. Lee was on probation from that point on, but thanks to Dad, he kept his job.

Mr. Gordon was a nice guy and a good barber. Despite that, Dad decided he was going to save some really big money by going into the hair cutting business himself, at least for us boys. After receiving a hand-operated clipper through the mail, I was to be his first customer – sort of like being a guinea pig. It was terrible; getting scalped couldn't have hurt more. It felt like my hair was being pulled out by the roots. I howled, flinched and cried out, until he finally slammed the clipper down in disgust, threw me a quarter, and sent me to the barbershop. I remember clearly how embarrassed I was walking in with half a haircut. Everyone in the shop, except me, thought it was pretty funny.

At the back of the cream station was a large room for buying poultry, mostly chickens. They were kept in what we called "batteries." Each battery had twelve metal cages with feed troughs attached and slide-out trays to catch the droppings. It was my responsibility to clean the trays every few days and to feed the chickens. They were fed a commercial mash mixed with water. They not only loved it, they couldn't gobble it down fast enough. Watching those chickens devour that wonderful smelling feed was so intimidating, I got a spoon and ate some myself. It wasn't too bad, tasted a little like Cream-of-Wheat. Beside mouse droppings, God only knows what all was in it.

The City Café, owned by a Chinese family, served only American food. The manager hired me to butcher eight chickens every other Saturday. This included picking, cleaning, cutting up, and delivery. I was paid seven cents a chicken or $1.12 a month — a lot of money back then — but I earned it. The cook was a wizened-up little Chinese guy named Lum Hing. When I delivered the finished product, Lum scrutinized and smelled every piece of chicken, then inventoried all the parts. He couldn't speak a word of English so far as I know and looked as though he'd never see eighty again. My estimate of his age may have been a slight miscalculation as I learned later.

A classmate of mine, Pat Leer, was walking through the alley on his way to school one day when he stumbled across a dead cat. He picked it up by the tail, swung it around above his head, and then let go. The cat, according to Pat, accidentally sailed right through the back door of Lum Hing's kitchen. One second later, Lum came charging out the door full speed brandishing a giant meat-cleaver. Pat was a fast runner, but he said Lum not only stayed right behind, but also appeared to be gaining ground, screaming Chinese all the way. Fortunately for Pat, Lum ran out of gas about a block from school, or it's anyone's guess what might have happened. Pat was so scared and out of breath it was several minutes before he could coherently tell us how he came to within just a few feet of being hacked to death.

The telephone office was on the second floor of the European Hotel, just up the alley. Not many people had telephones in those days, so if a long distance call came for a person without a phone, the operator called the cream station for a messenger. If one were successful in locating the person we were paid a dime, otherwise we got nothing. It was an exciting job, one I took great pride in doing. It wasn't unusual to be called once or twice a week. Sometimes the recipient of the call paid us as well, but not more than a penny or two. Once I was given a five-cent pool hall chip.

Philip delivered the *Liberty* magazine each week to about thirty customers. When he wasn't available, I took over. We made two cents per copy. Not much, but with all our other jobs, it kept us in spending money. There was a Mrs. Lynch on the route who asked me to leave the magazine but to collect from her husband, a prominent and wealthy

LaMoure attorney. Mrs. Lynch was a young, attractive woman, in her thirties while Mr. Lynch was nearly sixty. I knocked on his office door and when he answered I could see he was having some sort of meeting. I barged right in anyway and said, "Mr. Lynch, your mother told me to collect for the magazine." He went into hysterics and paid me an extra dime. I didn't have the faintest idea why. I told Dad about it and he explained that I shouldn't refer to a man's wife as his mother, especially when she's almost thirty years younger than her husband, as in the case of Mrs. Lynch.

I was a little mixed up about a lot of things. One evening my parents were in a discussion regarding an acquaintance they judged to be a good nurse. I interjected that my classmate, Irene, would really be good at a job like that. When they inquired how I'd reached that conclusion, I stated the reason being that she already had large breasts, and was still only in the fourth grade. "What on earth does that have to do with being a good nurse?" Dad asked. With great difficulty I tried to explain that I thought a nurse's job was to breast feed babies. Wrong! That was almost as bad as my Aunt Lenore – until well into her twenties, thinking that if she were to be married and have children, they would be born through her belly button.

⇒◆⇐

The railroad depot was prominently located in the very center of town, just half a block from one of the main thoroughfares. It was an attractive building with a full-length brick platform in front, and an elevated wood platform in back. Both made excellent racetracks for bike riders, though we were strongly discouraged from using it for that purpose.

Looking back, I realize how important the railroad was to kids my age, and how closely much of our entertainment was associated with it. One major event each fall, soon after a killing frost, was the arrival of the "weed-burner." Dead grass and weeds alongside the track were extremely hazardous due to tiny bits of burning ash escaping from the smokestacks of steam engines. The noise made by the weed-burner was deafening; it sounded much like the blowtorch my father used in soldering, only magnified a thousand times. We kids followed behind as closely as possible. All of us were fascinated by the fiery power of this grotesque monster as it incinerated every blade of vegetation in its path. The section crew carried shovels and pails of water, putting out any fires that were in danger of spreading.

In winter, I looked forward to the first blizzard. If there was a significant amount of snow on the ground, the giant rotary snowplow wouldn't be far behind. The snowplow wasn't quite as much fun to watch as the weed-burner. But it did shoot streams of snow high into the air, which was exciting. The engine pushing the plow was always busy going back and forth, hissing steam and puffing black smoke into the air. Sometimes it was forced to take a run at some of the higher drifts.

During sheep-shearing season, usually in early spring, the wool buyers were allowed to utilize the railroad freight house for their headquarters. Giant sacks of wool, eight- to ten-feet long, would be stacked in rows awaiting shipment to the mills back east. After school, when no transactions were taking place, we'd head for the depot. It was great fun leaping about the sacks of wool, with little danger of being injured.

In late June, most kids my age headed for the river. It was a welcome relief from the hot summer sun that beat down day after day during the drought of the '30s. There were no sandy beaches and few trees, but there was a railroad bridge, which we used as a diving board and bathhouse. A rickety ladder had been nailed to one of the pilings and served as a means to both enter and exit the river. It was about a twelve-foot jump from the top of the bridge, but only the bravest dared to do so. The rest of us had to use the ladder.

The downside of climbing the ladder, or even swimming close by, was the disagreeable act committed by the town bully, who seemed to take great pleasure in peeing on those of us who were smaller and unable to defend ourselves. Once he had emptied his bladder, however, we felt reasonably safe, but had to be prepared to leap back into the water at a moment's notice.

A much greater danger was the presence of snapping turtles. We felt reasonably safe swimming from the bridge, since most of the snappers stayed nearer the shore. There was a case when a turtle got hold of a boy's toe and wouldn't let go. Once a snapper gets hold of you, it hangs on until the most extreme measures are taken.

Few kids had much in the way of toys when I was growing up so we engaged in other activities, such as rolling old car tires around town, pretending we were driving cars.

A favorite game, one seldom seen today, was playing "Cowboys & Indians." It sometimes lasted for days. While it was great fun, it led to many heated arguments over who had been killed and who was still alive. There were always one or two who refused to fall down and play dead.

Later, we graduated to rubber guns, which were more realistic than toy guns or, as in many cases, just using our fingers. Rubber guns were simple in design; a two-foot long stick with a spring-loaded clothespin secured to one end. Rubbers were cut from discarded automobile inner tubes and resembled large rubber bands. Teddy Skovgaard, a boy from the farm, invented a machine gun that would shoot four rubbers in rapid succession, a significant leap forward.

One pastime we engaged in occasionally was exciting, but downright mean. Next door to the Community Building was a dry-cleaning business operated by a middle-aged, foreign-looking man named Phil Aman. Phil had emigrated from Denmark some years earlier, and could speak little English. He lived alone in the back of his shop and never bothered anyone. But because he dressed differently and spoke with an accent, neighborhood kids, including me, singled him out for special attention, making him the target of our little pranks. Quite by accident we discovered Phil didn't appreciate us knocking at his door. He reacted exactly as we wanted by chasing after us. We could easily outrun him, however, so there was little danger of getting caught. But that was about to change when my friend, Kelly Shockman, came to visit.

With little else to do, it seemed like a good time to introduce Kelly to the door-knocking game. I explained the procedure and he was immediately interested. Perhaps I was a little hasty in my instructions, or else he didn't fully understand what was going to happen. He walked up to the door and began pounding away. I watched in horror when he failed to run. About the third knock, the door flew open and Aman's big arm shot out grabbing Kelly by the scruff of the neck, jerking him inside. I went into a panic, imagining he had been dragged into some sort of evil torture chamber. As fast as I could go I ran for home, explaining to Dad what had happened. We rushed back to Aman's just in time to see a dazed Kelly stumble out the door, his hair standing on end and his shirt torn down the back, but otherwise unhurt. Aman had shaken him up good, wrote down his name and address, but that was it. It was the last time I went near Phil Aman's back door.

Each weekday during fall and winter there was a race to be the first one home from school. That lucky person took possession of the prized seat, a well-worn footstool in front of our small Philco radio. The best programs began at 4:30 P.M. and lasted until mealtime. Most were just fifteen minutes long, including commercials. The radio signal was often so weak, that in order to hear, one had to have an ear pressed tightly against the speaker. Many times, right at a critical moment, the sound would fade away completely. Our favorite programs were "Orphan Annie," "Jimmy Allen," and "Jack Armstrong the All-American Boy." Orphan Annie was sponsored by Ovaltine. For sending in a special label, the makers of Ovaltine offered a free "break-proof" plastic cup with Orphan Annie's picture on the outside, one of the first plastic cups made. We hardly had ours out of the box when Philip decided to test it by dropping it on the floor. It broke into a hundred pieces.

David was six years younger than I, much too young to participate in any of my exploits, which was all the better for him. His laid-back personality didn't lend itself to the type of activities Philip and I engaged in. He did, however, learn to smoke at a tender age, along with his friend, Jackie Weiler. On the south side of the cream station was quite a nice yard with a double row of lilac bushes. The lilacs had over-grown each other, leaving an ideal place in their center for kids to play, or perhaps to have a smoke. The smoke was beginning to thicken when Dad came running with the hose shouting, "Fire, Fire!" He soaked them good and then apologized, explaining he thought the lilacs were on fire. It was one of the few times I ever saw my brother David angry.

In the dead of winter, David's friend, Jackie, stuck his tongue on an iron railing on his way to school. Of course his tongue froze to the metal pipe rendering him helpless. No one knows how long he stood there before a woman on the second floor of a nearby building recognized his problem. She rushed down with a glass of warm water and set the poor boy free. He was late for school but still had his tongue.

The James River provided unlimited opportunities for swimming, camping, and fishing; and it was only a half-mile from where we lived. It was fun to walk along the bank and observe the many kinds of wild life. Several boys, including Philip and I, planned a camping trip for the next Saturday afternoon. We took along meat to cook over an open fire, potatoes for roasting in the coals, and peanut butter and jelly for sandwiches. Most important, though, was a can of Prince Albert smoking tobacco. Our sister Genevieve asked to go along, but we couldn't allow that. She couldn't keep a secret and our smoking and swearing would be reported to higher authority. This was to be a big camp-out, similar to the Lewis and Clark Expedition.

Nearly a mile up river was a small grove of trees. It was close to the road and had a small, spring-fed brook, a perfect place to make camp. After unpacking and arranging our supplies we set out on an exploratory trek further up river. We returned one or two hours later and started a campfire, and after a sumptuous meal, we all sat back in warm anticipation of a good smoke. When we opened our can of Prince Albert, however, we were stunned to find thick, gooey peanut butter mixed in with the tobacco. A monstrous joke had been perpetrated upon us, practically ruining our camping trip. We were absolutely mystified as to how such a horrible thing could have happened, and didn't learn the truth until the next day.

Early the next morning Dad asked if anything unusual had happened on our camping trip. It was at that precise moment that everything became crystal clear. Both he and Genevieve thought it was a big joke and laughed about it for years afterward. Believe me, it wasn't very funny to us at the time it happened. It remained the subject of conversation among our companions for some time. Philip and I never dared disclose the fact we had solved the mystery. Dad had meant it as a form of punishment, I'm sure, for refusing to take our sister along.

While the rest of the family always gave the peanut butter story top billing, Philip and I never did see any great humor in it, even years later.

Sandy loved tagging along wherever we went, he wanted desperately to be a part of every adventure, but there were times when it just wasn't practical to take him with us. In those instances, which were rare, we'd order him to stay home. When that happened, he'd put his tail between his legs and slink away like we had seriously hurt his feelings. If it were possible for him to cry, he would've shed giant tears. Sometimes we couldn't stand it and let him come anyway. Then he'd bound after us with his tail wagging, licking our faces to show his appreciation.

One of our more daring adventures, and one of the times Sandy had to remain home, was when we braved the storm sewers on the north end of town. They were just large enough to crawl through comfortably and spanned three or four city blocks. The Foran boys and I made our plans several days in advance, stockpiling all the necessary provisions such as tobacco, matches, and flashlights. We began at one end, crawling on all fours in complete darkness, except for an occasional flicker from a flashlight. It was certainly not a place for one with a morbid fear of the dark or of being in tight places. We became the most fearful after reaching the halfway mark, and that lasted until we could see the first speck of light at the far end. Once we emerged safely there was a rush of exhilaration, perhaps similar to one reaching the top of a mountain. Had a sudden rainstorm come along, we could have all drowned. We made this journey two or three times each summer.

An interesting footnote to this event happened while I was visiting with a physical therapist, Bruce Hocking, at the home of my sister in 1999. Bruce was a former resident of LaMoure and he related that he too had made the famous trip through the sewers, along with several of his friends.

Another challenge facing kids my age was climbing the city water tower. It was against the law but that made it all the more tempting. The tower stood atop a hill on the north end of town. It was a formidable undertaking for kids our age, most of us not yet teenagers. No one dared display the least sign of fear or hesitancy. The day we picked was not the most suitable for climbing; it was both cold and windy. It was when we neared the top that the wind seemed to grow stronger and our hands became stiff with cold. Once we had reached the topmost rung of the ladder, there was a walkway and railing encircling the base of the tank.

It was said to be a beautiful view, but by then I was so terrified I can't remember looking. The whole structure seemed to lean with the wind, which felt stronger with each passing second. I couldn't wait to get down. What a relief it was to feel solid ground under my feet. That was the first and last tower I ever climbed.

Dad didn't appreciate Philip and I hanging around the cream station unless we had work to do. As a result, he was constantly thinking up ways to keep us occupied. One afternoon he took a pair of six-foot two 2 x 2's and quickly put together a pair of stilts. It was a huge success and we soon had half the neighborhood learning how to walk on them. Then he decided to make a second pair and we held races and other events. We had to put them away after a boy fell and broke his arm.

The old community building was the hub of city life in LaMoure. That is where all the important meetings took place, in addition to the county basketball tournaments. Our cream station was right next door so we seldom missed anything of importance.

⇒◆⇐

When I was in the third grade, the entire school participated in putting on an Easter Operetta at the Community Building. I was a rabbit along with most of my classmates. Our job was to hop merrily up and down rows of upperclassmen while they sang songs. The downside of being a rabbit was our inability to extricate ourselves from our costumes without help. We were both sewed and pinned in, and expected to stay that way until we had completed our portion of the program. As is usually the case, the curtain didn't go up on time, forcing us to wait.

Finally, the singing started and we began hopping. However, during an interlude between numbers, a mysterious puddle had appeared quite suddenly beneath a fellow rabbit, and directly in our path. Naturally, as soon as we reached this unmentionable obstacle, we were obliged to take a giant leap as opposed to an ordinary hop. The audience became ecstatic, especially those in the front row. I never learned the name of the offending rabbit.

One chilly Sunday afternoon in late September of 1936, Dad was invited on a pheasant hunt with a group of friends. He was not an avid hunter but decided to go anyway. They drove to a cornfield a mile from town where pheasants were plentiful and began the hunt in the traditional way, beginning at one end of the field and walking through to the other.

Not until he got home did Dad discover his billfold missing. He thought he had lost it while hunting. For some unexplained reason, he had taken with him a substantial amount of money, most of it belonging to North American. I could see from Mom's reaction that this was a catastrophe of major proportion. Darkness had already fallen so there was nothing to be done until the next day.

The following morning Mom went into action. She marched us to the church where we made a novena to St. Anthony, the patron saint of lost articles. Afterward, we picked up a few neighborhood kids and drove to the cornfield. It was a military-style operation with each of us assigned two rows, beginning at one end of the field and ending at the other. About a third of the way in, a wounded pheasant jumped out in front of me with a squawk so loud it scared me half to death. I forgot all about the task at hand and began chasing the pheasant. By the time I caught him I was completely winded, and had to sit down. Voila! Just a few feet from where I sat lay Dad's big brown billfold. It was a miracle, or the closest thing to it. St. Anthony had outdone himself; we hadn't been searching more than half an hour. Dad wouldn't believe it until I produced the billfold. Oh ye of little faith!

Earlier in the summer there had been a major crime wave in LaMoure. Most were solved in short order and justice meted out on the spot. Hardly any reached the level of law enforcement, in sharp contrast to the way it works today.

A doctor's teenage son and two friends took a revolver from one of their parents, walked next door to a service station and held up the owner. They hadn't bothered with disguises or making get-away plans. All three were caught in short order with the proceeds from the stick-up in their pockets, a little over four dollars. They had been listening to a radio show and were under the impression that anyone with a gun could get by with this type of behavior. The parents and the service station owner worked it out together without involving the police.

The LaMoure Community Building

NOT VISIBLE IN THIS OLD PHOTO IS THE NORTH AMERICAN CREAM STATION just across the alley behind the Community Building. Also not visible is the city jail, constructed in the middle '30s, to house the village drunks until they sobered up. One Saturday night the noise made by those in jail became intolerable. So Dad went over with a crowbar and sprung the lock, letting everyone out. The police chief never did find out how they had escaped. The Community Building was replaced in the 1980s, but the small jail remained for several more years.

*A*POPULAR SUBJECT AMONG NEIGHBORHOOD KIDS back in the '30s was how to get something for nothing. One afternoon two of the older and smarter boys in the community agreed to let the rest of us in on their latest scam, "how to outwit the new candy machine on the second floor of the courthouse." The more experienced of the two criminals explained how he had taken a washer, about the size of a nickel, and filled the hole with tinfoil, thus somehow fooling the machine into ejecting a candy bar. It sounded so easy that Dick Foran and I couldn't wait to get in on some of this free candy. We quickly prepared two washers and made our way to the courthouse. I knew it wasn't entirely legal, but it didn't seem like stealing either. More like us being smarter than the machine.

We inserted the first washer, turned the knob, and bingo, out came a candy bar, then another. It was like magic. However, before we had time to take one bite, all hell broke loose. People came running out of every office on the second floor. One guy grabbed us while another opened the machine revealing our two washers. I felt weak, sick to my stomach – where had I gone wrong? It was obvious I'd have to quit associating with those criminals out at the stockyards.

As soon as our guilt was firmly established, the county auditor came out and took over the investigation. He took down our names, addresses, and all other pertinent information, then asked where we had learned to "bamboozle" LaMoure County like that. We were completely truthful, explaining about the washers, everything we knew. At that point, I was firmly convinced we were about to be marched away to jail which was located just two floors below. The county auditor gave us a long sermon on what happens to criminals, but after just a few additional admonishments, and to our great relief, he let us go. Later that same afternoon, the boys that had so obligingly given us all that good information were caught near the candy machine with a handful of washers and made to sit in jail for a few hours.

Another serious crime, in which I wasn't involved, happened one summer afternoon right under the nose of the county sheriff. A local merchant had been robbed of his new gum machine. He wasn't concerned about the money or the gum, but he did want his new machine back. The sheriff inspected the scene of the crime, got in his car and drove off. Just three blocks away sat three young boys on the curb, all chewing gum and blowing bubbles. After a brief interrogation, they confessed to the crime, including the destruction of the new gum machine. Another case where the parents had to pay the damages, but no one went to jail.

My brother Philip began driving the family car when he was a fifth grader. He was quite mature for his age and only associated with older kids. Twice a week we drove to the Brunsoman Farm, a mile from town, to buy milk. Philip was usually entrusted with this little chore, for which he was more than happy to oblige. My job, and the only reason I was asked along, was to hold onto the pail of milk while he spun around the corners. One fine spring day while on a milk run, Philip's success as a race driver came to an end. After spinning out of Brunsoman's yard at a high rate of speed he nearly missed the first turn, then overcorrected after which we flew into the ditch and tipped over, all in less than two or three minutes. It felt like the end of the world. I lay on top of Philip screaming, but somehow had managed to hold onto our pail of milk. More than anything else, I was worried about the car and what might happen to us when we got home.

Philip remained completely calm, like nothing untoward had happened. While the ditch was deep, the ground was quite soft and moist, and the car had merely tipped on its side. The two Brunsoman boys were tall and husky, and with their help we were easily able to tip the car upright and get it back upon the road. While one of the boys jumped on the bent front fender, the rest of us cleaned the dirt and grass from the side of the car. In just a few minutes we were ready to drive on with little evidence of an accident. Our old Chevy was well built, nearly indestructible. Not a drop of milk had been spilled and the folks never learned of our accident until we told them years later. The one small dent was blamed on Mom.

———❖———

Prohibition encompassed the years 1920 through 1933, when it was repealed by the Twenty-first Amendment. Minnesota was one of the first states to license the sale of hard liquor after repeal, but it remained illegal in North Dakota until later. It was during that interim that my father and his friend, Bill Billstein, decided to go into the bootlegging business.

So early in 1934, Dad went to Valley City and made a deal for a brand new, black Ford sedan with a V-8 engine. He stored it in a friend's garage some distance from the cream station to allay any suspicion from our neighbors. During the next week I made several trips to this garage where I was able to climb through a window and sit behind the wheel of that beautiful machine, enjoying it's sleek appearance and the smell of its newness.

My fun behind the wheel was to be short lived, however. Dad and Bill set out for Minnesota a week later for their first load of merchandise. They drove south and east toward the border, avoiding major highways, hoping to bypass any law enforcement officials on the lookout for bootleggers.

Unfortunately, and for them almost fatal, Dad and Bill had taken along samples of the very merchandise they were going after, and had apparently over-indulged along the way. It's anyone's guess what happened exactly, but I can imagine Dad was showing his friend Bill how easy it would be to outrun any lawman with this new, high-powered car. In any case, when they came to a fork in the road near the town of Milnor, only fifty miles from home, instead of turning either right or left, Dad took the middle. After nearly severing a telephone pole, the car rolled several times. Both were injured, but not severely. The car, however, was a total loss, as were their dreams of getting rich in the bootlegging business.

After getting patched up by a doctor, Dad called home with the bad news. Mom was so angry she refused to go after them, leaving it instead to Mrs. Billstein. Philip and I rode along and were able to see the crumpled remains of that once beautiful automobile. It was a miracle either had survived. Dad had a few bumps and abrasions and a long cut on his neck, which had required several stitches. Bill looked as though he had come through the ordeal without a scratch. He had, however, suffered a severe neck injury from which he never recovered. His neck was permanently stiff, and he was unable to turn his head thereafter. Mom said it was good for them, she had been opposed to the idea from its inception. The word bootlegging was never mentioned around our house again. Incidentally, the word "bootlegging" came from a time long ago, when the purveyors of this illegal merchandise carried it concealed in their boots.

⪼◦⪻

A month before school was out, a friend of Dad's from Grand Rapids offered us the use of his ornery little pony and four-wheeled cart for the summer. Dad took us to the man's farm, and Philip and I drove home in the cart. There was an abandoned livery barn nearby where we stabled the pony. In no time at all we became expert horsemen, the envy of every kid in town. On our forays about the neighborhood we were usually accompanied by an entourage of friends, most of them on bicycles, but some that were content to tag along on foot. A small box behind the seat was utilized for giving rides to those we considered worthy, and for storing crab apples.

The pony was broke to ride, but due to his ill temper we seldom did so. We soon learned his favorite tricks. The one he seemed to like best was to bite us in the leg while we were trying to mount, or failing that, to quickly brush up against a fence, building, or anything else in sight to rid himself of our body. His preferred method of discharge, once we managed to get on, was to run full speed, then stop short, causing us to fly over his head. He was not above adding insult to injury by nipping us in the hind-end while we lay incapacitated on the ground before him.

In spite of our warnings, Genevieve insisted on taking him for a ride. Ten minutes later she came home in tears, with bruises all over an arm and leg. In between sobs she said, "The pony tried to jump over the train, and I fell off."

⪼◦⪻

Every town and village had a stockyard, which provided endless forms of entertainment. One game we played was called "Timber Tag." It was patterned after the traditional game of tag except that it was conducted along the topmost timbers of the pens and gates. We became so adept at this game, that in no time we could run full speed. It was both dangerous and exciting, and there were mishaps, but none that were very serious as near as I recall.

Whenever cattle were in the pens awaiting shipment, we'd stage our own version of a rodeo. Our favorite method of getting on a critter was to drop on their back from atop the corral fence, or to leap on them while they were lying down. We felt the wrath of the railroad section-foreman more than once.

——————

My brother's friend, Jackie Weiler, seldom, if ever, got in any sort of trouble. He didn't have to, trouble had a way of finding him. On his way to school one day he got the surprise of his young life. Ernie Engel had parked his horse-drawn milk-wagon in front of the cream station while he delivered our daily supply of milk and visited with Dad a few minutes. Jackie stopped to admire the horse when curiosity got the best of him. He walked to the open door and then made the mistake of stepping inside, whereupon the horse started down the street.

By the time Ernie was ready to leave, Jackie and the milk-wagon were turning the corner two blocks away. Fortunately, the horse stopped at the next house on the route. Ernie caught up all out of breath, not realizing someone was inside until Jackie stepped out and sauntered off toward school without so much as a word.

Later, Jackie explained that he just wanted to see what the inside looked like when the blamed horse started off down the road.

The weather had warmed considerably the last week in March. Most of the snow had melted, and spring was in the air. Dad was good at coming up with ideas to get Philip and me from under his feet. With the advent of spring, he suggested we take Billy Kranz on an outing in the country, perhaps on a hike to Grand Rapids and back. That suggestion, I'm sure, was made to keep us occupied for most of the day, and it did sound like a good idea.

We packed a light lunch, dressed in warm clothing, and started out about ten o'clock that morning. A hike to Grand Rapids and back, about fifteen miles, would take a considerable amount of time at the speed we traveled. We took the most direct route, which was a trail running adjacent to the railroad track, and made good time on the forward part of our journey. We arrived in Grand Rapids in early afternoon and ate our lunch on the depot platform. On the return trip, we decided to walk east toward the river, stopping a few minutes at Elmwood Farm, where Mrs. Cloke gave us each a big molasses cookie.

From Elmwood Farm we made our way toward home walking along the James River, which was still covered with a reasonably thick layer of ice. The first mile was slow going since we spent a lot of time exploring along the riverbank. We wasted a lot of time and the sun was getting lower in the west, causing a rapid drop in temperature. I was poking about with a stick when I heard an ear-shattering scream behind me. I turned my head just in time to see Billy's body bob up through a hole in the ice. He was hollering and thrashing about like a snared alligator. Philip rushed toward him and was able to get hold of an arm, and between the two of us we managed to pull him to safety. In spite of the fact the river wasn't more than four or five feet deep where he had broken through, it could have ended in disaster.

Billy, who was big for his age, sounded like a week-old lost calf. He was bawling loud enough to raise the dead. Giant tears streamed down his cheeks accompanied by an unsightly flow of green mucous from his nose. Then his clothes began to stiffen from the dropping temperature, turning him into a giant icicle. I knew we weren't far from Melitta Hennings' farm, so I suggested we move along quickly before he got pneumonia. Trying to get Billy to hurry, though, was out of the question. We had to literally drag and push him every foot of the way. The situation wasn't funny, but I couldn't help but be amused at the way that kid could howl.

It seemed like an eternity before we finally reached the bridge leading to Hennings, though I doubt we had walked more than a quarter-mile. By this time, his clothing was almost frozen solid and we had to lift him bodily up the riverbank, all the while listening to his incessant moaning. Once we arrived at the farm, Mrs. Hennings took charge. She quickly got him into dry clothes with the result that the howling gradually subsided. Fortunately, Mrs. Hennings had a telephone from which we were able to call home.

"The Storyteller & Actor"
Bill Kranz (seated) shares a memory with the author.

By the time Bill senior had arrived at the farm, young Billy was in a cheerful mood, in sharp contrast to just an hour earlier. He showed few signs of having suffered such a traumatic experience. Mr. & Mrs. Kranz were extremely grateful that their only child was safe, largely through the efforts of Philip and me. We were subsequently invited to dinner, and best of all, treated to a movie afterward.

Bill Kranz senior was a great actor and storyteller. Most of his stories were true, albeit somewhat exaggerated. He had the uncanny ability to make the characters in his stories come alive by contorting his facial features to closely resemble those he was talking about. And he was able to imitate their voices and physical characteristics as well. The more often he told a story, the funnier it became.

One of Bill's stories, and the one I always liked best, was the time he and his wife were invited to a card party at the Ballweg home. Al Ballweg and his wife had gotten married late in life and subsequently had two children, both boys. They were doting parents that coddled and spoiled their sons to the point they had lost all semblance of control. All during the card party the boys, ages four and five, made a general nuisance of themselves by crawling beneath the tables, and playing recklessly with their vast array of toys.

Floyd Leehan, Bill's whist partner, was having a difficult time concentrating on the game, due to the competition from one of the boys trying to crawl beneath his table. Floyd was a tall, middle-aged, enigmatic man who had the look of a habitually ill person. He was well over six feet tall, with long skinny legs that barely fit beneath the card table. His most prominent feature, however, was an oversized Adam's apple which danced up and down his elongated neck in sync with each syllable he spoke.

At the precise moment he was contemplating a strategic play, the boy beneath the table took his hammer and struck Floyd a sharp blow on his spindly shinbone. Floyd screamed out in pain, the blood draining from his already pallid face. No words came out, but his giant Adam's apple began bobbing up and down his neck like a yo-yo. He struggled to his feet and proceeded to dance around the room on his good leg, while embracing the injured one in his arms.

Bill and the other guests were mystified by Floyd's bizarre behavior and decided he must be suffering some sort of seizure. They were about to throw him on the couch when the pain subsided long enough for him to explain what had happened. His Adam's apple continued trembling, however, until Mr. Ballweg gently removed his son from the room.

—＞◇＜—

NP agent, Frank Bauer, was Bills' boss at the depot. While Bill was only the telegrapher, he had to do all the office work as well, while Frank strode about town dressed in the latest style suit visiting with all his cronies at the local bar. Bill was perfectly content with this arrangement so long as Frank stayed away and didn't interfere with the internal affairs of the office.

Frank envisioned himself a "Lady's Man" and spent much of his time entertaining at a roadhouse he owned at the edge of town. He and a partner had renovated an old railroad passenger coach they named the "Chicken Shack." Frank's flamboyant lifestyle, however, was costly and as a result he was habitually in debt, borrowing heavily each month against his railroad paycheck. People he owed were constantly coming to the depot inquiring as to his whereabouts or wondering when his check would be arriving. Frank, on the other hand, became more and more adept at avoiding them, always keeping a wary eye out. On payday he'd sneak in through the freight house in an effort to avoid his numerous, and sometimes indignant benefactors.

The "Chicken Shack" was not doing well, resulting in Frank sliding further into debt. In addition to that, his creditors were becoming more determined than ever to collect, even resorting to hiring spies to watch the depot on payday. On one occasion, just as Bill handed him his check, Frank looked out the window just in time to see two men coming toward the office. He grabbed his hat and locked himself inside the women's restroom, begging Bill not to reveal his hiding place. "Please knock on the door when they're gone," he pleaded.

"I let the bastard sit in there for two hours," Bill said.

Frank enjoyed being in the public eye, so when he was asked to ride on the Fireman's float in the Independence Day parade, he was ecstatic. With a fireman's hat firmly on his head he crawled to a bench near the front. Each man carried a flag in one hand and waved to the crowd with the other. Frank was a little wobbly after a pre-celebration party with his buddies, so when they turned a corner rather abruptly, he lost his balance and tumbled over the side. He was nearly killed, but Bill hadn't seen the last of him. Three weeks later he was back living it up as before.

⟨⟩

I never learned where "Crab" Townsend got his nickname; he was the contracting drayman for the railroad, and therefore hauled most of the freight arriving in LaMoure by rail. One day he was preparing to unload a carload of brick when Bill asked him to hire a starving bum that had just jumped off the local freight that morning. Crab gave the poor man enough money for lunch and told him to report back afterward. The first thing the bum did after coming to work was drop a brick on Crab's toe, not only causing him unbearable pain, but a trip to the doctor as well. The bum's employment began and ended the same after-noon, and he barely escaped a good thrashing from Crab.

Going "Snipe Hunting" was an age-old prank occasionally played on the unsuspecting. Harry Ellison became a leading candidate shortly after joining the LaMoure Civic Club. Bill Kranz and two other club members decided Harry should to be invited to one of their famous hunts. Harry accepted the invitation with enthusiasm and they agreed to meet at midnight — the ideal time to hunt snipes. Harry was told to bring along a large burlap sack and a flashlight, explaining that he would need the flashlight to light the opening of the sack for the snipes, while he walked slowly through the weeds calling, "Here snipe, snipe. Here snipe, snipe."

The spot where Bill and his fellow conspirators planned to take Harry hadn't seen a snipe for the last thousand years. And even if it had, there was no way a snipe would be stupid enough to walk into a burlap sack, with or without a flashlight. They stopped the car in an isolated area about three miles from town where Harry was instructed to take the lead. The trick, of course, was to drive off, abandoning the snipe-hunter in the middle of nowhere. What they hadn't counted on, however, was the fact that Harry wasn't nearly as gullible as they had at first believed. When they were about to begin the hunt, Harry suddenly remembered he had forgotten his flashlight in the car. The last Bill and his friends saw of Harry that night was the lights of the car as he drove off, leaving them stranded. Bearing the brunt of their own joke was a painful experience for all three, but most of all for Bill, who prided him-self on his ability to plan the perfect prank. That was the last time he or-ganized a snipe hunt.

———⪼◆⪻———

Nic Cruden managed the Downing Farm, one of the last "bonanza farms" still in operation. Located two miles northeast of LaMoure, it was only a half-hour's walk from town. Nic Cruden's son, Jerry, was our age and a good friend. When the weather was nice, Philip and I some-times walked to the farm to spend the afternoon playing with Jerry. There were three or four giant horse-barns, a long, low-roofed cow barn, and numerous other buildings, including a large house that looked like it might have as many as six or eight bedrooms. Just east of the house, protected by a high woven-wire fence, was a large orchard with a wide variety of fruit trees. Adjacent to the orchard was a sizable vegetable garden. The barns, however, were the most interesting.

At the far end of the main horse-barn was a large enclosed stall with vertical iron bars across the upper half. Locked inside was the biggest, meanest looking stallion I'd ever seen. He must have weighed over 2,000 pounds. His thick neck and massive head were covered by a long shaggy mane that nearly hid his eyes. The minute we got close, he began snorting, pawing the floor, and kicking the walls with his hind legs. His nostrils flared as he shook his giant head from side to side. We all three ran from the barn, thinking he might escape at any minute. It was a frightening experience.

The horse-barns were built on high ground adjacent to each other, perhaps not more than twenty meters apart. A high board fence closed off the open area between the barns, and a huge water tank was centrally located in back. The low-roofed barn, used exclusively for milking, was also just a short distance from the water tank. Late one afternoon, several hired men were busy milking cows and had refused to let us inside. To retaliate for this rude behavior we began throwing rocks at the barn. One of the men appeared in the doorway and threatened us with bodily harm if we didn't leave at once. Since Jerry didn't slack off at all, Philip and I remained reasonably confident nothing bad was going to happen, so we continued hurling rocks as before. Then, from out of nowhere, and running at full speed, one of the men came after us. Philip and Jerry managed to escape, but I was cornered between the side of a barn and the high board fence. This big gorilla grabbed me by the seat of my pants and carried me to the water tank where he threw me bodily into that slime covered water, and held me submerged for what seemed an eternity.

I was too busy kicking my feet for my life to flash before my eyes, but I definitely thought my days on this earth were ending right then and there. When he finally pulled me out and threw me to the ground, I was coughing up water and screaming as loud as I could. Jerry's mother rushed to my rescue, took me to the house, and gave me a hot bath. All the while I kept on howling. When I got dried off and into some of

Jerry's clothes I felt a little better, but it was a terrifying experience, one that remains as vivid today as the day it happened so many years ago.

We seldom told our folks about these incidents, primarily because we generally received little or no sympathy. But in this case I had no choice — I had Jerry's clothes on. It was clear to my folks that the stone throwing had a direct bearing on my unscheduled baptism in the water tank.

I didn't disclose any details either about the day I got caught lighting a match on the school ground and had to write 500 times, "I will not light matches on the school ground again." I had found the match just outside the door, and it had seemed a waste not to light it.

⋙◆⋘

Living in the business district of LaMoure was not a healthy thing for our dog, Sandy. There was considerable traffic in and out of our alley, territory he intended to protect. Consequently, when a truck, car, or a team and wagon passed through, Sandy chased after them. This behavior was especially irritating to the mailman on his frequent trips to the back door of the post office. During the winter months we kept him inside as much as possible, but he spent the summers outdoors. Several attempts had been made to poison him, but in each case he had survived. I knew he'd been sick a few times but I had no idea what had caused it.

Then one fateful day in the early spring of 1935, Sandy was missing. I looked and searched everywhere. We all did. I rode around town on my bicycle for hours calling to him, all to no avail. He was simply nowhere to be found. The next day I went down the basement for something and found him beneath the stair; he had been dead for one or two days.

It was my first close encounter with death, and I was devastated. I cried when I found him, and every night thereafter for weeks. I prayed and prayed he would come back to life though I knew deep down that wasn't likely to happen. My loyal friend and protector was gone, and the loss was deep and painful. It was an experience that took me a long time to deal with.

~=>-◇-<=~

Two relatives from Minneapolis stopped in LaMoure and offered to take me with them to Bowman, where they planned to visit Dad's sister, Mame Stinchfield. Aunt Mame and Uncle Mark had invited me to spend the summer, so it was an opportunity for me to get away and forget about losing Sandy.

The Stinchfields lived some twenty miles southwest of Bowman in one of the most desolate and remote areas of North Dakota. Conditions were made worse by the continuing drought. Uncle Mark farmed a few acres with horses and ran a few head of cattle and sheep. Due to the dry conditions, forage for the livestock was extremely sparse. There

The hot summer of 1935 on the Stinchfield Farm
Lenore West and the author on "Topsy"
Standing (from left), Robert (Tag) Stinchfield,
Daryl West, and Joe Stinchfield
This picture illustrates the severity of the drought & depression.

was, however, an abundance of cactus and rattlesnakes. We had to be constantly alert for rattlers.

Mark and Mame raised six children, four boys, George, Kenneth, Joe, and Tag, and twin girls, Dorothy and Doris. The twins were both married with families of their own and the eldest boy, George, was away at summer school. Kenneth worked for a rancher some distance away, so we seldom saw him. The rest of us, with little else to do, spent every spare minute wallowing around in a slough a short distance from the farm. By midday the temperature was usually in the high 90s, and we couldn't wait to escape the unrelenting heat by immersing our bodies in that dreadful mud-hole.

Two weeks of Bible school began the middle of July, a welcome diversion from the incredible monotony of our daily routine. Four of us walked the five or six miles each day to the "Cave Hills," a quiet little valley surrounded by trees and picturesque hills. It was a perfect setting for the small church, classrooms, and a few cabins. The first day of our journey we took turns riding the Stinchfield horse, "Topsy." But so many arguments broke out over the length of riding time, we decided it was best to leave her home. The time passed quickly and before we knew it Bible School was over.

⎯⎯⊰◆⊱⎯⎯

It is impossible to make a realistic comparison between conditions in the '30s and the colossal affluence of today. I don't recall any of us feeling deprived, however. Every other Saturday, and most Sundays, the entire family crowded into their old Model T for the trip to Bowman. We followed a trail for about five miles and a narrow, bumpy, graveled road the rest of the way. Rattling along at about fifteen miles per hour took like what seemed an eternity to reach town. Saturday was grocery shopping and visiting day, almost like attending the county fair; everyone was excited about going to town. Every Sunday we went to church and afterward visited one of the twins.

Despite the dire poverty and depressed conditions, we managed to have a reasonably good time. Summer was drawing to a close, however, and the day finally arrived for me to return home. I was homesick, and anxious to get back to my family.

Aunt Mame and Uncle Mark took me to the railroad station and saw me safely aboard the train. When Mom met me at the station in Aberdeen, she screamed, "Robert! What on earth has happened to you?" My meager diet, in addition to spending most of the summer in the water, had reduced my already slim build to skin and bone. Though my ribs were clearly visible I hadn't noticed anything different.

A great tragedy took place later that fall with the sudden death of George Stinchfield from meningitis. George was the pride and joy of his family. His untimely death brought unimaginable sorrow to them. He had been attending school at New England and was doing so well. Aunt Mame and Uncle Mark had sacrificed a great deal for his education and had high hopes for his future. Aunt Mame suffered terribly during this time. Like others before her, she was sustained by a steadfast faith in God.

———⋙◆⋘———

It was wonderful to be back with my family, except I once again missed Sandy. It hadn't bothered me much while I was away, but now that I was home I continued to be troubled by his death.

I hadn't been home more than a week when Dad decided to take us on an overnight camping trip. He knew a place along the river near Elmwood Farm that would be perfect.

We loaded up the car with food, blankets and an old canvas tarp. Dad took along his shotgun in the event we were attacked by robbers or Indians. Dad made our adventure sound a little ominous. Philip and I weren't afraid, but Genevieve and David were apprehensive.

It was late afternoon when we arrived at a beautiful spot atop a grassy knoll, just a few feet from the river. The campsite was almost completely surrounded by trees. The first order of business was to build a fire and store enough wood to last the night. By the time we finished our meal it was nearly dark, and the night air was beginning to feel damp and cool.

Dad rolled out the tarp and placed the bedding on top. The only light came from the stars shining through the overhanging branches, and from our dwindling campfire. We crawled beneath the blankets fully clothed, except for our shoes, while Dad piled a few more logs on the fire.

The ground beneath the tarp and bedding felt cold and hard, but we didn't complain. Dad told us stories of his youth, about how he and his father often walked along the riverbank when he was our age, over the very spot where we were camping. He related how Grandpa Cunningham loved to go hiking and how he always carried a walking stick.

With the onset of darkness, the flames from our campfire cast long shadows that danced about our small enclosure. There were intermittent crackles from the burning logs accompanied by an occasional shower of sparks. Except for the fire and chirping of crickets, it was deadly quiet.

After several minutes of complete silence, we were all startled when Dad said, "I think we should go home!" There was an almost immediate chorus of agreement, going home sounded like a good idea. We were disappointed, however, that we hadn't heard what a gunshot sounded like. So, just before we left, Dad aimed the gun in the air and fired. It sounded like a cannon going off. Soon we were home in our own beds and happy to be there.

⋙•◦•⋘

The Roxy Theater was a major source of entertainment in LaMoure. Movies, shown every night, cost ten cents for children and twenty cents for adults. Unfortunately, few could afford even that small price, so we seldom got to go. One Christmas day, after attending church and opening our gifts, which didn't take long, Dad gave us each a dime for the afternoon matinee. I remember thinking it was the best Christmas I'd ever had.

Mrs. Klien, wife of a local businessman, owned and managed the theater. During the hot summer nights, just after the movie had started, she would tiptoe down the aisle and quietly open the emergency exit for better circulation. That open door was an invitation for those of us with no money, to circumvent the ticket window. One by one, we'd slither over the threshold on our stomachs and gently ease ourselves into a front seat. Mrs. Klien must have had x-ray vision, because within seconds she'd run down the aisle and throw us headlong out the door. Seldom did we succeed in watching for more than two or three minutes.

————≫◦◦◦◦≪————

In 1936, after a great deal of resistance, the government agreed to pay the veterans of WW I a bonus. Those that had been in combat overseas received a greater amount, so Dad received near the maximum. I could only guess how much it was, perhaps around $1,000. I remember him showing me a sheaf of negotiable certificates that looked like savings bonds, only larger. It was a great day when the bonus money came, and there were lively discussions about how it should be spent. Mom wanted to put most of it in the bank but Dad had other plans.

The major purchase was a new car. Dad ordered a 1937 Deluxe Chevrolet right from the factory. Mom and I caught a ride to Fargo, where it had been delivered, and drove it home. She had been against spending so much money on an automobile, but secretly I think she liked it as well as the rest of our family. It was a beautiful car, one that served us well over the next eight years. Mom got a new dress and a pair of shoes, but her pride and joy was a nine- by twelve-foot Oriental rug, which remained in our family for nearly four decades. How beautiful she looked in her new blue taffeta dress, with its small cluster of red cherries at the collar.

We were proud of our new car. Few people could afford one back then. Dad kept it parked in front of the cream station for everyone to see, sort of like displaying a medal for having served his country in the "Big War." That's the way Dad saw it.

————≫◦◦◦◦≪————

Our little brother, Douglas Terrence, was born in Doctor Ribble's office on February 2, 1936, about a block away. Dad brought Mom home in the car a week later. Then he and I took an arm-full of blankets, ran the one block through an alley full of snow, and brought little Doug home. We decided to call him Terry, a shortened version of his second name, Terrence.

Doc Ribble had delivered all the Cunningham children except David, so he and Dad were on a first-name basis. One day a woman was brought in with a broken leg after falling off a wagon and Doc needed help setting it. The first place he called was the cream station. Dad held her by the arms while Doc pulled on the leg for all he was worth; it was like a tug-of-war, with the poor woman in the middle, screaming at the top of her lungs.

After more than six years in LaMoure, Dad was offered the job managing a larger cream station in Edgeley, about nineteen miles west. I had learned to love LaMoure and wasn't looking forward to another move.

Douglas Terrence Cunningham,
called Terry by the family

LaMoure to Edgeley

Chapter V

Packing Up for Edgeley

PACKING DISHES, SILVERWARE, AND OTHER OBJECTS considered valuable was a task shared by the entire family. We double-wrapped everything in old newspapers, carefully placing them inside apple boxes, washtubs, and any other containers we could lay our hands on. Once the packing was completed we again awaited the arrival of Lee McCann and his truck. Carrying the heavy furniture down the long stairway was the most difficult part. That's when Lee's great strength was an enormous help.

So, in late summer of 1937, we were on the move once again. We left the familiarity of LaMoure to face the ordeal of establishing new friendships in a strange town. It was distressing and uncomfortable being thrust into another unknown environment. Perhaps I'm the only one that felt that way; I was always shy around strangers. I'm sure my parents also had regrets after having lived in LaMoure for six years.

Despite my anxiety, there was the pleasant prospect of moving into a home with a decent bathroom and a bedroom for Philip and me that included a little privacy, like a door. And Genevieve, at long last, would have her own bedroom. It wasn't a new house by any stretch of the imagination, but it was a palace compared to the second-story living quarters above the cream station.

By the time we got settled school was ready to begin and I had managed to make a few friends. An Irish family named Donegon lived only three blocks from our house. There were eight Donegon children, all at home except for the eldest son. Donald was my age; both of us were in the seventh grade. We became good friends, though we had a few differences of opinion later on.

Mr. Donegon was a tall, lanky man with a long, craggy face, who seldom smiled and always appeared to be deep in thought. Like many men in those days he didn't have a steady job — he worked only when he could find something. He did carpentry and was a self-taught veterinarian. How he managed to feed and clothe his large family borders on the supernatural. He spent a lot of time in a rocking chair reading and smoking his pipe, which wasn't terribly unusual in 1937.

Above all, the Donegons were good people. All the boys worked at some sort of job around town. They shoveled snow and coal in winter and sold newspapers the year round. Donald was the most enterprising, always looking for ways to earn extra money. He was the youngest of the boys and the final recipient of hand-me-downs. By the time the clothes got to him they were almost transparent. My own were but a shade better, for I had to wear all of Philip's outgrown clothes and those that had been passed on to us by relatives.

I didn't notice at the time, but we lived in the lap of luxury compared to some of our neighbors. Many families were dependent on friends and relatives for survival.

Life in Edgeley soon settled into a routine, and I was beginning to like it more with each passing day. The cream station was much larger than I had anticipated, and there was a 1925 Chevrolet delivery truck. In addition to buying cream, North American was licensed as a wholesale outlet for beer. Philip and I became experts at driving the truck and were occasionally called upon to make emergency deliveries. Otherwise, we used it for joy riding around town.

Donegons owned two cows they kept in a small barn two blocks from their home. A big manure pile had accumulated over the past two winters and the two older boys offered me $5.00 to haul it away. That amount of money was too good to pass up so after surveying the job, I accepted their offer. It would be easy money now that I had the use of a truck — not more than two or three days hauling I reckoned.

I got up early the next morning full of enthusiasm, and by mid-afternoon had hauled five big loads to the city dump. Then, after a second survey, I discovered those five loads hadn't made so much as a small dent in the manure pile. Beside that, I was all tired out and my enthusiasm for the job was waning. It dawned on me that this was not the moneymaker I had at first envisioned. In fact, it looked more and more like I had been taken for a ride. So, after hauling more than half a day, and wasting my hard earned money on gas, I decided to tell the Donegons' to haul their own manure. Since I hadn't completed the job they refused to pay me anything. But I had learned a valuable lesson, and I would never to be that gullible again.

After the manure-hauling fiasco, I was a little depressed, so I sought solace in a weed patch out behind the cream station. I planned to buoy my spirits by smoking the Elmo cigar I'd found outside the hotel the day before. It was a beautiful cigar wrapped in silver foil. Man, it looked and smelled good enough to eat. After puffing away a few minutes, I began to feel rather poorly. Everything was moving in circles. I mean, I was sick. In my vast experience smoking tobacco, I'd never been this sick before. It was awful. I threw up for half an hour and was so dizzy I couldn't stand upright. After suffering for an additional half-hour, I staggered home and went to bed, promising myself never to smoke again.

My next big job opportunity came a few weeks later and proved to be considerably more successful than the manure hauling business. A farm auction was being held west of town the next Saturday, and Dad suggested it would be an ideal opportunity to sell ice-cold drinks. I loaded the truck with several cases of pop, plenty of ice, and a metal tank — along with ten cases of beer from which we had removed the labels. Offering alcoholic beverages for sale without a license was risky. Once those farmers discovered what I was really selling, business picked up considerably. It was a hot day and I could hardly keep up with demand. There were more people gathered around my cold drink stand than there were watching the sale, which wasn't appreciated by the auctioneer.

In just a few hours I was completely sold out, and my pockets were stuffed with money. When I returned to town, Dad was surprised at how well I'd done. He donated a share of our profits to the Boy Scouts in case the sheriff came around asking questions. To be successful in the '30s, one had to be not only innovative, but a wee bit of a crook as well.

———⋙⋘———

The local Rexall Drugstore was the sponsor of a widely advertised contest. A free bicycle was to be awarded the person selling the greatest number of pocket combs over a period of six weeks. The bicycle was prominently displayed in a front window surrounded by thousands of multicolored combs. It was a real beauty, red with white trim. Every kid in town wanted that bike, myself included, and at least half signed up. The combs sold for a nickel, and the sales people were required to pay the druggist up front, thus eliminating a sizable number of salespersons. If you quit, or just couldn't sell your combs — too bad, you were stuck.

Success depended on total commitment to the cause. I could see early on, I wasn't going to make it, even though I had made a respectable beginning. My friend, Donald Donegon, however, was determined to be the top comb salesman, not just in Edgeley, but in the entire United States. He made up his mind he was going to have that bicycle come hell or high water. He mobilized all his relatives into an army of comb-sellers, and even skipped school to go on selling trips, never missing an opportunity. He walked around with his pockets stuffed with combs of every color. No one was safe from the comb-sellers; they were everywhere, like locusts. The citizens of Edgeley were so aggravated there was talk of running the druggist out of town.

When the final results became known, Donald had won hands-down. Most kids had sold combs in the hundreds, but Donald was in the thousands. Everyone was amazed except me. It was a tribute to his tenacity and determination. One of his relatives revealed that Donald was still trying to sell combs a year later. It is a little ironic that he chose barbering as a vocation in life.

＝＞◆＜＝

One Sunday afternoon I decided to hike out to the city airport. I took my 22 rifle along in case I saw a gopher. Near an old hanger sat two abandoned airplanes, their cloth covering hanging in shreds. It was fun to climb into the cockpit and imagine flying to some exotic place. The old biplane had one tire still partially inflated. That seemed an injustice somehow, so I backed away about thirty feet and fired at it with my 22. At almost the precise moment I pulled the trigger, there was a light slap against my chest. Then I discovered the lead from the spent cartridge had ricocheted back and had fallen into my shirt pocket. It was still warm. So help me God that is exactly what happened. Back then, airplane tires were made of genuine rubber.

Carl Wilkie was a prominent area pilot and owner of a large grocery store in Edgeley. He also owned a new Stinson airplane. Flying was still a novelty in the '30s, prompting people to run outdoors whenever a plane flew over. Right then, in front of my very eyes, Carl came in for a landing with that beautiful Stinson. Moments later a car drove up and out jumped the two Anderson girls, both in their early twenties and good looking. Carl had promised to take them for a ride and they were all excited.

Carl was a handsome man, sort of an adventurer, but for some reason he had never married. He was a veteran of WW I, much older than the Anderson girls, but that didn't seem to matter. It was interesting that while in the store business, Carl sometimes delivered his rural sale bills by air wrapped around a candy bar. That was one reason everyone ran outdoors whenever they heard a plane fly over. As a result of this innovative method of advertising, he became both popular and successful.

It was obvious the Anderson girls wanted to go for a ride, yet for some reason they were a little hesitant. Carl coaxed and cajoled until they finally agreed to go, but only on condition that I come along. I couldn't believe my good fortune when Carl asked if I'd like to go flying. Moments later we thundered down the runway in a cloud of dust, then sailed into the air like a giant bird. What a thrilling experience it was. The girls laughed and giggled the whole time. Carl enjoyed their company immensely, explaining the intricacies of flying a plane, even offering them the controls. It was fun watching people run out of their homes to wave.

———⟫◆⟪———

Miss Stapelton was my seventh grade teacher the fall of 1937. She was an excellent teacher, and I liked her a lot. She was responsible for getting me interested in reading. An avid reader herself, she tried to instill in her students a love for books. Each afternoon, for fifteen minutes, she read to us from a novel. I'm not sure how many books Edgar Rice Burroughs wrote, but I'm sure she read them all to our class. On one occasion I just couldn't wait for the next installment, so when she left the room I took the latest book from her desk and began reading the next chapter. I was so engrossed I didn't notice her come up behind me. She was furious, and I paid the price for my indiscretion by staying after school a few nights.

Friday afternoon was a special time in our room. It was reserved for special events, like birthday parties and having Miss Stapelton read to us for an additional fifteen minutes. Whenever a classmate had a birthday, we'd celebrate the occasion on Friday afternoon by holding an apple shower. Those that could afford to do so brought an apple to school, and when a signal was given, we simultaneously rolled them up the aisle toward the front of the room. Miss Stapelton always acted surprised, and maybe she was. It was always a thrill to see the expression on her face. All those apples rolling at once made a tremendous noise. The girls would then gather them up, cut them into small slices, and divide them equally, whether or not you had brought one.

In 1938 the Nash Coffee Company advertised an opportunity to enter an unusual contest. The school saving the most metal strips from the covers of their coffee would be awarded a floor-model Philco radio. Miss Stapelton put the question to us, and we were all in favor; everyone loved a contest. She brought a large cardboard box to school in which to deposit the metal strips and placed it in front of her desk.

The coffee promotion was very similar to the bicycle contest. We enlisted the aid of our parents and all our relatives and friends. Every family in town had to switch to Nash Coffee whether they liked it or not. Fortunately, the contest ended shortly before Thanksgiving. Our room had saved over 1,500 strips, and two weeks later we were notified we had won. Shortly before Christmas our beautiful radio arrived. We were very proud of our accomplishment. One of the first programs we listened to was an ominous sounding speech by Adolph Hitler, translated into English. Until that day I had never heard of him, nor had any of my classmates. It was the first hint that I recall, concerning the possibility of war. Miss Stapelton felt it was important for us to be informed on world events.

We left Edgeley two years later. I've often wondered what became of our beautiful radio. Perhaps it's still around somewhere.

It was customary in Edgeley for the freshmen class to initiate seventh graders into the eighth grade. It was generally a harmless exercise as long as one cooperated, not so harmless if there was resistance, and worse yet if one tried to avoid it entirely. In the case of Robert Donegon, it turned out to be the latter. The day after initiation, Robert came to school with a three-inch wide strip of hair cut from the center of his scalp. He resembled a Mohawk Indian, except his scalp was shorn of hair down the middle, instead of on the sides. In addition, there were large chunks of hair missing from the back of his head. We all felt sorry for him after he spent most of one morning sobbing, his head buried in his arms, embarrassed at the way he looked. There had been an unsuccessful effort to learn the identity of the guilty students, but none came forward, and Robert refused to name those responsible.

—◆—

Old man Kipp was the only undertaker in town. He ran his undertaking business from the back of his jewelry store. When he finished embalming a body, he moved it out front for viewing by family and friends. If one happened into the jewelry store on business, it might become necessary to skirt around the open casket to reach the counter. The first time I saw a dead body was at Kipp's. A three-year old girl had accidentally fallen into a horse tank and drowned. Most of the kids from school marched through the store to see her, mostly out of curiosity. It was a sad and depressing sight.

The embalming room had both a window and door facing the alley. Donald and I happened along one evening after dark when the light was on, and we discovered that by climbing a tree next to the window that we could see the embalming table. I was the first to climb the tree to investigate. It was such a gruesome sight I nearly got sick to my stomach. When it came Donald's turn to crawl up the tree we apparently made too much noise, because, without warning, old man Kipp came charging out the door with some sort of club in his hand. It happened so quickly I didn't have time to shout a warning – only a half-hearted scream as I ran down the darkened alley. Fortunately, old Kipp's eyesight wasn't too good and he completely missed seeing Donald up in the tree. Despite our narrow escape, we returned several times over the summer.

For the most part, Donald and I maintained a good relationship. We did a lot of things together without having any major disagreements. There were times, however, when our friendship became a little strained. One of those occasions took place toward the end of the school year when we were marching from room to room viewing art exhibits. It began with Donald giving me a good-natured push, then quickly escalated into a shoving match. I finally turned around and landed a well-directed blow to his nose with my clenched fist. That took care of the situation for the time being, but I knew it wouldn't end there. The very next afternoon, Donald was waiting for me just off the school grounds. The minute I came within range, the fists began to fly. Early into the fight I heard a popping noise after he had landed a blow to my cheek. A giant goose egg emerged almost immediately just below my left eye. I thought I'd been seriously injured and went howling home with what later turned out to be a beautiful black eye.

A few days later all was forgiven, and we were once again the best of friends. We had other disagreements later, but none that were serious or long lasting, and we always managed to become better friends afterward.

There were two barbershops on the main street of Edgeley, one of which doubled as a poker room in the evening. Bill Brady was not only a good barber, he was reported to be an excellent card player. He and his friends gathered after dark one or two nights a week for a little game. Neither my friend, Corky, nor I could see what was going on inside, though we suspected it was something illegal. But through a small crack in the shade, Donald saw five men huddled around a table. Corky thought it would be interesting to knock on the window and see what would happen. We found out in a hurry. Two men bounded out the back door and almost caught little Corky.

That method of harassment was much too dangerous, so Donald suggested we tie a long rope to the door and bang it a few times from a safe distance. I rode home on my bike and brought back a ball of twine, which we soon had strung from the screen door to a location between two buildings across the street. After a few bangs, the same two men came running out. It was too dark for them to see the twine, causing some bewilderment. About the fourth time, however, they discovered the twine, and we had to run for our lives. Man, could those old guys move.

<hr />

During the summer months the town filled with people on Saturday night. There was little for kids to do unless one had money for a movie. Dropping water balloons from atop the cream station was a lot of fun, and it caught the attention of the country kids. It made them positively furious. As soon as one came within range, it was bombs away. It didn't take them long to locate our ladder at the back of the building. What they didn't know, however, was that we had a second ladder for making an escape. While they were coming up the one in back, we were descending near the front. It was a dangerous game, one where perfect timing was all important.

Once cold weather set in and snow began to fall, it was a totally different world. Winter was almost as exciting as in summer, with many interesting activities for kids my age. Most were related to school in some way. During noon hour we played "Tin-Can Hockey," much like regular hockey except we played with a tin can. Any old club served as a hockey stick. There were few rules and the game was fast and rough. After only a few minutes play, the can was reduced to the size of a golf ball. From the many bruises acquired I once ran a fever, the Donegon boys usually aimed for the shins.

Town kids weren't allowed back inside the school after lunch until the bell rang at 12:55 P.M. This was especially irritating after the temperature dropped to below zero. To vent our fury over this disagreeable rule, we bombarded the front door with snowballs. The janitor was an ill-tempered little man with a bad limp, an imperfection that didn't improve his disposition in the least. When the noise from the snowballs became intolerable, he would pop his head out the door and yell for us to stop, shaking his fist for added emphasis.

What happened next was a miracle of sorts. I had lobbed a good-sized snowball high in the air at the precise moment the janitor's head popped out. He got as far as "you boys," when, SPLAT! — a direct hit, right on top of his bald head. The door slammed shut just seconds before an additional volley of missiles landed. When the bell rang, we were ordered to the assembly and subjected to a stern lecture from the superintendent.

All was not fun and games; there was plenty of work to be done, especially in winter. A particularly disagreeable task, one I hated the most, was cleaning the clinkers from inside our furnace and carrying out the ashes. Of course, most winters there was plenty of snow to shovel, both at home and at the cream station. That was in addition to all the other snow removal jobs that Donald and I competed for around town.

It seems that every kid, at some point during their lifetime, takes a job selling papers, and I was no exception. The Sunday edition of the *Minneapolis Star Journal* was a popular paper, nearly an inch thick, and it sold for ten cents a copy. Ten cents doesn't sound like much today, but in 1938 it was a lot of money. My commission for each copy sold was three cents. If I managed to sell my entire allotment of forty papers, I made $1.20. That rarely happened. I regularly sold about thirty-five papers, but then I had to deduct from my commission the losses incurred by people who never paid.

Every Sunday, regardless of the weather, I began my route right after we returned from church. If the snow was quite deep I hauled the papers inside an apple box on my sled, otherwise I used a wagon. After serving my regular customers, I'd hang around the restaurants, hoping to sell any that were left.

A few of my customers were disagreeable deadbeats and some were just plain mean, but most were honest and friendly. Mrs. Davis lived a lonely life in a tiny brown house two blocks up the street, the third customer on my route. She was quite elderly, perhaps in her middle eighties, and I considered her my good friend. It seemed as though the major event in her life was when I came with the Sunday paper. She always insisted I come inside to rest or to warm up in winter, while she rummaged about the pantry in search of a cookie. Then there were always a few small chores for me do, such as taking out the ashes, filling her coal pails in winter, and running some little errand in summer. It occurred to me to be a calculated plan to keep me there as long as possible. I was happy to help her; she seemed so frail, and was always so appreciative. Once I had finished the chores, she made an extensive search for the ten cents, generally paying in pennies, counting them into my hand one at a time, as though they were pieces of gold.

It was little wonder then, that when she died the next spring I was overcome with grief. Not since the loss of Sandy had death affected me so deeply. Perhaps it was the interest she had taken in me or her always inviting me in to warm up in winter. Whatever the reason, I took it very hard, and it was a long time before I could walk by her house.

Convinced I needed it in my business, I made the mistake of buying a bicycle on the installment plan. My weekly payment left little money for any other purpose, such as for movies or candy, and nearly cured me from ever charging anything again. The bike was black and white with a headlight, a horn, and a small compartment for concealing valuables, which I don't recall ever using. I hadn't had the bike more than a couple of months when I suffered a terrible accident. It was always a challenge to see how far I could ride with my eyes closed until one day I was nearly killed when I strayed off the road and hit a culvert. In addition to my bruised body, the bike suffered significant damage. The fork was bent so badly it took a garage mechanic to repair it. I decided to ride with my eyes open thereafter.

One of the regular customers on my paper route was Mr. L.H. Brown, owner and publisher of the *Edgeley Mail*. He was the father of the famous movie star, Angie Dickinson, known to us back then as Evangeline Brown. I seldom saw Mr. Brown, but when I'd deliver the paper, Angie and her sister were usually playing on the long stairway leading to their apartment. They were born in the small town of Kulm, but grew up in Edgeley.

My first love affair was with a girl down the street named Mardell. She came each year to spend the summer with her grandparents. I nearly wore out my bicycle riding past her door, making sure my hair was always neatly combed, and that I had on my best looking pair of trousers. While I did manage to stop and talk to her a few times, I was too shy to stay long.

Summer was a time for revival meetings. I'm not sure of the denomination, but the first week in July my friends and I watched as a large tent went up on a vacant lot near downtown and prayer meetings were scheduled every night for the next two weeks. There was a stage at one end where the minister did his preaching. It was there that those most recently saved would join him. We watched the proceedings through a small opening near the back. The services were quite different from any we had seen before, so we naturally viewed them with suspicion.

There were two ministers, both attempting to preach at the same time, like they were having a contest. One was young and handsome, while the other was old and balding. It was fascinating watching the women, especially those on stage, hollering "Hallelujah!" and "Amen," then swooning into the arms of the good-looking young preacher. Even at my tender age this appeared to be a little unorthodox. While the young preacher seemed sincere and tried his best to avoid them, there was little the poor man could do short of letting them fall to the floor.

Once the women had reached the frenzied stage, their "Amens" grew closer together. It was at this point that Donald, unbeknown to Corky and me, had pitched a three-inch magnum firecracker inside the tent. When it exploded there was immediate pandemonium. People were yelling and running for the exit, trying to escape what they must have thought was "Armageddon." I was caught completely off guard, and while attempting to flee the area, I accidentally tripped over one of the ropes anchoring the tent. Donald and Corky got away, but I was held firmly in the grip of a muscular churchman. Once the smoke had cleared and order restored, I was escorted inside and made to listen to the balance of the sermon. I had no choice in the matter. As soon as no one was looking, I made my way out the exit.

⇒◇⇐

That fall, Mom took us to LaMoure for a day at the County Fair. My attention was directed toward a tent where a barker was introducing a professional boxer. It was announced that he was taking on all comers. Anyone able to last three rounds would be paid the grand sum of $10.00. By the time I had my ticket and got inside, one victim had already succumbed to this young, experienced fighter. But there was another challenger in our midst determined to win the money. Homer Gibbons was the town bully, a Saturday-night brawler. He removed his shirt and stepped brazenly into the ring. Never in my life have I witnessed such a beating. By the end of the second round, poor Homer had been knocked senseless and was covered in blood. His relatives had to drag him from the ring. That was the day Homer received his well-deserved comeuppance.

⇒◇⇐

In late November of 1937, Terry was almost two years old when he came down with pneumonia. He was a very sick little boy, and the doctor warned us he might not live. Mom wanted to take care of him herself, so we kept him at home. He lay in his small bed for days hovering between life and death, both eyes were stuck shut with a brown, syrupy-looking matter. We took turns swabbing his eyes with boric acid water and applying cold compresses to his forehead.

Finally, after a three-day vigil, and for the first time since he had become ill, his eyes began to open, and he showed the first real signs of recovery. It took several weeks for him to regain his body weight, but with

Mom's excellent care and us kids hauling him about the house, he soon returned to normal.

—=>·◦·<=—

Early one spring Mom had me out digging horseradish. It was growing everywhere out near the garden and was always best when little green shoots first began to appear. After helping her make a few jars, I came up with an idea I felt was a sure-fire winner, the "horseradish business." I was all enthused and began digging at once, three pails full. That was the easy part. I gathered all my meager resources and bought the other necessary ingredients: sugar, salt, and vinegar. By the time I'd finished grinding up all those roots, there wasn't a tear left in my entire body.

The rest of the family was skeptical. They could envision a supply of horseradish lasting several years. What a bunch of doubters! As a matter of fact, it turned out to be my most lucrative business venture since I'd been in the beer- and pop-selling business. My first batch yielded about fifteen pints. At twenty-five cents a pint, it sold like hot cakes. By the time I finished my third batch, I was rolling in money.

My good fortune wasn't to last, however. As soon as Donald Donegon heard about my success, he began his own horseradish business. In addition to that, he undersold me by five cents a pint, undermining the entire operation. The town was pretty well saturated by then anyway, so I was content with the money I'd already made. Donald went into it in a big way, as usual, and was left with a sizable inventory. Toward the end he was offering a free comb with every jar.

—=>·◦·<=—

The Mathson boys from out in the country drove a nice little Model T Ford to school. Every kid in town admired that car, and we were all a little jealous. One afternoon, while they were on a field trip with a crop-judging team, Donald and I decided to take their car for a little spin. They wouldn't be back for two or three hours, so we had plenty of time. A key wasn't necessary to start it, so Donald did the cranking while I managed the controls.

We took turns driving down a country road, but we had driven less than a mile when we became frightened and decided to turn back. I'm not sure if Donegons' owned a car or not. If they did, Donald sure hadn't learned much. In his attempt to turn around he somehow got into the ditch and we couldn't get out; the car just didn't have enough power. In a panic, I ran back to town for help. After being assisted by three classmates, we got the car back on the road and arrived at the school just in time to be welcomed by two angry Mathson boys. They threatened us with all sorts of bad things, including jail, but in the end they let us off with a warning never to do it again.

⟾⟾◆⟽⟽

Philip was afforded many privileges that did not extend to me, such as being allowed to take the car for a drive and to stay out later at night. This led to some resentment on my part, but I learned to accept it without a great deal of protest. The folks had no idea where Philip and his friends went; they mostly accepted whatever story he gave them, and it was usually a good one prepared well in advance. As I mentioned earlier, Philip fraternized with older people, including girls. While still an eighth grader, he began driving to LaMoure on school nights to visit a girl. I don't know how, but Dad discovered she was several years older than Philip, and a divorcee to boot. In desperation he wrote the woman a letter pleading with her to break off the relationship, pointing out that Philip was still in grade school and staying out nights interfered with his homework. The love affair came to an abrupt end. Philip was furious, but he soon got over it.

I devised a method for getting the car that worked like a charm so long as I exercised good judgment and limited my driving to early afternoon, a time when the folks were unlikely to be going anywhere. I learned to copy Dad's handwriting so well Mom couldn't tell the difference. When conditions were right, I'd write a note requesting her to give me the keys, saying I was to deliver the car to the cream station. It never failed, though I was careful not to overdue it. After buzzing around for half an hour or more I'd return home and park in the usual place, with no one the wiser. For fear of discovery, I never offered to take anyone along, and I never got caught.

———⇒•⇐———

In the late summer of 1938, Barnum and Bailey Circus was coming to Jamestown, forty miles north of Edgeley. Carl Wilkie was handing out free tickets to some of his customers, and because he liked me, I was given two. My folks refused to go, so I had less than a week to find a way to see the biggest circus in the country. I scoured the town, asking all my friends if they were going, with no luck.

The Midland Continental Railroad ran a daily freight train between Edgeley and Jamestown, up one day and back the next. If we could ride the train to Jamestown, I was confident we'd be able to bum our way home. At that point I was considering asking the conductor for a ride in the caboose. While I was weighing the feasibility of doing that, my friend Corky came by. He too wanted to take in the circus but hadn't the vaguest idea how to get there or how to get home. We walked to the depot where the train was about to leave. We had to decide quickly. In a moment of bravado I marched up to the conductor and asked for a ride. He promptly ran us off the premises, shaking his fist and warning us to stay the hell away. What an ornery old bastard he was.

We weren't licked yet, however. The moment he looked away we crossed to the opposite side of the track and walked back along the train. Luck was with us, and we came upon an open boxcar with six or seven bums inside. We told them of our encounter with the conductor, and one of the older men invited us in, offering to hide us if anyone came by.

Ten minutes later we were on our way, too late to change our minds. One of the great shortcomings of my character, at least up to that point in my life, was my inability to consider consequences. My primary focus was getting to the circus, and I gave little thought about how we were going to get home. My dad used to call that going off somewhere "half-cocked."

The trip was tiresome, hot, and mostly uneventful. We stopped at every station along the way, so it was late afternoon when we approached the outskirts of Jamestown. We stayed out of sight toward the back of the boxcar as much as possible for fear of being discovered, and some of the bums didn't appear too friendly. I was afraid to ride the entire way to the depot, so when the train stopped at a switch, Corky and I thanked the bums for their help and bailed out. We were about a mile from town, and it was an additional two miles to the fair grounds. Our feet were hot, and we were dirty and thirsty. I had fifty cents, but Corky, naturally, didn't have a red cent. We cleaned up the best we could, had a bottle of pop, and made our way to the giant tent, just in time for the evening performance. What a spectacular circus! It was well worth the effort we had made to take it in. We would have enjoyed it even more had we not had to worry about a ride home.

It must have been at least ten o'clock when we emerged after the final act, and it was totally dark. We scanned the crowds of people coming out, hoping to see a familiar face, with no luck. Shortly thereafter, the very real possibility dawned on me we might be stranded. Corky was absolutely no help at all — in fact, he was more of a hindrance. He had no money and no ideas. It would have been significantly simpler had I been alone. Having given up on getting a ride, we walked the two miles back to town and I made a collect call home. To my surprise, Dad didn't seem too angry. He gave me the address of some people he knew that might put us up for the night.

We were unsuccessful in locating the friends Dad had told us about, and though it was early in September, the nights were getting chilly. Walking along Main Street we passed the Pulsher Hotel. It looked like a nice place, so we decided to go in with the idea of sleeping in the lobby. At least we'd be out of the cool night air. We had just sat down when I recognized the night clerk, a former teacher from LaMoure. Once I explained our predicament, he suggested we take a room and Dad could pay for it when he came to pick us up. Both of us were exhausted, so we slept until late the next morning. Dad didn't show up until mid-afternoon, and he found us wandering around in front of the hotel. He paid for the room, three dollars, and said little about the circus or anything else. The curious aspect of the entire episode was that Corky's parents never missed him. His mother was an alcoholic and his father unemployed. There was always some question as to the identity of his biological father. Corky was short, almost a midget, with curly brown hair. His brothers were all six feet tall with dark hair.

＝＞•◦•＜＝

"Turkey Days" was the most exciting time of the year at the cream station. North American began buying and processing turkeys just prior to Thanksgiving, usually in late October, and this went on for several days. It took a lot of work and manpower. Dad hired both men and women, most of them local farm families. There were openings for turkey-stickers, scalders, and pickers. Women did the picking for five cents a turkey, the rest were paid twenty-five or thirty cents an hour. The entire basement of the cream station was utilized for this operation, giving it a carnival-like atmosphere. There were as many as fifty or sixty people employed. The pay wasn't great, but most were grateful for the opportunity to make a little extra money before Christmas; and it was great fun, at least for me.

To give the turkeys a finished look, I was given the job of wrapping the heads in wax paper and stacking them on pallets in an outer room to cool. I wasn't paid for the work I did, but I didn't mind.

The turkeys remained on the pallets until Lee McCann picked them up on his way to the plant at Oakes; there they would be readied for distribution to various parts of North Dakota, South Dakota, and Minnesota. I felt really important during this time because my Dad was the boss.

During "Turkey Days," local merchants bought dozens of live turkeys and released them, one at a time, from the roof of a store on Main Street. Those lucky enough to catch one had a free bird for their Thanksgiving dinner. I felt sorry for the turkeys, however, since while some flew quite well, others crashed headlong into the buildings on the opposite side. Two city blocks had been cordoned off earlier in the day, and the street was full of people. Every time a turkey was released the crowd went wild. There was pushing and shoving and an occasional tug-of-war, with the poor turkey in the middle. Even a few fights broke out. In later years, that part of the festival was discontinued.

⇒·◇·⇐

Once or twice a year, the big bosses from Oakes made an unannounced inspection of the cream station. One such visit came during the summer of 1939. Lee McCann, the truck driver, had been staying over night in Edgeley twice a week. It was the midpoint on his route, and he was paid an allowance for expenses. But due to their long friendship, and Lee's large family, Dad gave him permission to set up a cot in the basement of the station, thus allowing him to pocket the small amount he received for lodging, which, of course, was strictly against company rules.

By the time the inspection team arrived it was too late to remove the cot, and it didn't take long for them to figure out who was sleeping there. They may have suspected something, or another employee may have tipped them off. In any case, when Dad was confronted with the obvious, he tried to minimize its importance, pointing out Lee's struggle to provide for his large family. A.B. Carlson, the boss of North American, was in no mood for excuses. I wasn't present to see what actually happened, but by piecing together conversations in subsequent years, I concluded Dad had lost his temper, threw the keys to the station on the floor, and stormed out the door. That ended his long relationship with North American.

Of course Mom was angry and worried — what were we to do? There were five children to feed and clothe and no pay check. She became gloomy and depressed. It was curious how little it seemed to affect us kids. I was completely oblivious of the magnitude of our predicament, and yet I recall an indistinct feeling of discomfort, knowing something dramatic had happened.

Ernie Engel had sold his dairy business in LaMoure and taken a position with the Kidder County Farm Security Agency in Steele. On his way there, he stopped to visit Dad. When he learned of our plight, he suggested we move to Steele where an elderly man named Anderson was looking for someone to lease his hotel and café. I'm not sure, but I think Dad had been toying with the idea of moving back on the farm.

That was his ace in the hole in the event he ever lost his job. With little or no savings, however, that seemed out of the question.

We packed up and were on our way to Steele two weeks later, without the help of either Lee McCann or the North American truck. It was to be an experience we wouldn't soon forget.

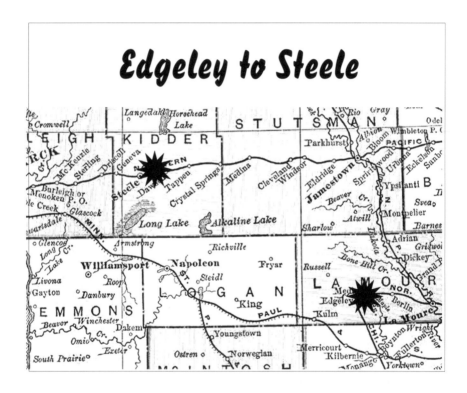

Chapter VI

An Adventure in Steele

IT WAS LATE SUMMER OF 1940, and I had entered my sophomore year at Steele High School. Growing older seemed to make it easier to accept change. I wasn't nearly as concerned about moving as I had been while still in the grades. Steele was a nice town, slightly smaller than either Edgeley or LaMoure, but with plenty of things to do, and close to Bismarck, the state capital.

The brick exterior on the front of the Grand Pacific Hotel belied a dilapidated interior, which was all but falling apart. It needed extensive repairs, in addition to cleaning and painting. We were happy to have a roof over our heads and food on the table, but none of us had the least idea how much work lay ahead to make this business successful. Our location just across the street from the courthouse was a major asset.

Grandma Larson and my brother, Terry,
out back of the G.P. Hotel in 1940

That gave us access to all the personnel working in the county offices, in addition to those having business to transact.

Grandma Larson wrote that she would be glad to come and help, so we immediately drove to Marion and brought her back to stay with us. Both Grandma and Mom were excellent cooks, so in just a short time business picked up substantially. The hotel boasted a large dining room, an adequate hotel lobby, and a small lunch counter in front. The Lion's Club met each month for dinner, which was good for business. This wasn't going to be a gold mine, but it had starvation beat. Dad signed a one-year lease and paid Mr. Anderson at the end of each month. Unfortunately, by the time the bills and rent were paid, there was little money left.

Everyone pitched in and did their part. We hauled out junk, repaired the furnace, painted rooms, scrubbed floors, and did everything else that seemed urgent and necessary. There were bed bugs in some of the rooms and cockroaches in the kitchen. We fumigated and sprayed and did more fumigating. Before long, we had six or seven rooms that were freshly painted and bug free. This was during the days when there was a community bathroom at the end of the hall, and each room had a dry sink with a pitcher of water and a wash bowl. Rooms rented for $2.50, $3.00, and $3.50, depending on size and condition. Those with bed bugs were only $2.50.

Cockroaches were the big problem. The principal reason they were almost impossible to eradicate was due to our grocery suppliers. They had them in the warehouse and brought more in with each delivery. Dad tried every conceivable method to rid the place of those pesky creatures without success. Cockroaches, however, are allergic to light, so they make themselves scarce during the day; but once the lights were turned off at night, they were everywhere. If one turned the lights on after they'd been off for a while, literally hundreds would scurry for cover.

One terribly embarrassing incident regarding those god-awful cockroaches happened one afternoon when a group of well-dressed, elderly tourists stopped in for lunch. After their meal, each one ordered a piece of Mom's delicious apple pie. After serving the pie I had started for the kitchen when one of the women called me over. I walked to their table with a concerned look on my face, hoping I hadn't forgotten something important.

She looked up at me and said, "There is something on my pie!" I took a look but didn't immediately see anything. Then she raised her long, bony forefinger and pointed to the syrupy part along the crust. There, in deathly repose, lay the granddaddy of all cockroaches, a real monster. I stood dumbfounded, my mouth hung open, but no words would come out, and my face got redder and redder. She finally said in a quivery little voice, "Young man, just bring me a different piece of pie." What a relief! Mom had been watching through the window in the kitchen door but didn't know, until I showed her, what all the commotion was about.

When her eyes focused on that big cockroach she screamed, "Are you completely blind, why didn't you see it?" I immediately asked why she or Grandma hadn't seen it when they cut the pie and put it on the plate. Grandma stood back with her hands on her hips, murmuring to herself. We laughed at that most embarrassing experience long afterward.

Friday and Saturday night I had to work until all the customers had been served, usually around nine o'clock, after which I could join my friends. On one particular Saturday night we were busier than usual. I remember it well because a classmate of mine came in for a hamburger about the time I was ready to leave. He had on a beautiful light blue suit and was planning to attend the dance at the town hall. I noticed he was having trouble getting the ketchup out, so in my impatience I decided to help him out. I gave the bottle a good slap, after which the front of his nice blue suit was covered with bright-red ketchup, and I got ready to run for my life. Even though I cleaned him up the best I could, he left in a huff.

When I was finally able to sit down and contemplate the sorry state of my life, hunger pains began gnawing at my insides. Then, like a thunderbolt from on high, an awesome thought came to me. I decided that for once in my life, I wasn't going to eat leftover food. Grandma had already retired for the evening, and Mom was busy cleaning up the kitchen. I marched through the swinging door with great bravado and called out, "One T-bone steak!" Mom seldom came into the dining area so I felt reasonably safe. I set up a place in the lobby, just off the dining room, not visible from the kitchen. All the time the steak was frying my mouth watered in anticipation. I had never eaten a T-bone in my entire life, though I'd served quite a few.

I had just taken a generous forkful of that delicious steak when there was an ear-shattering scream. "Robert!" Mom yelled, "what on earth are you doing?" The fear of God settled over me as I sat there with a large chunk of steak in my mouth, unable to answer. Maybe she was more surprised than angry. Fortunately, she got over it in a short while. Though tempted several times, I never tried that little stunt again.

The G.P. Hotel became a popular place to meet friends for coffee. The court house crowd were our best customers. And when court was in session even more people came for lunch and dinner. A full meal cost fifty cents, and for those that weren't too hungry, we offered a half-order for thirty-five cents.

Genevieve and I had to run home from school every noon, put on our aprons, and help out in the dining room. It was exciting, and I didn't mind the work at all.

⟨―⧫―⟩

Prior to our move to Steele, Philip had already fallen in love several times, or so he thought. After meeting Juleen Hanson, however, his previous girlfriends were soon forgotten. They both had been smitten by the love bug at the same time, and there was to be no recovery. Right from the start, they became inseparable, walking to and from school, arm in arm, every day. The minute he finished his evening meal, Philip retreated to the hotel lobby to begin an interminably long, whispered conversation on the telephone, which lasted sometimes for hours. His constant use of the phone often provoked serious arguments with the rest of the family.

Philip, David, and Dad behind the G.P., 1940

Each time Philip got into one of his long-winded conversations, Mom would mutter under her breath, "What on earth can they find to talk about all that time?" Thank God, shortly after Philip was inducted into the army, Juleen became Mrs. Philip Cunningham. She was a bastion of stability, which Philip sorely needed. Had it not been for her, his life would have been quite different, I'm sure. She was a welcome addition to our family.

Girls didn't play a significant role in my life while we lived in Steele. I did go out with one or two, but I wasn't attracted to any that I recall. There were more important things in my life right then. Shortly after enrolling in school, I renewed an old friendship with Billy Engel, whom I had known in LaMoure. We began spending a lot of time together when I wasn't working. Neither of us owned a car, of course, nor did we have access to one. As a consequence, we did a lot of walking and hitch-hiking. We often thumbed our way to Bismarck, narrowly making it home a couple of times.

Billy's parents were leaving on a train trip for a couple of days, so Billy and I immediately began making plans to take his Dad's car on a little trip of our own. We decided to skip school Friday afternoon to give us plenty of driving time. Dawson, eight miles east, was on our itinerary, since Billy claimed to know some girls there. The superintendent, E. J. Totdahl, lived just a block west of Engels, and we were deathly afraid of him. He had an almost perverse aversion to students that played hooky. For that reason, we wanted to make absolutely certain we didn't get caught. There was a gas station strategically located along the route leading to school where we were able to monitor each passing car. He was due back from his lunch break about 1:15, but when two o'clock rolled around and he still hadn't appeared, we began to think we had missed him.

Billy finally decided that, for some obscure reason, Mr. Totdahl must have taken an alternative route. We began walking furtively across the street to an alley, ready to run at the first sign of his car. The gods of chance were against us on this day, however. Midway across, Superintendent Totdahl came roaring around the corner from out of nowhere, nearly running us over. Clouds of dust mushroomed into the air as he braked to a stop. It was too late to escape, and we had but a few seconds to think up a plausible excuse for not being in school.

This guy was definitely psychotic. He was already screaming when he leaped from his car, demanding to know where we thought we were going. I was so scared I couldn't think of a thing to say. Totdahl was at least a head taller than I, and I was concerned that, in his anger, he might resort to violence.

Billy, on the other hand, was calm as could be. He took me completely by surprise as he related an astonishing story detailing all our plans for the afternoon. I was amazed as he described how we had intended to load up some of his Dad's goats and haul them to Dawson. It sounded like a reasonable story to me, but only seemed to infuriate Superintendent Totdahl, prompting him to grab both of us by the neck and fling us bodily into the back seat of his car. By this time, Totdahl's blood pressure was mounting, and his face was flushed with anger. The blood vessels in his neck were beginning to pulsate. Shifting into a forward gear, he let the clutch out with a bang, landing Billy and me against the seat with such force we didn't notice our classmate, Forest Hanson, sneaking across the road just a block ahead. When Totdahl spied Forest he became apoplectic — it was like he was going to explode.

The car slammed to a halt a second time. At this point, Totdahl was beyond asking for alibis. He threatened to, in his words, "parade us around town." The three of us were dumped at the front door of the school and ordered up to his office. Forest spent more time in that office than the superintendent. Well over six-feet tall, he was thin as a beanpole, and looked as though he might break into tears any minute. In addition to zeros, we lost some privileges as well. The goat-hauling episode was soon forgotten, however, and we moved on to more glorious endeavors.

⟫◆⟪

Early in June, Dad had received a letter from our former parish priest in Edgeley, asking if he would hire a wayward girl for the summer. Two weeks later, Caroline came to live and work as a waitress at the G.P. She was a happy-go-lucky girl but for some reason, her parents were unable to keep her on the straight and narrow. She was a good worker, and everything went fine for the first few weeks. It was suspected sometime later, however, that she was having an affair with a young man rooming at the hotel. I doubt that Dad knew, but it was common knowledge among us kids that Caroline and this guy were a little too friendly.

Genevieve and a friend, Ruby Merkel, decided to do a little detective work in order to determine the exact nature of this illicit affair. The meeting between Caroline and her paramour generally took place early in the evening. The two detectives slipped into her room and hid beneath the bed. After spending an hour all cramped up, they were finally rewarded with the sound of footsteps and laughter. Then came a lot of small talk and giggling, but none of the heavy stuff they had suspected. Caroline must have heard movement beneath the bed. She leaned over and looked directly into Genevieve's face. Caroline demanded to know what they were doing. Genevieve answered in a weak voice, "Just resting." It was the only explanation she could think of on such short notice. A week later, Dad returned Caroline to her home, and she was never heard of again.

I loved the excitement at the G.P. Banquets and special dinners kept us busy throughout the holidays. And, of course, waiting on table had some benefits. During the tourist season there were occasional small tips, but seldom more than a nickel or a dime. Local customers never tipped, so I always kept an eye out for people that looked like travelers. On my most successful day I amassed a small fortune of thirty-five cents, a tidy sum in 1940.

Even with extra kitchen help and an additional waitress, working seven days a week was taking its toll. Such a pace could not last indefinitely.

⋙◆⋘

In mid-summer of 1940, Philip and I went to work for a farmer from near Napoleon named Nels Stukey. Mr. Stukey was elderly, or at least he appeared so to me, perhaps because of his snow-white hair. His wife was in a rest home after being seriously injured in an accident, and he needed help on the farm. In retrospect, it seems likely that he was looking more for companionship than anything else.

Philip was hired for fifty cents a day, and I for a minuscule twenty-five cents. I don't recall how we got into this predicament, but shortly after arriving, we decided someone had made a dreadful mistake. Here we were, nearly forty miles from home, living with a complete stranger, and the money not exactly piling up. Philip worked in the field with Mr. Stukey, and I was delegated to be the maid and cook. The first week was a disaster. I knew nothing about cooking, so the principal fare was soup and sandwiches. In an effort to please them and to demonstrate my culinary ability, I decided one day to surprise them by preparing something special. From an old cookbook I stirred up a batch of baking powder biscuits. Unfortunately, I forgot to add the most important ingredient, "baking powder." When I took them from the oven they resembled undernourished golf balls and were hard as rocks. Nels was very patient and understanding, however, and settled once again for soup. Philip complained about my cooking, but there was little he could do about it.

When Saturday came, Nels drove to town to visit his wife and stock up on groceries, mostly bread, breakfast food, and canned soup. It was a serious mistake not taking Philip and me along. As soon as the breakfast dishes were done and the place tidied up a bit, I was on my own. For lack of anything better to do, Philip had been out cranking up the old McCormick-Deering tractor, fully intending to take it for a ride. It had huge, steel-lugged wheels and was not exactly suited for joy riding. Top speed was three or four miles per hour, but when one is going wide-open in a tight circle, it seems much faster. I hung on for dear life while the inside wheel dug a huge crater in the earth resembling the crash site of a UFO.

A few days later Nels discovered the odd-shaped craters and was completely baffled. If he ever figured out where they came from he never said, and we were certainly not about to provide any explanations.

Dad and Billy Engel drove down to see us the middle of August in Engel's 1935 Ford coupe. Just a few miles from town they hit loose gravel, went into the ditch and tipped over. They both escaped serious injury, but the car was a total wreck. Philip and I didn't hear about their bad luck until Dad came to get us a week later in the 37 Chevy. We packed up our belongings and said goodbye to Nels, for whom we had grown quite fond. I think he learned to like us too, and he seemed genuinely sorry to see us leave.

On the way home Dad told us, quite casually, he was thinking of moving back to the farm in the spring. It was like a bombshell. Philip and I were taken completely by surprise. We contemplated the impact of this news in silence for the remainder of the way back to Steele.

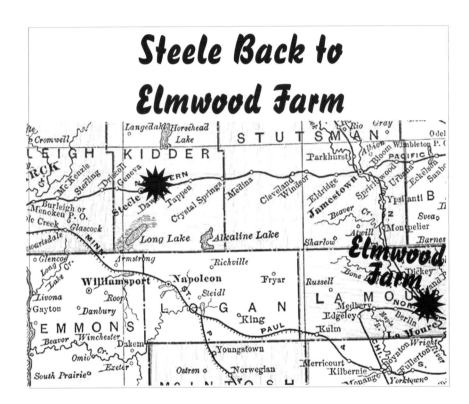

Chapter VII

Elmwood Farm

HEN MY FATHER FIRST SUGGESTED WE MIGHT MOVE BACK TO THE FARM, I wasn't convinced he was serious. But as the days and weeks went by, such talk became more urgent, and I listened more attentively. The most illogical aspect of such a move was our complete lack of resources. It would have surprised me if my parents had more than two or three hundred dollars in the bank. Dad didn't believe in saving for a rainy day. Without machinery or livestock, such a venture seemed risky at best. We didn't have the ability to plow a garden, let alone a field.

I must admit, moving to the farm had an appealing ring to it. But Dad was almost fifty years old and about to embark on a venture that would require excellent health, unlimited stamina, and more importantly, money. The hotel and café business, however, was not a realistic alternative for the long term. In any case, the die was cast, and it was only a few months until our lease was up. Realizing there were hard times ahead, I began saving every penny I could lay my hands on.

A Hungarian family named Zokema had been renting the farm for several years. They liked living there and were reluctant to leave. Dad nearly had to call the sheriff and have them evicted. Finally, the last of April they moved out.

Beginning with the first weekend in May 1941, Dad and I began making a series of weekend trips to the farm, taking with us as much as we could pack into the 37 Chevy; tools, cleaning supplies, extra clothing, food and bedding. The house was in dreadful condition. It smelled bad and was downright filthy. The walls were dirty, there were holes in the linoleum, and all the window shades were missing. The bathroom, just off the kitchen, hadn't been functional for years. But instead of hauling water from the well for bathing, Zokemas had used the tub to raise baby geese and chickens, leaving straw and feathers everywhere. Mrs. Zokema had apparently helped with the fieldwork at the expense of her household chores.

To see this beautiful home in such a state was positively demoralizing. We spent half a day just getting the old kitchen range cleaned up; it was full of soot, ashes and grease. Dad didn't want Mom to see how the house had deteriorated since the time they had lived there following their marriage. Once the windows were washed, the shades up, and a new kitchen rug put down, it began to look habitable. Rural electrification wasn't available yet, so we had to rely on kerosene lamps for lighting. When nightfall came, we made our beds on the floor. I thought it was exciting, sort of like camping out.

The distance from Steele to the farm was roughly one hundred miles and required some three hours or more to get there. Highway 10 to Jamestown was paved, but beyond that it was washboard gravel. We'd pull off the road near some trees to eat our lunch, never stopping at a café. Dad talked at length along the way about his years growing up on the Cold Spring Farm. The more he talked, the more convinced I became that we were doing the right thing. Admiration for my father increased substantially during those trips; his tremendous optimism was both encouraging and reassuring.

We had hired a truck for the bulk of our furniture and had borrowed a two-wheel trailer for the small items, especially those that would be needed immediately upon arrival, such as eating utensils, bedding, towels, water pails, etc. In addition to all that, we had along a box of fifty baby chickens that everyone took turns holding onto. The trailer was overflowing with incidental pieces of furniture tied down with binder twine. Half way to Jamestown, people passing us kept pointing frantically at the trailer. I pulled to the side of the road to investigate and found the ball of twine had jiggled out of the trailer and was bouncing along a half-mile behind us, one end still tied to an old chair. With a face sticking out every window, our entourage must have resembled the family of Ma and Pa Kettle.

Everyone gave a sigh of relief when the last of our worldly possessions had been carried into our new home. Elmwood Farm was such a beautiful place one couldn't help but love it. We were surrounded by tall elm, ash, and cottonwood trees. The James River, with an abundance of trees on either side, ran close by the house. At daybreak, we were awakened by the gentle cooing of morning doves. To this day, whenever I hear that mournful call, I am reminded of the farm.

One of the Shockman boys came to our place just a few days later and plowed our garden with a walking-plow and team of horses. Dad built a dock out into the river from which we could fish, and our neighbor, and Dad's old friend, Bill Lawson, lent us a milk cow. We named her "Blondie" because of her giant white head. She gave us a pail of rich milk twice a day. Without a doubt, Blondie was our salvation. We not only had all the milk and cream we could use, but plenty of homemade cottage cheese and butter as well. We treated Blondie like a queen.

A week later, Dad came home with a baby pig we named "Emily." We put her in the barn from where she escaped the very first night. Being so tiny, leaving the barn door open just a crack was all she needed. The entire family gathered to conduct a search, but there were so many weeds near the barn it became an impossible task. We were all depressed over our loss but Dad gave us a ray of hope. If we left the barn door open she just might come back. Philip and I rushed out early the next morning, and there she was, inside the barn waiting for something to eat. She soon became a family pet. During her lifetime, Emily gave birth to fifty or sixty baby pigs.

She had the run of the farm, so we paid little attention until one day we couldn't find her. I thought she may have fallen into the river and drowned, but Dad seemed to think she had gone somewhere to have her latest family of baby pigs. A few days later, while walking after the cows, I thought I heard grunting noises near an old straw pile. Emily had burrowed deep inside and had eleven little babies at her side. She was a gentle mother and raised them all.

The years 1940-41 brought an end to the drought that had plagued much of the country during the Depression. When the rains finally came, they lasted for days, falling gently over a wide area. It was an enjoyable experience going to the attic, listening to the raindrops being whipped against the roof by an occasional gust of wind. Then, when the sun came out, there was beauty everywhere. During the rains, our barn stayed nice and dry, providing a cozy home for Emily, Blondie and our fifty chickens.

With the end of the drought came the prospect for improved crops, and Dad was anxious to get our fields seeded. He drove to LaMoure and applied for an FSA loan, which was approved in record time. It was a meager amount, however, with many mindless restrictions. For example, we were prohibited from buying a tractor. Instead, we were required to buy horses and horse machinery, mostly from farmers that were hastily converting to mechanized equipment. That regulation placed us at a terrible disadvantage, and seriously affected our ability to succeed. If it hadn't been for our neighbors and the beginning of better times, we would have failed miserably.

The old methods of farming were familiar to Dad, so we plugged along the best we could. It was demoralizing, however, having to plow a field with four horses on a gang-plow while our neighbor across the river covered four times the ground in half the time with his tractor and three-bottom plow. The only thing that sustained me those first two years was the fact that I loved working with horses, although some we had could be better described as "nags."

Dad took on a plowing job for a neighbor in exchange for the use of his tractor, and we both shocked grain and hauled bundles that fall to earn extra money. Back then, most grain was cut with a binder, which tied the grain into bundles, dropping them in neat rows to be gathered up and placed in round shocks for curing. After a few weeks, the shocks were loaded into hayracks by bundle-haulers and pitched into a threshing machine. It was hard work, but I looked forward to that time of year. The threshing crew Philip and I worked on that first fall went from farm to farm until school started. The only time we had to catch up with work at home was after church on Sunday and on rainy days. During threshing season, meals were nothing but the best, and it wasn't unusual for the women to bring us lunch both morning and afternoon. The long days and hard work kept us continually hungry.

The second year, and for several years afterward, I hauled bundles on a threshing rig owned by our neighbor, Shorty Seefeldt. He and his wife were always good to me, and I liked working for them. They owned a large farm with a bunkhouse for the men just a mile north of Grand Rapids. Our bundle crew generally walked the mile into Grand Rapids every evening for a little entertainment, mostly to drink beer and play cards. The Else brothers, however, always refused our invitation to come along, so on our way home one night we decided to play a little trick on them, sort of retribution for being nonconformist. In reality, the Else boys had more sense than the rest of us, opting for a good night's rest instead of carousing in town.

We crept into the bunkhouse shortly after midnight in our stocking feet. Then, with great fanfare, we lit the lamp and pretended to be dressing, preparing for another day of hard work. Since it was always dark when we arose, and there were no clocks, our plan worked to perfection. The Else boys jumped from bed, dressed, and hurried to the barn to feed and harness their horses. The minute they left, of course, we went to bed.

No one knows how long it took before they discovered they were victims of a fiendish prank and that it was actually only a little after midnight. The next morning we complained about the noise they had made tramping around in the middle of the night. The Else boys, however, never said a word.

Elmwood Farm

By the end of August we were milking about a dozen cows. None except Blondie gave much milk. Though most cream-checks were small, they were an enormous help to my parents. The money I had saved was long gone, and there were few jobs available after harvest. Philip and I suffered from serious financial hardship, but we soon devised a plan to remedy that situation, a plan whereby we could raise enough money to at least cover the bare necessities of life, such as candy and smoking tobacco. We tied a rope to a small cream can and hung it from a branch overhanging the river, where it remained out of sight in the water below. Each time we separated, a small amount of cream was added to our can. In no time at all we had accumulated two or three gallons. Payday was at hand! An old burlap sack served as an inconspicuous means of transporting our ill-gotten goods to town via our old mare. Philip rode in front and I in back holding the sack. Ludwig Amundson, owner of the store, didn't seem at all suspicious and promptly wrote us a check, which we cashed on the spot, dividing the proceeds.

Delighted with our initial success, we looked forward to the next trip, which we reckoned to be the next Saturday. But we had failed to take into account the fact that our sister, Genevieve, was home for the weekend. She eyed us suspiciously as we mounted up, trying our best to conceal the sack. When she challenged us and we were unable to come up with a reasonable explanation, she gave Mom a full report. That evening, our scam quickly unraveled and we made a full confession. Genevieve reveled in the fact that it was she who had found us out, much to our chagrin.

In the fall of 1941 we began school in Grand Rapids. It was my junior year, and Philip was a senior. David and Terry were in the grades and Genevieve went to Marion High School, rooming with Uncle Connie and Aunt Amanda. The Marion school offered a more extensive curriculum, and Mom wanted Gen to have a good education.

After graduation, Philip spent most of his time away from home. One summer he worked on a sheep ranch near Bowman and later for a farmer near LaMoure. This was a suitable arrangement so far as he was concerned. He disliked milking cows and being under the watchful eye of our parents. After that first year we seldom saw him; he came home only when he happened to be in the immediate vicinity.

———◆◆◆———

Adolph Hustman was a typical small-town school janitor who took his job a little too seriously. One noticeable flaw in Adolph's personality was his inability to find anything the least bit humorous. That became an invitation to make him the brunt of our dirty tricks. Adolph was a big man with a giant bump on top of his bald spot. When he stood near the open stairway, he became a perfect target for an eraser attack from above. In the event of a direct hit, especially on his bump, he would treat us to his rendition of the bull-elephant mating call and then come charging up the stairs.

Commodities were just beginning to be introduced into the public school system by the government, supposedly to promote a balanced diet. First to arrive at our school was fresh squash. Mrs. Hustman prepared a huge kettle full, enough for the entire town. Though it was completely lacking in taste, we were expected to eat it, without even the most basic seasoning. We simply couldn't get it down, and the entire batch had to be thrown out, except for one small portion.

Donald Axelson, a studious and unpretentious upper classman, took that one small portion and deposited it in a neat pile just behind the ping-pong table which stood propped against a far wall in the assembly room. Then a suitable supply of toilet tissue was placed alongside, after which we held our noses and hollered for Adolph. Adolph's face turned several different shades of red while he shuffled about waving his hands in the air. He could even smell it himself. Before cleaning it up he threatened us with all sorts of disciplinary action, demanding to know the perpetrator of this vile act. It hadn't occurred to him that it might be a joke. Most of these shenanigans took place during the cold, stormy days of winter, when we had to remain indoors with little to do.

Our school received a shipment of apples the middle of December. They were kept in a closet in the basement where there was less chance of them freezing. It was Adolph's job to hand each student one apple every other day. He had great difficulty with this task due to his lack of mathematical skills. Some students were given two apples while others went without. To compensate for this inequity, we went to the basement during noon recess and helped ourselves. Then, to aggravate Adolph, we'd deposit the cores in a pile on the basement floor.

After a few days of helping ourselves, Adolph announced with a wide smirk, "That monkey-business with the apples is at an end!" Then with a key he'd gotten from the superintendent, he locked the closet door. The very next day, however, one of our classmates brought a skeleton key to school and we once again helped ourselves to an apple, depositing the cores on the floor. Adolph was furious, and with great fanfare reported this depredation to the superintendent, after which an unsuccessful search was made for the skeleton key.

On our trip to the basement the next day we found that a hasp and padlock had been installed above the door lock. This required a more innovative approach in order to get in, but nothing a screwdriver couldn't handle. In no time we had the door off its hinges, and more apple cores were piled on the floor. To say that Adolph was angry just doesn't do justice to the frightful bellowing we heard after he discovered the closet had been breached once more.

It was pretty well known to Adolph which students were responsible, so when we arrived at school the next morning, he announced in his customary, overbearing manner, "Well boys, no more apples for you, I've got you this time!" When the noon bell sounded, we all rushed to the basement and were appalled to find hasps and locks on both sides of the door, with absolutely no way of getting in short of bashing the door down. We weren't quite licked yet, however. I ran to the store for a sack of apples, and after eating them we deposited the cores in the usual place. As soon as we had returned to class, Adolph made a beeline for the basement. The echo from those basement walls could be heard all over the school. "Jesus Christ! How did they do it?"

A week or two after the apple incident, Keith Johnson brought some firecrackers to school, and lit one in the basement. The noise created by that explosion reverberated throughout the entire building, causing a furor among the faculty. Keith was called into the office almost immediately and punished. Our classmate, Calvin Fossen, was believed to have been responsible for his almost immediate apprehension.

Keith was a genius of sorts; he could make almost anything related to explosives, all with his small chemistry set at home. Still smarting from his recent punishment, he came to school the next week armed with a twelve-inch fuse attached to a huge firecracker. We got together and arranged an elaborate ruse, coaxing Calvin to the basement. The timing of the explosion wasn't perfect, but close enough for Calvin to be caught racing up the stairs two steps at a time. He convinced the Superintendent he was the victim of a conspiracy, but not before he was roughed up by Adolph.

To say that our sister Genevieve was out of touch with farm life was putting it mildly. One Friday afternoon, right at milking time, David and Terry were sweeping out the haymow in preparation for the new hay crop. The noise was deafening and Genevieve, on one of her rare visits to the barn, asked what it was. I explained that, due to a shortage of space, we kept some of our cows upstairs. She was a little skeptical, however, and said, "I guess I'll go up and see."

The next afternoon Gen volunteered to help shock grain, but in spite of our warning, she insisted on wearing shorts and a halter-top, just in case some neighborhood boys might stop by. Thirty minutes later she was covered with dust and barley beards and nearly in tears. After we rushed her home, she decided to stay within the confines of the farmyard.

Philip and I regularly engaged in milk-squirting fights. But the cows he milked seemed always to be located at just the right angle, placing me at a distinct disadvantage. As a consequence, I always got the worst of it, with the result that my face and body got saturated with milk. There was one spot, however, where I was able to get even, and that was when he milked the cow next to mine. At the appropriate moment, I'd grab my cow's tail and whip it against the back of his head. "Make your cow quit that!" he'd whine. I insisted it was the flies. I'd wait a few minutes and then let him have it again. It was the only time I ever came out on top, but I didn't dare tell him.

———•◦••◦•———

The first two winters on the farm we couldn't afford to buy coal. Fortunately, there was a vast supply of timber along the river, and we took full advantage of it. Even on the coldest days, whether a holiday or not, we had to hitch a team of horses to the lumber wagon and head for the woods. When it was extremely cold, Dad would build a fire of brush and small branches while Philip and I sawed down trees that were either dead or dying, mostly cottonwood. We preferred ash, which was not too plentiful, because it burned longer and hotter and was especially useful for banking the fire at night. Dad was skilled with an ax, so while he trimmed a felled tree, Philip and I were kept busy sawing the larger logs into manageable lengths with a two-man crosscut saw. Dad enjoyed reminding us of the old adage that "one is warmed twice by every piece of wood — once when it is cut, and once when it is burned." I still have nightmares about running out of firewood during a winter storm.

In order to stay warm on the way home, we took turns driving the horses. While one of us drove, the other two walked. The most difficult job still lay before us, that of sawing the logs into lengths we could split with an ax. That first winter we went for wood about every other day, including Thanksgiving and Christmas. But by the second year we were able to afford a load of coal over the holidays. Sometime later Dad bought a circle saw powered by a 6-HP stationary engine. Then, in one day, we were able to saw enough wood to last a week or longer.

———•◦••◦•———

In late spring of 1942, just before school was dismissed for the summer, several classmates and I were on our way to a school picnic. Calvin, Lenore Carson, I, and another girl whom I can't recall, were in the back seat engaged in conversation, happy the school year was nearly over. Calvin, always the great lover, cuddled up to Lenore for what he had hoped would be a romantic interlude, casually putting his arm around her neck. That seemingly innocent act became the catalyst for what happened next. Lenore turned abruptly and slapped his face so hard it sounded like a bomb going off. We were all shocked at her explosive reaction to what seemed like a mostly innocent gesture. The camaraderie we had been enjoying ended in a stony silence while we watched Calvin's face turn different shades of red, except for the imprint of Lenore's hand, which remained a brilliant-white for several minutes. It was one of the few times I felt sorry for Calvin.

Few people visited the Grand Rapids Memorial Park during the middle of the week, so I and my friend, Billy Wilson, felt perfectly safe going for a swim in the nude, as we had done on many previous occasions. Lenore Carson lived with her parents on the Cold Spring Farm, just a stone's throw away. Billy and I were splashing about when, from the corner of my eye, I noticed movement on the riverbank behind us. I looked up just in time to see Lenore running away with all our clothing tucked beneath her arm. Billy remained submerged, but I scrambled up the riverbank in full pursuit. We were both running full-speed when she looked back. When she saw me, perhaps thirty feet behind her, she let out the most blood-curdling scream I'd ever heard and threw the clothes high in the air. Then, in an incredible burst of speed, she vanished over the next little knoll. At a class reunion, some fifty years later, I was surprised when she whispered confidentially that she'd always had a crush on me. That's when I recalled how she had slapped Calvin's face.

———◦•◦•◦———

Our old mare was the most aged animal on our farm, maybe in the whole country. Her legs were stiff and she had difficulty moving faster than a trot. My brother, Terry, and his second cousin, Larry Jorve, spent one whole summer walking her up and down the fields and around the farmyard. She seemed perfectly content with both of them on her back, moving at her own pace.

Larry was a quiet boy, not given to doing or saying anything that might be considered controversial, except for one time. His mother received a telephone call one afternoon from the school superintendent asking her opinion of the hot-lunch program. She was somewhat mystified and replied she had no knowledge of the program whatsoever and therefore wasn't able to express an opinion one way or the other. "Well," the superintendent said, "that's a little strange since your son, Larry, is circulating a petition demanding better food." She couldn't understand it; Larry had never eaten hot lunch in his entire life. When he arrived home later, he explained to his mother that his friends from the country had told him the food was real bad, so he decided to take action.

———•••••———

In winter, regardless of the weather, we were required to walk the one-half mile to school, despite the fact the bus went directly by our farm. It was a relatively short walk and we didn't mind except on days it stormed. The Hennings family, however, lived quite a distance away, and it was dangerous walking on cold, wintry days. Delores Hennings, still in the lower grades, usually took a shortcut through our pasture. One winter day, without warning, a snowstorm came up shortly after she had left home. Several hours later Mom heard scratching at the door, and when she opened it, poor little Delores fell in on the kitchen floor nearly frozen.

———•••••———

Friday night was dance-night in Grand Rapids. People young and old came to attend from miles around. Late in the afternoon, Philip and I began rushing around in an effort to get our chores done early so as not to miss any of the fun. Philip agreed to go after the cows while I did the feeding. When he decided to ride the old mare, however, I argued against it, reasoning that it would be infinitely faster on foot rather than herding that arthritic old nag all over the pasture. The more I tried to dissuade him, the more determined he was to ride. He leaped on her back and started down the lane, spurring her on with a barrage of kicks to her flanks. Instead of speeding up as he had anticipated, she came to a sudden halt. Then, with great effort, she gave a little buck, just enough to send Philip flying headlong to the ground. He was stunned. How had that old crow-bait managed to unseat a veteran horseman like himself? He jumped to his feet with a bad case of horse-rage and began chasing her around the barnyard, yelling some pretty bad words all the while. Incredibly, no doubt fearing for her life, she somehow managed to out-run him.

I watched this scene unfold from the open barn door; it had any rodeo beat I'd seen up until then. Philip finally brushed the dirt and manure from his trousers and headed for the pasture on foot. What had made him so angry was the fact I had witnessed the whole thing. A little short of breath, the old mare shuffled to her stall like she'd just won the Kentucky Derby.

On dance nights, one could enjoy the entire evening for as little as fifty cents. Admission to the dance was a quarter, unless one waited until intermission, after which they quit charging. A glass of beer cost a dime, no identification required. In fact, few people bothered with a driver's license back then because getting one was too expensive.

Roy Morrell owned and managed the Grand Rapids Saloon, right next to the dance hall. Aside from his duties as a bartender, he was the village barber. A small section of the bar had been partitioned off for that purpose. One needed a strong stomach to sit through one of his haircuts, however, because Roy both belched and farted the whole time, sometimes managing to do both simultaneously. After a medical consultation about this embarrassing malady, the doctor told him he was a human dynamo with gas on his stomach and electricity in his hair.

Roy was an interesting man and generally well liked. He kept a violin behind the counter which he brought out when the mood struck him. The sounds he made more closely resembled a cat fight out behind the barn rather than any recognizable musical number. In spite of that, we encouraged him to play, mostly because it was so comical. Before long, the audience would become hysterical, and the concert would end abruptly.

Dad's old friend, "Wild Bill Lawson," lived with the widow, Melitta Hennings. I never did figure out the relationship between them and was too embarrassed to ask such a personal question. We put up hay with Bill and worked with him on other jobs. I often went by his place on my way to a piece of land we owned nearby. He and Melitta raised chickens and turkeys and milked a few cows on their small farm. Bill was plagued with chicken hawks carrying off his young turkeys, which, for lack of a better place, roosted in the trees at night. Vowing to end this depredation, he stood guard early one morning with his double-barrel shotgun. When the hawk came swooping down, "Wild Bill" blasted away. The final tally: zero chicken hawks, fourteen turkeys.

Bill's neighbor, Harry Kolberg, had a similar bad experience. Several dogs, including his own, had banded together and were attacking his sheep. Harry made the mistake of calling on "Wild Bill" for assistance in ridding his farm of those killers. Bill brought along his trusty double barrel, and the two of them drove to the pasture. It was yet another disaster — the only dog in the pack to get shot dead was Harry's prized German Shepherd.

Harry was a farmer and homegrown veterinarian. Above all, he was a good neighbor. He did have one peculiarity, however, that set him apart from what one might characterize as the more refined people of the community. This oddity manifested itself one summer afternoon while Dad and my brother David were visiting Harry and his wife out in their barnyard. During the conversation, Harry nonchalantly unbuttoned his pants and urinated, right in front of everyone, including his wife. He kept right on talking as though nothing unusual was happening. Dad and David were flabbergasted; they gave each other an embarrassed look and tried not to notice. They could hardly wait to get home to tell about this bizarre incident. In spite of that little episode, Harry was a good, honest person, and I liked him.

As the economy improved, demand for furs increased dramatically. Prices were good and there was an abundance of mink, beaver, raccoon, and other fur-bearing animals along the James River. Dad bought a few dozen second-hand traps and we set up a trap line. A good Beaver pelt brought between $35 and $50, and we had trapped five within just a few weeks. The first winter we took in the incredible sum of nearly $400, a tremendous help in supporting our family.

Checking the trap line each morning was exciting. When both Dad and I went, and the ice was thick enough, we drove the car. Otherwise I went alone, sometimes on skates if there wasn't too much snow. In just a short time I became a dedicated trapper.

—•◦•◦•—

Our well water was quite hard, and Mom complained it didn't get the clothes clean. So in winter she made us cut chunks of ice from the river and melt it in a copper boiler. Even on the coldest days she washed clothes out in the well house with our gas-powered Maytag. She made her own soap from rendered lard and lye. It was great soap for washing clothes, but it would burn the skin right off your hands. Cutting ice proved costly, however, as we were soon to learn.

By the middle of March winter gave way to signs of spring. The snow began melting along the warmed north side of the riverbank, making it an inviting spot for Emily's grown offspring to root for grubs. We had quite a few hogs that spring and planned on keeping about half for breeding purposes. It had not occurred to us they might wander out to where we had cut the ice. Then one afternoon tragedy struck. Eight full-grown hogs broke through and drowned. Since they were ready for market, it represented a substantial loss.

Dad cautioned us not to mention this tragic event to Mom. Things were bad enough without burdening her with the knowledge of such a loss. One important lesson I learned on the farm is to "never count too heavily on anything." It can be snatched away in an instant. Spring is a time of renewal, however, and it was just around the corner.

By the end of March, ice on the river began melting in earnest. And a few days later, from the heat of the sun, one of the drowned pigs popped up through the thinning ice. It was clearly visible from the kitchen window, and Mom asked what it was. Dad answered truthfully, but evaded the extent of our loss. Then, a few days later, two more pigs popped up. By now, Mom really became alarmed, so there was no more skirting the truth. By the end of the week all eight had emerged from their watery grave. It was a depressing sight, and we were sickened by it, but life goes on.

—•◦•◦•—

Toward the middle of April, water from melting snow up north was pouring into the James, causing it to rise at a rate of more than two inches an hour. Three days later the river began pouring over its banks, placing our buildings and livestock at risk. A thick, impenetrable fog settled over the entire valley. It was eerie waking up to a deathly stillness, except for the cooing of morning doves. Two days later, water was lapping at the edges of our barn and other outbuildings and only inches from our outside cellar door. Dad monitored the constant rise with a stick at the water's edge. We were soon surrounded by an enormous lake which had already inundated most of the adjacent farmland. We couldn't sleep nights worrying whether we might have to evacuate in a hurry.

Dad and I drove our cattle east along the road to the safety of the upper pasture. There was a wide expanse of deep water separating our farmyard from the ascending edge of the pasture hills but not more than a few feet over the roadway. Once the cattle and horses were safe, we hauled the sheep and calves in a grain wagon, one load at a time, to a neighbor's barn some four miles distant.

Returning from our third trip we watched in horror as a dramatic scene unfolded before us. All our cows had left the high ground and were swimming back toward the barn. Halfway through the deep water, Blondie got her leg caught in the wire of a submerged fence. She thrashed about for several minutes before finally freeing herself. We continued to watch helplessly as they swam through the swirling water. Exhausted, Dad once again led them up the hill, one cow tied behind the wagon, while I brought up the rear on horseback. We drove them to the neighbor's barn where they joined the rest of our menagerie. The horses were smarter; they chose to remain where they were, well away from the dangerous waters below.

The next morning we filled a few sacks with sand and piled them in front of the basement door. By late afternoon the water level began to stabilize, and by early evening it appeared our prayers had been answered. Dad wasn't positive, but it looked to him as though the river had crested. We checked every hour and, indeed, there had been an ever so slight drop below his last mark on the stick. By midmorning of the next day the level had fallen an additional two inches. We all cried for joy.

The high water remained far above flood stage for some time, restricting our visits to town. The road between our place and the bridge was under four or five feet of water, and the only way through was on horseback. A week later we made it with a team and wagon, but that entailed a degree of risk due to the strong current and huge chunks of floating ice. Only Dad and I were allowed to make the trip. I had a frightening experience a day later that nearly cost my life.

⬥⬥⬥

Roy Morrell and his wife drove to LaMoure nearly every Sunday evening to take in the latest movie at the Roxy Theater. They encouraged kids my age to ride along in case of car trouble. I was tired of fighting the flood and needed a little relaxation, so early in the afternoon I threw a bridle on Jane, our one-eyed mare, and rode to town. She was a big horse and easy to ride, but I was reluctant to use her because of her missing eye, I wasn't sure she could see that well. The river had dropped some, but the swift current and floating ice still presented a significant danger.

It hadn't occurred to me until I reached the bridge on my way home that I'd have to confront the flood in the dark of night. There was no moon, and the road ahead was completely obscured by overhanging branches. I had traveled this road nearly every day without a second thought, but on this night it had suddenly become totally unfamiliar. I was alarmed by my predicament, but there was no turning back.

I stopped on the bridge, peering into the darkness, trying to get my bearings. But I simply couldn't visualize at what point the road angled to the right. Without a saddle it was even more dangerous, and I became all the more fearful. Right then I wished I'd stayed home. Summoning all my courage, I nudged Jane along, one step at a time through the icy current. Midway through the deepest part, I must have pulled her too far left, and we both plunged headlong into the deep ditch. Instinctively, I dropped the reins and grabbed for her mane, holding on for dear life. She began swimming, first with the current, and then back toward the road. Jane may have had just one eye, but she knew exactly where to go. Before I knew it we were in front of the barn.

My body was drenched and I shook uncontrollably, more out of fear than from the cold water. When Jane was safely in her stall I walked to the house, shaking like a leaf. Sensing something wrong, Mom and Dad got up and listened in disbelief while I told them of my harrowing experience. Jane was my special friend from that day forward. Had I given her free rein at the outset, I'm sure she would have taken me home safely without suffering the indignity of getting soaked and nearly drowning to boot.

Later that spring, Jane crawled through a fence and got mired down in a sinkhole. By the time I found her she had been missing several days and was up to her neck in a slimy gumbo. We managed to free her, first by digging, then pulling her out a little at a time with a team of horses. In her effort to escape, however, she had thrown a hip out of joint, and we were never able to use her again. It was regrettable and I felt sorry for her but there was nothing to be done.

A few days after my dunking in the James River, there was a knock on our door about 3:00 A.M. Harry Cuyper, a young man from the neighboring town of Dickey, desperately needed help. Due to a washout, it became necessary for him to cross our bridge in order to get his girl friend home. I harnessed a team of horses to a wagon, hooked a chain to his car, and pulled him safely through the flood waters. It was a moonlit night, and I didn't have a problem. Harry insisted on paying me, but even though I wasn't a close friend, I refused. He stuffed a bill in my pocket and when I got home I discovered he had given me $10.00, an enormous sum back then. Harry was a real gentleman. Unfortunately, he died while still a comparatively young man.

Two weeks later we brought our livestock home, and everything returned to normal. The river retreated to within its banks and by the first of May we hardly knew there had been a flood.

I'd known Teddy Skovgaard since we were kids; he was a neighbor and good friend. Billy Wilson's sister, Jessie, was his fiancee. Teddy owned a new Dodge car, which made him enormously popular with the

girls, especially Jessie. Owning a new automobile in 1942 was unprecedented in a small community like Grand Rapids. Jessie refused to go
anywhere with Teddy, however, unless they were accompanied by at
least one other person. Billy and I were often the beneficiaries of this
rule and were thus privileged to attend many movies and dances because of it. I suspect Jessie was more enamored with the car than she
was with Teddy. I made a point of being near the Wilson home on weekends. Then, when Teddy drove up in his new Dodge, Billy and I would
pile in and wait for Jessie to decide where we were going.

One Saturday night she decided on the dance at Berlin, eleven
miles away. After a few drinks, Teddy went to sleep in a booth, while
Jessie kept herself busy by dancing with all the young men. I don't recall
either Billy or Teddy doing any dancing that night, but I do remember
Billy sticking several matches in Teddy's shoe and giving him a "hot
foot." Believe me, it was hot too. While still sound asleep, Teddy's foot
began to shake, just a little at first, until he finally leapt up and began
dancing around the floor on one leg, holding onto the other. That unusual spectacle drew a crowd of onlookers and was extremely funny to
everyone except Teddy. Billy turned pale when he saw the anger on
Teddy's contorted face. Fortunately, Billy never became a suspect, nor
did Teddy ever learn the truth. Had he found out, Jessie or no Jessie,
there would have been serious consequences.

Later that same evening a fight broke out in the street just outside
the bar. The two combatants were really mixing it up by the time Sheriff
Carl Lindbloom arrived. Carl was a real gentleman and a great diplo-
mat who tried his best to talk a little sense into people. He ordinarily
had a lot of patience, but on this particular evening, it was wearing thin,
especially after the fight began to escalate. Carl's average size and even
temperament belied a side to him few people knew about. With lighten-
ing speed he grabbed the two fighters and threw them into the back of
his car.

That would have likely ended the affair, except for the ill-conceived
benevolence of one "Buck" Kempler, who kept insisting one of the
fighters was innocent and should therefore be set free. Buck was well
known in LaMoure County, having once served as a police officer himself. The sheriff listened to his pleading for a few minutes, then pointed

out that he, Sheriff Lindbloom, was in charge, and he alone would decide who was or was not going to jail. That little speech didn't seem to
register with Buck, who kept right on agitating. Then, in a flash, Carl's
beefy arm shot out and grabbed Buck by the collar. "I've had enough of
you!" Carl yelled, "you're going to jail too," whereupon he threw Buck
in with the others.

Then everything quieted down, the crowd dispersed, and Sheriff
Lindbloom left town with his prisoners. I saw Buck the next day, and he
laughed as he told me how the sheriff had let them out down the road,
telling them they'd likely be sober and less in a fighting mood by the
time they walked the nearly three miles back to town.

Recalling the beautiful summer nights of our youth.

In Summer

The days drift by – as ships drift out to sea
Morning, high noon, twilight's tranquility.
And then – the peace the honeyed evening brings
With the large moon and old rememberings.

Old memories, old raptures, old desires,
Old joys return, and youth's immortal fires;
Old loves that still around the spirit lie
And whisper of long Summer days gone by.

O rapture of the world that crowds tonight
About my soul, and brings back lost delight,
Bid me farewell when the last stars awake,
Or else my wounded heart will break, will break!

Charles Hanson Towne

The Big Flood of 1942

Elmwood Farm after the water began to recede

The Northern Pacific train plowing through water
a mile south of Grand Rapids

LUDWIG AMUNDSON'S STORE was the second most important business in town, ranking right behind the pool hall. Students with money to spend walked the two blocks to the store nearly every noon. Even without money, it was a welcome diversion from school, especially in winter.

The expression on Ludwig's face never changed, like it was etched in stone. He was a six-foot five-inch mustachioed giant, thin as a rail, with a large, bony frame. His trousers were always too short, the hem being four or five inches above his shoes. And he could cover the entire distance up the aisle of his store, about a hundred feet, in a dozen strides. Ludwig neither laughed nor smiled, nor did he speak unless you asked him a direct question. Yet, I always felt comfortable in his presence. He was an honest and upright man that went out of his way to be accommodating.

Mrs. Amundson was a sickly woman, short and plumpish, completely devoid of personality. I can't recall ever hearing her speak. Most days she sat propped in a chair near the heat register. A giant St. Bernard lay beside her slobbering saliva on the floor about her feet. She had one facial expression, which resembled that of a child sucking on a fresh lemon. I remember Ludwig best for his absolute devotion to her. He catered to her slightest wish; all she had to do was raise her hand, and he was there in a flash.

Near the front of the store was a long glass display case containing a wide assortment of bulk candy. Atop the case was an antique brass scale with a candy scoop. A favorite trick was to stick a few wads of well-chewed gum on the very end of the balance lever. Then one would be rewarded with a considerably greater portion of candy for the same amount of money. Ludwig became suspicious one day and shook the scale a few times. The gum fell off on the counter, and that was the end of our bargains. I expected him to explode in anger, but he never uttered a word, and his expression never changed.

Bill Shiek was another of the many characters living in Grand Rapids. He was a gruff old man who had worked hard all his life. He lived in a small, two-room shack behind the saloon. After he grew old and senile and unable to take care of himself, his nephew had him committed to the Jamestown Hospital, commonly referred to back then as the State Insane Asylum. Some weeks later the same nephew went for a visit and found that his Uncle's health had improved dramatically. He listened attentively as Bill exclaimed about the wonderful food, how clean the beds were, and how he had been working really hard out in the barns. Then, just as his nephew turned to leave, he quickly added, "But they don't pay nothing!"

———◆•◆•◆———

We had a rubber-tired wagon for hauling manure from the barn. My younger brother, Terry, wasn't quite old enough to help, but he enjoyed riding along. After climbing a small tree below where I was unloading, he began questioning my marksmanship with the pitchfork, doing so in a somewhat derogatory manner. After putting up with his taunting for several minutes, and just meaning to scare him, I hurled a forkful of manure toward the tree. It sailed through the air, and then, "Whap!" A direct hit. His face and glasses were covered with fresh cow pie. I was immediately sorry for what had happened and cleaned him up the best I could, promising him all sorts of things in order to redeem myself. That didn't end the earsplitting howling, however, which continued all the way home. It was weeks before he would come with me again.

———◆•◆•◆———

With the onset of World War II, rationing became a way of life, and it became increasingly difficult to acquire many of the things we were accustomed to having, such as, sugar, soap, butter, gelatin, toilet tissue, and a host of others. New automobiles, trucks, tires, batteries and tractors were unavailable, unless you could prove a compelling need and able to get your name on an eligibility list. Since we didn't own a tractor, Dad received a permit to buy one, and luckily, we became first in line. The International Harvester dealer in LaMoure was a good friend of my parents. He confided to them that a new "M" International tractor was expected any day, and that it would be ready for delivery soon afterward. It is impossible to put into words the excitement we felt, when a few days later, we were told to come in and sign the papers.

The big day arrived, and I was given the great honor of driving that beautiful machine home. It was the single most thrilling trip of my life. How proud I was. The "M" had a road gear capable of traveling fifteen or sixteen miles per hour, but I was careful not to go more than ten. In addition to its other attributes, it had lights and a starter. We soon became the envy of the entire neighborhood. The first thing I did was get some wax and give it a good shine. We had been elevated overnight into the modern age; no longer would we be forced to rely on horsepower to do our farming.

People began driving by just to get a look. The Shockman boys came over and wanted a demonstration. The youngest boy, Mickey, and my brother, Terry, had been riding around the yard on an old four-wheel dolly behind one of our horses. The dolly had been designed for moving heavy objects and was low to the ground with small, swiveling wheels at each corner. To test our tractor's agility, I suggested they tie their rope to the front and I would give them a nice ride by backing in a circle. Mickey, anxious to be first, climbed aboard and I began backing. In an instant, the dolly became airborne. In that brief moment, while trying to get shut down, all I could see was Mickey's little round nose, two big eyeballs, and his hair flying straight back in a jet stream. When he couldn't hold on any longer and had to let go, he shot through the air like a human cannonball, narrowly missing the corner of the barn. After he landed in a cloud of dust, I was certain he'd been killed or at the least seriously injured. By the time I got to him, however, he was on his feet dusting himself off. The whole episode took less than one or two minutes.

As the war progressed, the draft took more and more boys from around Grand Rapids. Dad and I had been fixing fence near the Hennings farm when Melitta's only son, Ashley, walked over to where we were working. He showed us his draft notice and said he would be leaving the following week. Ashley was a handsome boy about nineteen years of age. He had a husky build and beautiful, brown wavy hair. He was reluctant to leave home and apprehensive about going into the army. His voice trembled with emotion as he shook hands and said good-bye. It was the last time we ever saw him. He was killed six months later. James Shockman, Kelly's older brother, enlisted early on and was also killed in action. The war was taking its toll.

Philip graduated from high school in 1942 and was classified l-A by the draft board. He was called up a short time later. After basic training, he was transferred to Camp Claiborne where he married his high school sweetheart, Juleen Hanson. After he left for overseas, Juleen returned to Steele where she and her sister-in-law, Verna Hanson, took over operation of the family newspaper, the *Kidder County News*.

Scenes from Elwood Farm

My brothers, David & Terry, on the "M" International

Billy Engel (left) and the author on top of the hill at Elmwood Farm

*P*HILIP'S CLASS WAS THE LAST TO GRADUATE FROM GRAND RAPIDS. The school board had decided to discontinue high school with little warning to those affected. If we wanted to continue our education it was up to us; we were on our own. With little money and no car, I decided to work as long as I could that fall to save enough to finish high school the following year in LaMoure.

When work at home slowed, I spent much of my time at the Mike Shockman farm. Mike had a large family, but most of the older children were married with families of their own. Kelly was in my grade and a life-long friend. Whenever I stayed with him I helped with whatever work there was around the farm, like I was part of the family. One day we were repairing the pasture fence with the help of a school friend, "Squeaky Larson." A yearling steer kept nosing around, getting in our way and licking on our jackets. Trying only to scare him away, Squeaky took a hammer and tapped him between the eyes. We were all stunned when the steer slumped to the ground dead as a mackerel. Squeaky got so scared he jumped up and ran for home. We called Mike, and he butchered the steer.

Later that fall, Kelly and I were helping his dad put up a stack of hay two miles from the farm. When we had finished stacking, Mike decided to take a load home. Kelly and I hitched the loaded hayrack to the tractor while Mike crawled up and nestled down inside the hay. Kelly drove while I hung on behind, both of us laughing and joking along the way. When we reached the end of the field, Kelly turned the corner a little short, tipping the entire load into the ditch. We thought Mike had been killed, but he soon crawled out from beneath the hay, spitting and spluttering. At that moment I knew we were in big trouble. Once he got his breath he came charging toward us with a pitchfork, bellowing like a mad bull, and we had to run for it. A few minutes later he calmed down and we began to salvage what we could.

Kelly and I went somewhere nearly every weekend. If I couldn't use my parent's car, Kelly, or someone else, usually found a way. As a last resort we'd take Mike's old pickup, a 1932 Chevy with no side windows and nothing but bare springs for a seat. On the way home from a dance one Saturday night, the engine quit and we had to walk about five miles. The temperature was close to twenty-five degrees below zero. Luckily, there was no wind. Transportation was always a problem. We were never able to make any definite plans so far as dating girls since everything depended on the availability of a car.

The Anderson brothers, Curly and Roger, had pooled their money and bought an old Hupmobile. It may have been old, but it was one beautiful car. They were driving to the little town of Marion to a dance one night and invited along all their friends, including Kelly, Philip, Bill Wilson, and me. Four of us were on a crew to help a neighbor thresh flax the next day, so we had planned to leave for home shortly after midnight. For some unexplained reason — even to this day — Kelly took the Hupmobile and left town, abandoning the rest of us in Marion. We spent the night in the dance hall with no heat. Two sisters that owned the hall stayed with us, more concerned about the safety of the building, I'm sure, than for any charitable reason. If it hadn't been so cold it might have been fun. Fortunately, we caught a ride to Grand Rapids the next afternoon, but the threshing job had to be postponed until the following Monday.

❖◦◦◦❖

After spending a weekend with Kelly I came down with a mysterious rash that caused considerable anguish for me, my family, and later some of my relatives. The disorder in question was formally diagnosed as "scabies." Kelly had mentioned something about it but I hadn't imagined it was anything too serious, perhaps just the result of coming in contact with some noxious weeds. I soon learned differently. Within a few days I had it bad and soon passed it on to my entire family. Next, I gave it to Larry Jorve, my second cousin from Marion, and he promptly gave it to all his family. Everyone was so busy scratching there was little time for anything else. Eradicating that appalling itch took an enormous amount of time and effort, not to mention the monetary cost. On orders from our doctor, we had to boil all our clothing and bedding daily for a week — this in addition to smearing our bodies with gobs of a vile-smelling salve. One can imagine the work involved ridding ourselves of that miserable affliction, especially considering our antiquated method of washing clothes. We finally got over it, but I wasn't very popular for a long time thereafter.

———•◦•◦•———

To supplement the family income and to help with the expense of sending my only sister away to college, Mom began teaching at a nearby country school. Dad and I were home alone much of the time after that. I didn't mind, except both of us were lousy cooks. Fried eggs, sandwiches, and homemade cottage cheese made up the bulk of our diet. Mom generally took the car, so if Dad and I needed to go somewhere it became a logistical nightmare. We helped with the housework to the extent possible, but the bulk of the work awaited Mom's expert hands, and we were mighty glad when the weekend came.

In 1943 she was offered a substantial salary increase to teach a school near Jud, about twenty miles west of Grand Rapids. None of us foresaw what a burden it was going to be, especially for my mother. She suffered unimaginable hardship that winter. Due to the distance and poor roads, it was necessary for her to live at the school from Sunday evening until Friday afternoon. Mostly for company, she took along my youngest brother, Terry. Though only five years old at the time, he has vivid memories of the loneliness and deprivation. Mom had to haul coal for the stoves, take out the ashes, pump water, sweep floors, and prepare their meager meals. Friday was an intolerably long day, especially for Terry. In late afternoon he'd climb to a small loft and watch for Dad. In spite of all this, I never once heard my mother complain. It had been her decision and that was final. Genevieve repaid those many sacrifices after my father passed away by inviting Mom to live with her. That is where she wished to be, living the remainder of her life with the one she loved the most, her only daughter, Genevieve.

———•◦•◦•———

In the fall of 1943, Vincent Christ and I rented a room at a boarding house while we finished our senior year at LaMoure High. Vincent and I had been classmates together in Grand Rapids. The only redeeming feature of my association with "Vince" was his 1932 Chevrolet, an indispensable asset on weekends, Vince, however, soon lost interest in getting an education, and he did not attend classes on a regular basis. He missed a lot of school and constantly urged me to do likewise. It was a serious temptation at times. While I was off to school each morning, Vince would often remain in bed, sometimes until noon. He received an unsigned diploma at graduation, and I didn't have an easy time of it. Three girls living at our boarding house may have been an inhibiting factor.

It was somewhat more than a year earlier that Vince and I had been hired by his Uncle Fred to shock a field of grain. Vince was a heavy-set, muscular boy, but lazy. He loved resting so much he made a career of it, using the flimsiest excuse to sit down. If he wasn't resting, he was either getting a drink of water or eating a portion of his lunch. We were both sitting behind a shock of grain talking when I began to feel somewhat uneasy and decided it was time to get busy. I should have made that decision a few minutes earlier, for when I stood up, there was Uncle Fred standing not more than three feet behind us. He gave me a terrible fright, and I hurried back to work. Vince, however, still hadn't seen him, and he kept right on blabbing away as though he had all the time in the world. That's when Uncle Fred yelled, practically in his ear, "get to work!" It was like Vince had been struck with a cattle prod. He leaped to his feet and ran to the next row, nearly knocking Uncle Fred over on his way. Fred never said another word. He just shook his head and walked away.

—•◦•◦•—

One Saturday near the middle of December it had turned bitter cold with a light snow falling. That afternoon, Kelly Shockman and I put on our fancy clothes and caught a ride to LaMoure where we planned to take in the dance that evening. Others from Grand Rapids would surely be coming later, so we weren't concerned about a ride home. The dance never really got going good until after ten o'clock, so we planned to spend most of the afternoon and early evening at Witt's Pool Hall. I didn't know it right then, but for me, at least, that night would end in disaster.

The pool hall was crowded, with scarcely room to turn around. Every time the door opened a blast of frigid air would come rushing in, causing the place to steam up like a Turkish bath. In addition to that, the place stank of spilled beer and stale tobacco. The only restroom had but one stool and sink with barely enough room for one person at a time. One look inside was enough to make a person sick. The stench of urine was so powerful it made one's nose hairs tingle. The wall and floor were soaked, an indication aiming wasn't a high priority.

Despite the fact I was facing an emergency, there was no way I could stomach that terrible smell. So I slipped on my topcoat and ran across the street to the restaurant. It too was full of people, and the restroom had a waiting line. By then I had reached the panic stage. In desperation, I grabbed a few napkins and ran out behind a billboard just around the corner — not a second too soon.

The wind was blowing hard, and I nearly froze. After returning to Witt's I had to fight my way to the bar. Once I had warmed up, the guy to my right began sniffing the air, complaining about a terrible smell. I paid little attention until the person to my left noticed it too. A minute later there was a chorus of voices hollering, "Who in hell stinks in here?" I began to smell it myself. When it dawned on me who it was I could feel my face turn red.

I had no choice now but to make a dash for that terrible restroom, trying my best to look innocent. In assessing the damage I discovered it was a case of carelessness. In that moment of extreme urgency, I had accidentally gone on the tail of my coat. There would be no dancing for me that night. I removed my coat and cleaned it the best I could, exhausting the supply of soap and towels. All the time I was cleaning, people kept banging on the door, demanding to be let in. My evening was turning into a nightmare.

Thank God there were no further complaints, even though I wasn't convinced the smell was completely gone. By then, almost everyone in the pool hall had left for the dance, leaving me to languish alone. Near midnight I walked to the restaurant where I waited for the dance to end.

The time dragged, and the weather hadn't improved. Kelly finally came in about 2:00 A.M. with bad news. He hadn't seen one person from Grand Rapids, most likely due to the weather. Back in late September we had stayed the night in an abandoned granary, but now it was below zero and storming. In addition to our other problems, Kelly had spent all his money, and I had but a paltry $3.00.

Just across the street stood the old Windsor Hotel. We soon contrived a plan whereby I would rent a room for the customary $2.50 for a single, and Kelly, after a respectable wait, would join me. That would leave fifty cents for a modest breakfast in the morning. Our plan looked good on paper, and initially it was a success. Old man Hunt, the night clerk, appeared half-asleep most of the time, and it was doubtful he'd know what was going on.

Sunday Mass wasn't until 11:00 A.M., giving us plenty of time for a light breakfast. Afterward, we could ride home with our parents none the worse for wear. Everything was working out well; I took a hot bath, got dressed and paid Hunt the $2.50 on my way out. Pulling the wool over his eyes was much simpler than I had anticipated. Once again Kelly was to wait a few minutes before strolling casually out the door.

After a good night's rest I felt rejuvenated. I crossed the street to the restaurant in good spirits, sitting at the counter awaiting Kelly before ordering. Ten minutes passed, and he still hadn't arrived. I began to feel a little uneasy, it was taking longer than planned. After another five minutes I went for a look across the street. My God, I could see Kelly at the window beckoning like crazy, with Hunt's arm clearly visible around his neck. To save us from jail, I ran to the hotel and liberated Kelly with my last fifty cents. We went to church hungry, a suitable punishment for trying to outwit old man Hunt, whom, as it turned out, was smarter than we had thought.

Vince usually stayed in LaMoure on weekends, so every Friday after school I had to search for a ride home. One miserable cold and windy afternoon in April, I ran into Mike Shockman. He offered me a ride, but only if I'd steer his little John Deere tractor home while he towed it behind his car. I was dead wrong to think it would be a simple task. Mike drove like a crazy man over the washboard road without once bothering to look back to see if I was still there. I waved, hollered and screamed, trying desperately to get his attention. Several times I was nearly thrown from the seat. I was tempted to jump more than once as the tractor bounced back and forth across the road like a "jumping jack." When at long last we pulled into his yard, I was frozen stiff and could barely loosen my fingers from the steering wheel. It was the most terrifying ride of my life, and I considered myself lucky to be alive.

Not owning a car was a distinct disadvantage, especially when dating girls. My parents were always generous letting me use the Chevy, but that was of little help when I was away at school. I never owned an automobile until many years later.

Virgil Beem, Northern Pacific Agent in Grand Rapids, was addicted to gambling. Whenever it rained and we couldn't work, several of us would meet at the depot for a game of cards. Virgil was nearly always broke, partly due to alimony payments to his former wife. He was a good friend, however, and always repaid any money he had borrowed. When his losses became extensive, he simply opened the safe and wrote out a Railway Express money order. I'm not certain how he managed to reconcile this practice with the Railway Express Agency, but it continued for as long as I knew him.

Some years later, after we had left the farm, Dad and I were driving through Grand Rapids when I decided to stop by the depot to say hello. Dad was dressed in a suit and tie and had never met Virgil. When we walked into the depot it was mid-afternoon, and Virgil was stretched out on the waiting-room floor fast asleep. When I nudged him with the toe of my shoe he awoke with a start. When he had reached a sitting position, I introduced Dad as the trainmaster from Jamestown. Virgil jumped to his feet, still half-asleep, and did everything but grovel at our feet. The stunned look on his face melted to a grin when I told him it was all a joke. The next summer he resigned from the railroad and moved to California. I didn't see him again for thirty-five years.

At the tender age of four, my Aunt Lenore began picking out tunes on the piano. She knew at that early age what her vocation in life would be. Though never married, she had been engaged while in her early twenties. Her social life had been limited due to the poor health of her mother, Grandma Anna Cunningham. After Grandma's death in 1939, Lenore began to enjoy life and was able to do some traveling, most of which was related to her profession, teaching piano.

Lenore was eight years younger than Dad, but in spite of this disparity, they were extremely close throughout their lifetime. This fact sometimes proved to be a thorn in the side of my mother, who may have been a little envious of the mutual admiration Dad and Lenore had for each other. Even Dad acknowledged that Lenore lived in comparative luxury while Mom struggled to raise a family, most of the time under difficult conditions. Lenore always drove a late model car, lived in a nice apartment, wore beautiful clothes, and was never without what were considered to be the "finer things" in life.

It was customary to invite her to all our family gatherings; she was nearly always present for major holidays, especially when we lived at Elmwood Farm, her childhood home. When Mom planned a big meal, she expected everyone to be punctual, seated at the table, and ready to eat at the designated time. There was nothing more frustrating to her than not having a meal begin on schedule.

As meticulous as Lenore was, she seldom arrived on time for dinner. Only once though, and that after a lengthy wait, did we finally begin the meal without her, and she was furious. On the many times we waited for her, the younger kids would establish a vigil, one at each window, vying for the dubious honor of announcing her arrival; then we'd rush out with a hearty welcome and escort her in. The only thing she brought along for dinner was her holiday specialty, a small tin of plum pudding and a jar of lemon sauce. She made it sound like her pudding was infinitely more important than anything else on the table, and it was her customary excuse for arriving late.

Aunt Lenore was a contrast in personalities. She was loving, highly ethical, and dedicated. On the other hand, she was conceited, egotistical and self-centered. She was never able to see or understand the plight of our family during the "hard times." She had been the center of attention from the time she was born, and planned to remain that way forever. She took exception to those who disagreed with her and scowled at anyone with the audacity to do so.

She drove into the farmyard one Thanksgiving in the early '40s with a new Plymouth car. Naturally, we kids wanted to get inside and look it over. She watched closely while each of us was permitted a quick peek. The car was always parked near the kitchen window where she could keep an eye on it at all times. When the meal was over and we were about to retire to the living room, my brother David chanced to look out the window. He quite suddenly yelled at the top of his voice, "Dad, the billy goat is on top of Lenore's new car!" Lenore paled, then led the charge outdoors with a broom. The goat received a severe lashing and was thereafter banished to the barn.

At Christmas, in addition to the plum pudding, she brought along several boxes filled with gifts she'd received, almost all of them from her students. There were scarves, perfumes, lotions, hankies, stationery and a host of other items. This was in stark contrast to the meager one or two the rest of us had under the tree. While Lenore daintily opened each package, we painfully exclaimed over each one. Never once did she offer to share something with Mom, who had so little. In addition to that, I can't recall that she ever brought a gift for us kids. She may have reasoned the pudding was gift enough. This was a side to my Aunt Lenore few of our relatives knew about, and one I did not become aware of until I was much older.

In spite of her shortcomings, however, we all loved Lenore and looked forward to her visits. She was a gifted teacher who was loved by her students. During the '30s she often gave free lessons to several talented students that lacked the ability to pay. She taught at many small towns in close proximity to Valley City. On one occasion she had a flat tire several miles in the country. She walked to a nearby farmhouse and was met by the father and his two husky sons. After they changed the tire she asked what she owed. The only pay they would accept was for her to play a few numbers on an old piano in their parlor. She was delighted to oblige.

Life on the farm was always interesting, with new challenges every day. When our toilet plugged up, Mom borrowed a plunger from our friend, Nick Weiler. The next week, after the toilet had been successfully unplugged, Mom became anxious to return it. So the next Sunday, as we were preparing to leave for church, Mom said, "Robert, we have to return that plunger today, so don't forget it."

It was a bitter cold morning, well below zero. Whenever there was a significant drop in temperature we kept the car inside the barn. Otherwise, we'd have to hitch up a team of horses and drag it around the yard until it started. After a few nights inside, the car took on a pungent barn smell, so by the time we arrived at church, our clothing, too, exuded the delicate odor of a cow-barn. At least half the families in church were farmers, so many of them smelled the same as us, and for the same reason. There was some satisfaction in knowing we weren't alone in stinking up the place. Fortunately, those of us infected the worst couldn't smell it.

With the plunger safely by my side, I backed the car to the house for everyone to pile in. Mom got in front with me, David, Terry and Dad squeezed into the back. The heater in our 37 Chevy worked well enough to keep us from freezing to death, but the windshield was something else. With five people breathing moisture inside such a confined area, it became impossible to keep the windows clear of frost.

All the way to LaMoure I was busy rubbing my gloved hand against the windshield. We had already given up on the side windows. Once I had the church in sight I slowed the car to a crawl, hoping to spot Nick Weiler. "Do you see him yet?" Mom kept asking. Finally, just when we were about to give up, I spotted Nick's green sedan just ahead. Mom wrenched the plunger from my hand and ordered me to drive alongside. I pulled up and stopped while she banged the business end of the plunger against his window. After a second look, and to her absolute horror, Mom saw it wasn't Nick at all, it was someone else, a complete stranger. She jerked the plunger back inside, rolled up her window as quickly as she could, and then yelled at the top of her voice, "That's not him you fool, drive on!"

We managed to locate Nick after church and return his plunger, but I was blamed for this embarrassing fiasco long afterward. We never learned the name of the frightened stranger in the green sedan. The "plunger story" became a favorite, one that I told at my mother's ninetieth birthday party using real props, and she loved it.

———•••••———

As I mentioned earlier, many of the necessities required for day to day living were rationed during the war. Farming was considered a vital industry, however, and that gave us an advantage, but in many cases we still needed a special permit. Car batteries were one of many things hard to get. During the summer of 1942 the one in the Chevy gave out. It held a charge great enough to run the car but not enough to start the engine. Until we could get a new battery, we had to remember to park on an incline wherever we went, unless there were plenty of pushers along, in which case we could park most anywhere. It was a little embarrassing if the engine accidentally died on Main Street, requiring everyone to get out and push. It was some consolation knowing that we weren't alone, that most families faced similar problems.

Genevieve and my younger brothers took Grandma Larson, who was then well into her seventies, to Grand Rapids to buy groceries. When it came time to push the car, Grandma insisted on doing her part. Once the car started everyone was to jump in, but nearly a block down the street, Gen looked back in horror to see Grandma still running alongside, one hand holding desperately to the door handle. After coming to a stop she jumped out to help poor Grandma in, who by then was gasping for breath.

As she grew older, Grandma became more and more forgetful. On one occasion she came down from her bedroom complaining that her girdle was missing; it had completely disappeared. We began an immediate search, but after turning the house upside down, Mom discovered Grandma had it on.

My father had only a passive interest in politics, but after receiving an invitation to a meeting in LaMoure, he decided to attend. The evening of the meeting, however, conflicted with plans Mom and Grandma had made to use the car. The ensuing discussion wasn't exactly heated, but there was a measure of hostility. Grandma made her displeasure known when she said for all to hear, "Well, you may as well let him go.

Maybe he'll be president some day!" Dad was furious, scarcely able to control his temper, and he had a hard time overlooking Grandma's ill-timed remark. Speaking thus was so completely out of character for her, we were all shocked.

Sometime later, Grandma moved back to Marion to be with my Aunt Amanda. One afternoon they were invited to a tea party at a neighbor's home, just a few blocks away. Grandma's hearing wasn't good, so she was content to sit in a rocker and read while the rest visited. On the way home she related an astonishing story. All the while she had been sitting in the rocker, a mysterious woman sat alone in the bedroom. Each time Grandma gazed in at her, the woman looked back and smiled, but never spoke.

The mystery deepened after Aunt Amanda called some of the other women and they too were puzzled. Determined to get to the bottom of it, she finally went to the neighbor's home and confronted her with Grandma's strange story. The neighbor was stymied for a moment, but then began laughing as she pointed to the bedroom door. Grandma had been looking at herself in a full-length mirror the whole time.

Our hog-house was just a stone's throw away from the barn. After separating, we carried the skim milk to the barn and fed the calves. Whatever was left over went to the hogs. Feeding the hogs was always hazardous. We learned from experience it was best to creep in as unobtrusively as possible and pour the milk into the trough in absolute silence. The slightest sound would awaken them and they'd come at you like a stampeding herd of buffalo. When that happened, one had to be a fast runner to escape being trampled to death. When our little brother Terry was about seven years old, he insisted he was big enough to feed the hogs. It was a disaster. Philip and I were in serious trouble after he ran howling to the house with his clothes all dirty and soaked with milk.

One hot summer day, Dad had arranged to have old Doc Clary vaccinate our hogs for cholera. Doc was a nice old guy who had been a veterinarian for more than fifty years, and he was a friend of the family. It wasn't a big job, except for the fact that Doc was nearly blind, leaving most of the work to me. He was a spindly little man in his late seventies.

He couldn't have weighed more than 120 pounds. I could most likely have managed without him if I'd had the serum. All Doc did was stumble around with the syringe in his hand while I grabbed the hogs, one at a time, and wrestled them to the ground. Then he'd totter over, peer through his thick glasses, and jab the needle into whatever body part was most accessible. During the melee, one of the larger hogs gave a sudden jump. Doc was caught off guard and gave me the shot in the hind end. Luckily, I didn't get sick, nor did I ever get hog cholera.

We had been waiting a week for "Wild Bill" Lawson to shear our sheep, between fifty and seventy-five head. Bill was never in a hurry and didn't believe in modern equipment; he brought along only the most rudimentary tools needed to get the job done. They consisted of a large shearing scissors, a sharpener, and a huge jug of disinfectant. There was good money in sheep back then — two crops every year, a lamb crop and a wool crop. But we had very little sheep experience, and learning along the way was expensive. The very first year — in the middle of May — many of our young lambs began mysteriously dying. We learned from the county agent, somewhat after the fact, that the leaves of chokecherry trees are poisonous in early spring, and that is what most likely killed them.

There were no woven wire fences on our farm, so the entire flock was continually crawling beneath the barbed wire and running away. First of all, you must understand that sheep are very stupid animals. They simply have no brains and have little or no ability to learn. Many times I walked, drove the car, or rode horseback searching for them. Neither the sheep nor anyone else had the vaguest idea where they were headed or why. They seemed not to care, only that they were moving as fast and far away as possible. The only explanation being that they must have known "Wild Bill" was coming with his shearing scissors.

Bill arrived early in the morning but didn't begin work until around 10:30 A.M. An experienced man, with good equipment, can shear 125 or more sheep a day. Bill was in the twenty to thirty range. When the day ended, the poor sheep were covered with cuts and gashes, several of them bleeding profusely. It was a terrible sight, and the last time we ever hired Bill. He should've been reported to the Humane Society and locked up. It was a big relief when we went out of the sheep business two years later.

———◆•◆•◆———

It was my responsibility to see that the corn was cultivated in a timely fashion using a one-row horse-drawn cultivator. It was a long and boring job, one at which I had to remain fully alert to keep from digging out the young plants. I was leaving for the field one afternoon when I noticed a package of "Beech-Nut" chewing tobacco lying on the seat of Bill's old car. He chewed two or three packages a day, stuffing huge handfuls into his mouth at once. Just watching him made my mouth water.

Bill was off somewhere so I helped myself to a small handful and stuck it in my shirt pocket. I could hardly wait to try it. After reaching the cornfield, I dug into my pocket for a chew of that delightful smelling stuff. Man it tasted good, nice and sweet, almost like candy. This was definitely going to ease the tedium of the job.

It seemed like I had to spit a lot. Then my stomach started feeling funny. Just a few minutes later, with still a long way to go on the first row, I became deathly ill. My eyes refused to focus and the corn plants were getting dug out right and left. Man, I was sick, sicker even than when I'd smoked the Elmo cigar. Beads of sweat broke out on my forehead and a thick, vile-tasting saliva welled up inside my mouth. I thought if I could somehow make it to the end of the field, I could lie down a few minutes.

I barely managed to get the horses tied to a tree before I came down with the dry heaves. Everything was going round and round. In addition to that, the heat was stifling, with little noticeable breeze. I had no choice but to lie there for as long as it took to recover or until I died. The latter seemed the greater possibility for the next agonizing half-hour. This was my second experience getting sick on tobacco; some lessons aren't easily learned. I continued to smoke cigarettes but never took a chew again, and I made sure I looked elsewhere whenever Bill took a chew of that awful tobacco.

————•♦••♦•————

In the spring of 1944, I graduated from high school and enlisted in the U.S. Navy along with my friend Billy Wilson. We were sent to San Diego for six weeks of "boot camp." After basic training I was assigned to the medical center where I was told to report to the laboratory, that part of the induction center responsible for determining the blood type of new recruits. In the next few weeks I learned a great deal about drawing and identifying blood.

All medical personnel in our department were instructed to wear white surgical gowns while on duty, so when the recruits came through our section, two or three at a time, they understandably assumed we were doctors. As a consequence, we were treated with great respect, which made me feel incredibly important. I even began to act like a doctor, despite the fact I hadn't received so much as one day of medical training.

Sometime later, on Tuesday and Thursday nights, I was assigned duty at the sickbay from 7:00 until 9:00 P.M. All personnel on sick call from our area of the base, other than officers, reported to me for treatment on those nights. It was my responsibility to diagnose and treat minor illnesses and to refer any serious cases to the U. S Naval Hospital in San Diego. The standard treatment for most of my patients was two aspirin and a glass of water. I took great pride in my job and doubt if a hospital corpsman could have done better. Those aspirin did wonders.

The most common illnesses I had to deal with were colds, flu, headache, scarlet fever and one called "crabs." Occasionally there were more serious maladies such as gonorrhea and syphilis. In the case of crabs, it was common to treat up to four or five men each duty night. Treatment was provided on the spot and included a trip to the shower room, just down the hall, with a generous application of "crab killer," a medicated powder that was highly effective. An interesting manifestation involving the treatment of crabs was that one could actually see them hopping about the floor following a treatment.

We processed one or two companies of recruits daily, anywhere from 125 to 150 men per company. It took three or four hours to run them through the laboratory and an additional two hours to type the blood and clean up. After that, it was "party time." There were two Navy Waves working with us in addition to five men, all but one older than I. There was a radio in back and as soon as we finished our work, the dancing started. We held a dance every afternoon until one day the Chief Medical Officer walked in unexpectedly and went ballistic. That was the end of the parties — and the Waves.

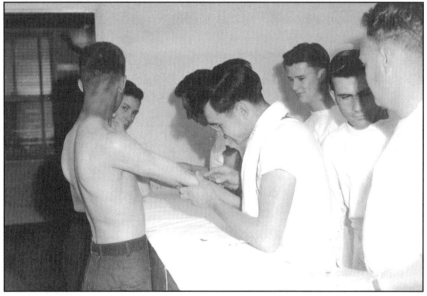

The author, fifth from the left
"Learning how to extract blood"

I WASN'T QUALIFIED FOR MOST OF THE ASSIGNMENTS given me in the laboratory. For the most part I learned by doing, guided by the hospital corpsmen, something of an on-the-job training. If the truth were known, someone would have likely been court-martialed for letting me make decisions I had been only marginally trained for. I gloried in the feeling of importance, however, and went about my work with great enthusiasm. I would have gladly stayed on indefinitely had the war not come to an end.

Most of the induction center staff was quartered in a barrack not far from the dispensary where we lived a pretty easy life. There were also various perks related to our jobs such as taking our meals ahead of the recruits and being allowed extra liberty.

One day after dinner, while taking a shortcut through the kitchen, a friend and I spied five giant batteries filled with fresh apple pie, just out of the oven. Minutes later we were back in our office enjoying all the pie we could eat. We gave some to a recruit after he promised to return the empty tins. Later we saw him double-timing around the parade ground with a seabag above his head. That was one example of the many hazards facing people in the military. Sort of like what happened to me when they asked for volunteers with a driver's license. I was assigned to a wheelbarrow crew, removing dirt.

There were four or five theaters on base, so each evening I either took in a movie or played cards. Just after payday I sat in on a poker game with a good deal of cash on the table, perhaps two or three hundred dollars. Suddenly, a member of the Shore Patrol came marching in. While gambling was against regulations, it was seldom enforced, so I was surprised when it looked like all our money was about to be confiscated. Just as the SP began to scoop up the evidence, a senior card player looked up and said, "Ed, what the hell are you doing in that uniform?" Ed's face turned beet-red. He dropped the cash and ran for the door. If this impostor hadn't been recognized, we would've lost all our money. It was a neat trick, but in this case, it hadn't worked.

One of my more notable experiences while serving in the Navy was meeting two of my Uncle Durward's children, Wilfrid and Laura. They had more or less dropped from sight during the '30s. Laura and her husband lived in Manhattan Beach, a suburb of Los Angeles. They invited me for a weekend and were kind enough to show me all around Hollywood. Wilfrid came by Saturday afternoon for a short visit. That was the first contact any of us had had with my Uncle Durward's family in over thirty-five years.

Shortly after the war ended I was sent to Fort Snelling and discharged a few days later. I was anxious to return home where the fall harvest was getting under way. I looked forward to my old job hauling bundles on Shorty Seefeldt's threshing rig.

One cannot imagine the joy I felt when the train pulled into Grand Rapids. No one met me at the station, since they had no idea when I'd be arriving. I left my sea-bag at Amundson's store and walked the half-mile home carrying my suitcase. Everyone was happy to see me. How wonderful it was to be back home at Elmwood Farm.

Unfortunately, my joy was to be short-lived. Less than a year later we lost the farm to foreclosure, largely due to unpaid taxes during the depression years. A bill passed by Congress had allowed farmers to re-deem their land, but because Dad's lawyer failed to observe a filing deadline, our application was denied. My father took it extremely hard, refusing to talk about this tragic event in his life for many years. Mom told us how he had often cried at night, blaming himself for what had happened. The anguish he felt remained with him until the day he died. Only on one occasion did he see Elmwood Farm after leaving there in 1946, and that was quite by accident.

The house on Elmwood Farm as it appears today
after being renovated in the 1980s and 1990s

That painful loss was shared equally by all of us. I loved Elmwood Farm more than most. It was not only beautiful, but a wholesome and wondrous place to live as well. I drive back every year to walk across the land. I recall with great nostalgia the exciting and wonderful times I had there.

The author, shortly before leaving Elmwood Farm in 1946

Things have a way of working out for the best, and I'm sure we would have faced difficult times had we stayed. Perhaps we were fortunate to have left with a measure of dignity before low prices forced us off the land, as in the case of so many others.

For my father, though, it was more the circumstances under which we had left that hurt him the most. He felt he had betrayed a trust. Elmwood Farm had been a part of his heritage to have for a while and pass along to his children. He never recovered from the feeling he had somehow failed his family. Few people understand the relationship between man and the land. It is not easily defined. Of the many descriptions of love, man's love for the land is perhaps the most obscure.

Chapter VIII

Leaving Elmwood Farm Forever

Our AUCTION SALE WENT MUCH BETTER THAN EXPECTED. A huge crowd had gathered and the bidding was lively. Many farmers had come with the intention of bidding on our "M" International tractor. The war had just ended and there was only limited production of farm equipment. Tractors, in particular, were still in extremely short supply.

In spite of a successful auction, there was, nevertheless, a great deal of sadness watching years of hard work and sacrifice evaporate before our eyes. Most upsetting to me was the sale of our tractor and giving away our faithful dog, Jeff.

Dad gave Jeff to a neighbor the day of the sale. Earlier that fall we had taught him to fetch the cows, quite a feat considering he had to climb the pasture hills and search them out. He had developed one little quirk, however. On his way, he'd always stop just before vanishing from sight, like he needed some sign of encouragement. One little wave and off he'd go; without the wave, he'd return home. He was definitely a farm dog and wouldn't have been happy in town, so we simply had to give him up.

Only a month earlier I had been plowing for our neighbor, Harry Kolberg, and, as usual, Jeff had come along. All the while I was plowing he ran along side investigating every suspicious looking hole. At the end of the day I unhooked the plow and started home on the tractor. Jeff was terrified of Harry's two vicious dogs and kept a wary eye out for them. As we neared the gate to Harry's yard, I could see Jeff trying to look as small as possible, running nearly unseen along the outer ditch. Harry's hounds came bounding out, however, and were about to pounce on little Jeff. I wasn't at all prepared for what happened next. In an unprecedented effort to save himself from sudden death, Jeff raced toward the moving tractor and took a giant leap, landing squarely in my lap. I could almost see the sweat fall from his brow as I held his quivering body in my arms. It was an extraordinary event.

We had been looking for a business to buy and were seriously considering a general store in Marion. It wasn't exactly what we wanted, more a temporary answer to an immediate problem, that of finding a means to earn a living. Dad bought it, and we moved two weeks later. Fortunately, the business included two apartments. We lived in one and rented out the other.

In spite of a monumental family effort, the business was only moderately successful. Cleaning the place up took most of one month. It was a typical small-town general store much like the one in Grand Rapids. We sold very little dry goods but made up for it with a thriving fresh meat and grocery business. There was a small back room where we bought cream and eggs and sold large quantities of chicken feed. Dad took care of the cream and egg business and I managed the grocery end.

During our brief venture into the store business there had been one potentially serious incident involving my brother, Terry, and his second cousin, Larry Jorve. Customers began returning boxes of breakfast food after finding shotgun pellets inside. After a brief investigation we discovered that Terry and Larry had been shooting their BB guns in the storage room, using cases of cereal for targets. Fortunately for us, no one suffered any ill effects.

From the outset, I had the feeling Cunningham's Grocery wasn't going to be a lasting enterprise, and I was right. A year later, in the spring of 1947, Dad began exploring business opportunities in the north-central part of the state near Garrison Dam, then under construction at Riverdale. It wasn't long before he found a small liquor store for sale in the attractive little city of Washburn, almost equidistant between the dam and Bismarck. Washburn was a progressive community built along the banks of the Missouri River, the county seat of McLean County. Highway 83 ran directly through the center of town, providing access to most of the traffic to and from the dam.

The store sold quickly, and we moved to Washburn a few weeks later. My parents were fortunate to find a place to live since housing was in great demand, especially in the smaller towns in close proximity to the dam. Workers with families wanted to live in towns away from the job site; Washburn was a good example. Every city and village for miles around were beehives of activity, all fueled by the construction going on at Riverdale.

Dad made Philip a partner in the business, so he too moved his family to Washburn. The interior of the bar was completely remodeled utilizing the latest fixtures. It was compact, attractive, and held a sizable crowd. "Cunningham's Bar" soon became one of the most popular stopping off places between Bismarck and Minot.

For the first time in years my mother could relax and take it a little easy. The house we moved into was small, but it had all the modern conveniences she had gone without for so many years, including a decent place to wash clothes. Two years later, my parents bought a larger home with a basement apartment, one block off Main Street.

There were enormous changes coming in my life as well. I began to realize that I needed to plan for the future rather than bumming around aimlessly, from job to job. I didn't know it then, but a significant event was about to take place that would change my life forever, and provide a compelling reason to add some stability to my life. I was about to be smitten by the love bug, something that hadn't happened to me before.

Shortly before this love affair began, I bought my first automobile, a 1939 Ford. It was a beautiful car, second hand, but like new. Full production of automobiles didn't resume until 1947, and not until 1948 were there any noticeable numbers available. My Ford car may have played a part in the initial success of my romance.

The first few months in Washburn were spent drifting from job to job, mostly in construction. My bank account wasn't anything to write home about, but I wasn't exactly in dire straights either. For that reason, I usually looked for work that appealed to me, staying until something better came along. If I became temporarily unemployed, I filled in as a bartender, giving Dad or Philip a break. Contractors were always short of help and one could quit a job in the morning and be hired by someone else in the afternoon. I always managed to find work, but I seldom let it interfere with my social life.

In addition to the dam, roads were being both built and rebuilt to accommodate the enormous amount of heavy equipment and construction materials being delivered to the dam site. To accommodate rail shipments, the Corps of Engineers began building a railroad spur from Riverdale to link up with the Soo Line tracks at Gateway. All this activity involved hiring thousands of laborers.

⟾⟾◆⟸

Hank Wahl's Barbershop, located two doors up from Cunningham's Bar, was a hangout for local storytellers. Hank was an excellent barber and father of four children. While waiting for a haircut one afternoon, Hank's daughter, Marilyn, walked through the door. One look at her, and a strange feeling came over me, one I had never experienced before. She had green eyes, ash-blonde hair, and nicely trimmed bangs across her forehead. What caught my eye in particular, was her beautiful skin and alluring smile. Once I learned her first name I arranged to have my younger brother hand-deliver a note to her at school with an invitation to a movie. She accepted, and from that point on we became inseparable. One could say it was love at first sight.

Work had tapered off that fall so I accepted a teaching position at a country school a few miles east of Washburn. My salary was only $165.00 per month. It wasn't a lot, but enough to cover my expenses, which had risen considerably since I had fallen in love. A good thing I owed nothing on my car and had no outstanding debts. In addition, I was living at home, which cut my overhead substantially. To compensate for my free room and board, I dropped Mom off each day at the school she was teaching. My only qualification as a teacher was my high school diploma, and a lot of help from others, including my mother. One embarrassing side to teaching was when my students hollered, "Hi teacher!" whenever they saw me in town.

Marilyn and I had a marvelous time over the next year and a half. We rarely missed a dance within fifty miles and went to many movies and parties in between. All this activity was a serious drain on my bank account, but nothing matters when one is in love. Unfortunately, while we had no immediate plans to get married, money I had put away for our honeymoon was being rapidly depleted by our extravagant life style.

During the years Garrison Dam was under construction, money flowed freely into the local economy, a natural result of all the extra employment. Also, the recent end to the war had released a pent-up demand for every kind of merchandise and piece of equipment imaginable. Everyone had money and was eager to spend it.

━━━◈◆◈━━━

Marilyn and I were invited to a party that was planned by a select group of high school girls. Most of them were our friends and Marilyn's classmates. It was a semi-formal affair chaperoned by several mothers. The girls had planned socializing and dancing with a light lunch afterward. The room was decorated with brightly colored crepe paper with long streamers descending outward from a chandelier. A large crystal bowl sat in the center of a cloth-covered table at one end of the room filled with a cherry-colored punch.

A few minutes into the party, three local boys home from college came to me with an interesting proposal: all of us should chip in on a bottle of gin. They reasoned it would accentuate the flavor of the punch and undoubtedly add a little excitement to the party. I was reluctant to go along until the banker's son and a few others joined in. There were two or three of us over twenty-one and knowledgeable about what to get. It was agreed that this part of the program be kept secret, especially from the mothers.

After one bottle didn't appear to have the desired affect, we bought another one. It was shortly after the second bottle that the girls began to laugh and giggle. But then some began to cry for no apparent reason. We decided they were suffering from a malady known as a "crying jag." It didn't take a brain surgeon to see that the party was getting out of control. Then, quite suddenly, all hell broke loose. Mrs. Tony Anderson came charging out of the kitchen full speed flanked by two stalwarts, all three shouting accusations, waving their arms, and pointing their fingers right at me. Seconds later, Chief of Police Houston came marching in with a billy club in his hand. Mrs. Tony pointed her short fat finger at me and screamed, "There he is, he's the one that did it, take him to jail and lock him up!"

The chief, thank God, wasn't prepared to make an arrest until he'd gathered all the information about who exactly was responsible for this debacle. The situation was chaotic to say the least — the girls crowded around, some still crying and the rest laughing and giggling. I could see myself being handcuffed and dragged off to jail.

Just as Chief Houston was about to arrest me, my fellow conspirators came to my rescue. Three of them stepped forward, including the son of the newspaper publisher, the school superintendent, and the states attorney. They told the chief exactly what had transpired. Faced with the prospect of having to arrest the sons of upper-crust society in Washburn, the chief quickly backed down. Mrs. Anderson stamped her feet a few times and then marched back to the kitchen in a huff.

We were all sorry for what had happened; none of us dreamed it would turn into such a complete disaster. Once things settled down the chief suggested everyone go home and all would be forgiven. I was more than happy to take that advice. Those of us over twenty-one could have had some serious charges brought against us. We hadn't considered the consequences until it was much too late.

One Sunday afternoon, just a few weeks after the disastrous party, Marilyn and I were cleaning the bar. After the work was finished we sat in a booth speculating about something interesting to do. For some time I had wanted to play a trick on Art Shelberg. Art was a greedy, loud-mouthed redneck with a cantankerous disposition. He was a tall, lanky man with a bushy, unkempt mustache which usually bore the residue of his last meal. A consummate gambler, Art had once bet ten dollars that the next car to drive by would be a Ford, and he won.

The local telephone operator, and a good friend of ours, played an important role in the conspiracy against good old Art. This was during the days when you needed the assistance of an operator to make a long-distance call. She rang Art's house and asked him to hold the line for an important long-distance call from a Bismarck radio station. In spite of Marilyn's uncontrolled laughter, I managed to disguise my voice and tell Art he was about to win a bucket full of money if he could correctly answer the question of the day. Art immediately got all excited, and I knew he was suckered. I asked the question, "What is the color of the Lone Ranger's horse?" When Art answered brown, I said, "Wrong, but that's the color of your prize. You just won a bucket of shit!"

There was a long pause, but just before I hung up, I heard Art bellow, "Who in the hell?"

Bright and early the next morning, Art came marching down town with Chief of Police Houston at his side, vowing to expose the dirty "son-of-a-bitch" responsible for what he described as "a stinking, low-down trick." He guaranteed frightful consequences for the guilty person, whoever it was. Naturally, the first place he began making inquiries was in the bar, his daily hangout. I was behind the counter when he and the chief walked in, and plenty worried they might somehow learn the truth. Art interrogated everyone present while the chief stood silently at his side. I pretended to be outraged that he would include me on his list of suspects.

Besides being habitually cranky, Art was a rude person, so I felt any risk I had taken was well worth it. He definitely deserved what had happened to him. There were added benefits to our scheme in the days following. His erstwhile friends kept asking him if he'd won any contests lately, after which he'd go into an earsplitting tirade, shouting his usual obscenities, still vowing to unmask the guilty person. The entire episode was soon forgotten, however, and Art resumed his ornery ways.

As my relationship with Marilyn grew more serious, I reached the conclusion it was time to consider an occupation that held more promise for the future. I had long been interested in working for the railroad, partly due to my admiration for Bill Kranz, our family friend. He had been employed by the Northern Pacific his entire life and had promised to help me if I ever needed him. After talking to Bill, I began looking for a railroad school. Both the Northern Pacific and the Soo Line were short of help and desperately needed telegraphers.

Newlyweds Robert & Marilyn, 1949

Aunt Lenore and her new car

The family of George & Myrtle Cunningham
Standing (from left), Philip, Mom, Dad, Genevieve
Seated (from left), David, Terry, Robert

Chapter IX

Working on the Railroad

WITH OUR UPCOMING MARRIAGE IN MIND, Marilyn and I drove to Bismarck one fall day in 1948 to pick out a ring. While the diamond didn't exactly blind anyone, it was a terrible shock to my bank account. Most people weren't unduly surprised by our engagement. Nevertheless, it caused quite a stir since Marilyn wouldn't graduate from high school until spring, and we were planning to get married before my school began.

I had received a catalogue and application from the Gale Institute, a school in Minneapolis specializing in railroad accounting, telegraphy, and teletyping. My application was accepted, and I was also approved for benefits under the GI Bill. Our plans were falling neatly into place, or at least we hoped so. Neither of us had the vaguest idea what to expect with regard to married life, or how far-reaching our responsibilities would be, especially for me. At the time, we could have cared less.

We entered into the state of holy matrimony on April 17, 1949, and I was scheduled to begin school May 1. Fortunately, I had already made a trip to Minneapolis where I had arranged for an apartment and acquainted myself with the logistics of getting to and from school.

The day we arrived in Minneapolis, our worldly possessions included a car, our personal belongings, and $36.00 in my checking account. Soon after getting settled in our new quarters, I found a part-time job at an appliance store. I definitely needed to supplement my income. The days were long for Marilyn, but before we knew it I was about to graduate.

A week earlier we had driven home on a long holiday weekend, giving me an opportunity to visit with my friend and benefactor, Bill Kranz. I left Marilyn in Washburn and drove to Cooperstown where Bill was the NP Agent. I spent two days copying telegrams and reviewing railroad procedures. Bill wanted to make certain I could pass a telegraph test before sending me for an interview with the Chief Dispatcher in Fargo.

After successfully passing the "wire test," my application for employment was quickly approved, and the chief instructed me to report to the agent at Buffalo for two weeks on-the-job training. Buffalo was located along the main line, thirty-five miles west of Fargo, at the end of double track. It was a busy station back in 1950, and I was terrified when, after just a few days, I was assigned the night job with no supervision. My hand shook so badly, the first train-order I copied was nearly illegible. Trainmen relied on telegraphers to copy orders with absolute accuracy; our jobs and their lives depended on it. A train-order was unacceptable if it contained any erasures or crossed-out words. I learned a lot from the agent at Buffalo. He had started many young men on their way to a career on the railroad.

When my training at Buffalo was over I returned to Washburn. My parents offered to let us live in their basement apartment until I was assigned a permanent position. For the foreseeable future, however, I would be relegated to the extra board working temporary vacancies.

Almost every position on the railroad, other than upper management, was governed by seniority. The longer one was employed, the greater the opportunity to be a successful bidder on a job opening. Employees high on the seniority list were said to have had "whiskers." One's ability to advance, therefore, was governed by seniority.

A somewhat reverse situation occurred when a job was abolished. Beginning with that position, all employees with lesser amounts of seniority were subject to the "bumping rule," resulting in a domino affect that ended with the lowest person on the roster. That man usually reverted to the extra board. Bumping was a disagreeable and disruptive practice, but one that was entirely necessary.

I bid on every job that was bulletined, but it was more than a year before I received a telegram from the Chief Dispatcher stating I was the successful bidder on the swing position at Steele. The swing operator was the least liked position since it involved three different shifts. Two days 8:00 A.M. until 4:00 P.M., two days 4:00 P.M. until midnight, and one day midnight until 8:00 A.M. While this wasn't ideal, it was preferable to the extra board, where I was assigned a different station every two weeks or so. Besides, unlike the branch lines, working on the main line of the Northern Pacific was one of the most exciting and rewarding jobs on the railroad.

My permanent position couldn't have come at a more propitious time. While on the extra board, two blessed events had taken place. Stephanie Ann was born October 26th, and a year later, on October 14th, Susan Kay arrived. I couldn't believe how quickly my family was growing. There was one consolation, the cost of having a baby back then was a bargain. In 1950 the bill for the birth of a child was around $100.00.

While living in Steele, Robert Gregory was born on February 2, 1952, "Ground Hog's Day." I recall vividly how disappointed I was when the nurse came into the waiting room early on that cold February morning to announce I was the father of a baby girl. Then, just seconds later, she came rushing back to say she had made a mistake, it was a boy.

I couldn't believe my good fortune. After having two daughters, I was delighted to finally have a son; despite the fact he bore a striking resemblance to a dried up prune and made more noise than a South

American howler monkey. He weighed just over six pounds at birth but grew into a good-sized young man. My friend, Kelly Shockman, was already the father of four children. He suggested we call the contest off. Apparently he never listened to his own advice since he subsequently became the father of eight additional children, twelve in all.

The Old Train Station
John Hagan

I see the old train station,
Its platform filled with carts,
Where once old friends and
    Neighbors stood . . .
Expectant joy in their hearts.

It seems I hear the laughter
That filled the waiting room;
I could swear I see bright faces
Still shining in the gloom.

How many joyous greetings there,
How many sad farewells,
Were muffled in the hiss of steam
Or the clamor of the bells.

All too many institutions
Such as this are fading fast;
These new modern innovations
Are blotting out the past.

But memory still gives to me
A most welcome invitation
To journey to a bygone day
When I see an old train station.

First Permanent Job at Steele

A FRIEND OF MINE OFFERED US THE USE OF HIS TRUCK to move our furniture. Three weeks earlier I had ordered a bedroom set, a desk, living room couch, and kitchen table from a catalogue, all on monthly payments. We rented the lower half of a house for $45 a month. There were two bedrooms, a living room, and a small kitchen – barely enough room for our budding family.

It was our first experience living entirely on our own and a welcome change from the small apartment in my parent's house. The down side of our new place was the family upstairs. They couldn't seem to get along and were hollering and fighting nearly every night. On one occasion the husband went after his wife with a butcher knife, chasing her up and down the stairs and around the yard. Several times we had to call the police. Afterward, she'd take her small children and temporarily move in with her parents. They always managed to get back together, but the fighting continued.

Two dreadful accidents happened in the small town of Steele while we lived there. During the holidays, a group of children were practicing for a church program that was to be held on the Sunday before Christmas. One evening after practice, the father stopped by the church to pick up his five children. He and the two youngest rode in the cab, while the three older children got in back. It was a bitter cold night and the windows were frosted over. The railroad crossing, which was protected by flashing lights, was only two blocks from the church.

No one knows with certainty why this accident happened. Despite warning lights and bells, the pickup began crossing the track and was struck broadside by the North Coast Limited. The three older children in back were killed instantly, but the father and two younger ones miraculously survived.

As a result of that incredible catastrophe, a pall of sorrow was cast over the entire town. There was a feeling of numbness during the holidays and for months afterward. It was as though everyone's children had been victims of this tragedy.

Telegraphers and agents were required to stand alongside the track and inspect every train that passed, reporting any abnormalities to the train dispatcher. The telegrapher on duty that night was struck by a wheel from the truck. In addition to other injuries, his leg was shattered. After many weeks of hospitalization he recovered; he was considered fortunate to be alive.

The previous summer, a carload of people approaching Highway 10 from the north failed to observe a stop sign. They crossed the highway at a high rate of speed, went through a ditch, and then literally flew over the main line track, landing on the other side. When they crossed the track, however, the car had struck and loosened one of the rails. Westbound train No. 603 came by minutes later and derailed, sending the engine and twenty-five to thirty cars careening off the track. One car broke open scattering lawn mowers more than a hundred feet along the right-of-way. Incredibly, the people in the car scarcely got a scratch.

———◇———

We were happy to be living in Steele. It wasn't entirely new to me having lived and gone to school there years earlier. Most of the people I had known back then, of course, were long gone. But in just a short time we had made several new friends, many of them fellow railroad employees.

What a pleasure it was to work on the main line of the Northern Pacific during the years when steam was still the primary source of power. It is difficult to describe the thrill one experienced, standing near the depot, watching a double-header fast-freight come thundering down the track toward you. When the engines were pulling hard they left a trail of black smoke and swirling ash and the whistle would be sounding with such an earsplitting shrillness, it caused the hair on your neck to stand on end. It took a while to get accustomed to the deafening noise. Until that time, such an experience could be very frightening.

The different shifts I worked were referred to as "tricks." First trick was 8:00 A.M. to 4:00 P.M., second trick 4:00 P.M. to midnight, and third trick midnight to 8:00 A.M. The telegraphers that manned these positions were called "trick-operators."

Mercedes Olson was the permanent second trick operator and estimated by my fellow workers to be well past her sixties. She was of average height with closely cropped hair dyed a glistening blue-black. The wrinkles on her face were well hidden by layers and layers of makeup. Despite her age, she entertained a boy friend two or three nights a week in the depot office. No one objected to her entertaining or her sharing a meal with him, but we did take exception to the mess she left, especially after frying fish on top of the stove. Fish bones and spatterings of grease were everywhere. She completely ignored our complaints, so we had no alternative but to retaliate in some way.

One of the trick-operators lived in a small trailer near the depot. From his dining room we could observe Mercedes through an office window. She never varied her routine once things quieted down. The lights would go off and out would come her giant jar of beauty cream. She'd sit at the desk like a queen, rhythmically applying generous portions of cream to her face and arms.

The Railway Express Agency furnished each office with a large container of glue. It was actually a combination of glue and paste that was opaque in color, with a consistency closely resembling Mercedes' beauty cream. It was so powerful we used it to mend the office chairs. Before she came on duty we removed most of her beauty cream and substituted Express Company glue. The glue wasn't guaranteed to remove wrinkles, but they sure weren't going to get any worse while she had it on.

A small number of operators gathered in the trailer for the event about to take place. Soon after dark, and right on schedule, all the lights went out except for the small bulb over the train-order desk. The main attraction was about to begin.

Her hands began moving slowly and gracefully in a circular motion as she applied generous quantities of what she thought was her miraculous face cream. It didn't take but a few seconds for her to realize something was wrong. Naturally, we were hoping her face would become so encrusted with glue that she wouldn't be entertaining the boyfriend for some time. Quite suddenly, the entire room was ablaze in lights, and we could see her at the wash basin, splashing her face with water. The more she splashed the funnier it became. One of the guys, Cas Budish, fell to his knees in hysterics, beating his hands against the floor.

Much to our chagrin, Mercedes never mentioned a word about her bad experience, nor did she alter her routine. We were reasonably certain she had guessed who was responsible, but she was careful not to give us any additional satisfaction.

Two years earlier, in the summer of 1948, there had been a robbery at the depot. Mercedes had placed $500 cash in the office safe, which was strictly against company regulations. The money mysteriously disappeared one day, nearly causing Mercedes to go into cardiac arrest. It was a considerable loss and caused an enormous uproar that reached all the way to the corporate headquarters in St. Paul. The agent was the primary suspect, but in spite of a thorough investigation, there wasn't enough evidence to charge him. He was severely reprimanded, however, for allowing an employee to keep personal funds in the company safe. This epic scandal was the top news item for weeks.

Mercedes made an error on a train order a few months after the glue incident and was allowed to retire without charges being brought. She and her boyfriend moved away and were never heard from again.

⇒◆⇐

Philip's wife, Juleen, had two brothers, Don and Harold. Harold was owner and publisher of the *Steele Ozone Press* and Don was a partner with his father, H.B. Hanson, in the grain and lumber business. Marilyn and I occasionally worked for Harold on weekends when he needed help with special printing jobs, mostly sale bills. It was interesting work, and Harold paid us well.

Old H.B. was an entrepreneur, always interested in new ventures. Long before entering the grain and lumber business with his son, Don, he had owned a small garage and gas station. A man of the old school, he practiced frugality to a fault.

A young man named Tilmer had been hired to help out at the station, mostly to run errands. He was a gangly, fourteen-year-old with enormous ears, and he was not known for his intelligence. But H.B. claimed he was a fast runner, which was what he had hired him for. Tilmer was instructed to alert H.B. whenever a car drove up. To facilitate that task, a whistle was hung around his neck, and he was instructed to blow it as hard as he could whenever a customer wanted gas. The whistle was barely in place when a car drove up, almost running them over. Tilmer looked up at H.B. and blew for all he was worth. "I see him, you damn fool!" H.B. stormed.

H.B. had devised an ingenious method of cooling pop. Instead of wasting good money on an electric cooler, he simply lowered a pail filled with soft drinks into a deep well behind the shop. Whenever a customer placed an order, it was Tilmer's job to run quickly to the well and pull up the pail. Everything went fine until the afternoon of the second day, when Tilmer accidentally dropped the rope and pail down the well, forty feet below. He wasn't given a going-away party, but he did get to keep the whistle.

H.B.'s son, Don, was like his dad in many ways — hard working and dedicated. He once told me that when he was about thirteen years old he yearned to be a cowboy. He desperately wanted a pair of woolly chaps like those worn by cowboys he'd seen in the movies. It was a goal that seemed beyond reach, especially for one with few finances. Don and two friends, also cowboys, considered the problem for a few days, then came up with a plan that very nearly got them in serious trouble with the police.

A farmer living at the edge of town, not far from the Hanson home, owned a dog with a coat of long, curly brown hair, closely matching the color and density of a pair of chaps worn by their favorite movie idol, Tom Mix.

Don never revealed how the three of them had managed to dispatch the dog. He did describe how they had hauled the remains to an old vacant garage and how they had skinned and nailed the pelt to an old bench. What they had failed to anticipate, however, was the hue and cry raised by the owner when his dog turned up missing.

An extensive search was conducted and a reward offered for information leading to the dog's return. The reward was later modified to include the return of the dog, dead or alive. After the police were called in, Don and his friends became alarmed. They realized they'd never dare wear chaps around town that closely resembled the hair of a certain missing dog, for which a sizable reward had been offered. Faced with this unfortunate reality they took shovels and, in the dead of night, buried the evidence. Don and his friends were so unnerved they completely lost their desire to become cowboys.

——◇——

Hesper and Temvik

IN THE FALL OF 1953, I became the successful bidder on the agent's position at Hesper, a small town south of Devils Lake on the Esmond Branch. I ordered a boxcar for moving our furniture — one of the few perks afforded employees of the railroad. Hesper was a typical small town, even smaller than most. There was an elevator, store, blacksmith shop and a garage. It wasn't much of a town, but there were living quarters in the depot for which we paid no rent. Anything not available at the local store required a trip to Maddock, six miles east.

Less than a year later I bid in the agency at Temvik on the Linton Branch. Once again I ordered a boxcar and we began packing. We were happy to be moving nearer our parents and other relatives in Washburn. When we visited Hesper some years later, we found it to be little more than a ghost town. Temvik suffered a similar fate not long afterward.

Temvik was named for two early residents, one named Larvik and the other, Templeton. It seems they couldn't agree on a name so they compromised. Temvik was considerably larger than Hesper with many more families, and a good school. Like many small towns, the elevator was the principal business. Grain shipments were essential to the well being of the railroad, and thus it's employees. Fortunately, Temvik had a thriving elevator that generated a lot of business. That first summer I decided to take advantage of the rural setting and began building a chicken house from abandoned railroad snow fences. The boards were so imbedded with sand and dirt, I wore out two saws. The next spring I bought fifty-three baby chicks, and that was the precise number we butchered that fall.

Soon after the chicken house was completed, I renovated an old garage for use as a barn and bought a cow. A friend of ours gave us a runt pig we named Clarence. He soon became the family pet, and with our expert care, he grew to quite large proportions. It was a sad day for the kids when they finally had to say good-bye to Clarence.

Marilyn and I made our own sausage and cured the bacon and hams in the freight house. It was a giant undertaking, but with the help of our neighbors, it was a great success. My friend, Frank Weber, let us use his smokehouse to give our sausage a little extra flavor. We ate well our second winter in Temvik.

Frank told me an interesting story about an incident involving a batch of homemade summer sausage he'd made. For some unknown reason the whole lot turned sour, smelling up the place something awful. He was forced to bury it out behind the barn. In spite of the fact it had been covered with a foot or more of dirt, the obnoxious stench refused to dissipate. Two days later, after the smell became intolerable, Frank discovered the sausage out behind the house under the protection of his black Lab. Now, desperate to rid the place of this incredible stink, he loaded it in his truck and dumped it in a ditch four miles away. Several days later the stink not only hadn't gone away, it seemed to be getting worse. Frank thought it was his imagination until he discovered his dog had once again dragged it all home. The final burial was ten miles down the road.

We didn't own a freezer so we improvised that second winter by storing our meat in a barrel out in front of the depot. After the trainmen discovered our good homemade sausage, and began helping themselves, we were forced to buy a chest freezer.

Temvik was a unique town, quite different from anywhere we had lived before, or since. The people there epitomized the words "good neighbors." There was no discernible enmity between the many families, and they exhibited genuine concern for each other. Several times each year the entire town gathered for a potluck dinner to socialize and discuss mutual problems. If there was a death or serious illness, everyone responded with assistance. Many times volunteers answered the call to dig a grave, even in the sub-zero cold of winter.

We were able to diversify our diet now that we owned a freezer. Frozen foods were being introduced more and more into the market, and we were thus able to take advantage of sale prices by purchasing larger quantities. We raised quite a large garden and stored the excess vegetables in a root cellar. The milk we couldn't drink was separated, and we made the cream into butter and the skim milk into cottage cheese. Marilyn canned jars and jars of vegetables and dill pickles. It was like being back on the farm.

We seldom locked our freezer until I noticed a box of Hershey bars missing and saw their wrappers strewn alongside the depot. The ensuing investigation failed to produce any knowledge of what had happened. When asked to explain the empty wrappers, our daughter Susan piped up, "The wind must have blown them down from Wudke's house." We didn't save any money on that deal!

Albert and Hilda Wudke were wonderful neighbors that lived just up the street, a block from the depot. Hilda often babysat for our children while we were away for the evening. They were humble people with little schooling; Hilda hadn't gone beyond the fifth grade. They had few material possessions, but were wealthy in so many other ways.

Their only income came from Albert's position as a contractor who transported the mail between the depot and post office in the trunk of his old Ford coupe. They raised rabbits, chickens, geese, and goats and raised a garden twice the size of ours, so they had a multitude of foodstuffs over winter. Their basement was filled with every imaginable kind of canned goods. Despite the fact they were considered "dirt-poor," Albert and Hilda always insisted on sharing what little they had with us.

We bought our first television set in 1955 and invited Wudkes' to watch whenever they liked. They came two or three nights a week, often staying until the station went off the air. Many nights, Marilyn and I went to bed, leaving them to lock up on their way out. "Liberace" was Hilda's favorite program; she wondered if he could actually see into our living room since he "winked" at her several times during the show.

Albert owned a small black dog named Pug. Pug was of unknown pedigree, but he made up for that lack with an uncommon intelligence. Ed Kist, a farmer living on the outskirts of town, had two vicious dogs that always chased along after his car on the way to the post office, just a block from Wudke's. Pug would lay in wait each day, barking furiously the minute the Kist dogs came into view. When they drew dangerously close he'd run to a ladder and climb to the safety of their roof. From this inaccessible perch, he'd continue his harassment in safety. The Kist dogs were always puzzled. They'd whine and bark at the foot of the ladder a few minutes, then leave.

I enjoyed watching this drama play out two or three times a week from the window of my office, always with the same result. Fortunately for Pug, the Kist dogs never learned to climb.

———⟫⋅◇⋅⟪———

Shortly before our daughter, Judy, was born in April of 1955, I took Marilyn and the kids to stay with her parents in Washburn. Dad had volunteered to take her to the hospital when the time came, and Mrs. Wahl agreed to keep the kids. There was some question about the wisdom of leaving Greg. Despite the fact he was only three years old, he had already acquired an incredible stubborn streak.

With all his experience raising a family, Dad was confident he could handle even the most difficult cases, but when little Greg had refused to remove his cap and coat, all that expertise failed. At the first sign of force, little Greg began screaming and yelling, holding unto his coat with all the tenacity of a baby possum. All the while this was going on, Susan kept hollering, "Take him to Grandma Grace, Grandpa, take him to Grandma Grace!" All our best efforts ended in failure. Defiant to the end, Greg spent most of the day with his cap and coat on.

When the uproar over the coat subsided, we decided definitely, he should return to Temvik with me. From the time he was able to walk, Greg loved staying with Grandpa and Grandma Wahl. So he was reluctant to return home, especially in light of the fact that the girls were being allowed to stay. In desperation I made several promises, one of which was to take him along to Reiny Merkel's bar for a beer. Going to Reiny's definitely appealed to him, and he decided to return peaceably.

Moments after we got back, Greg disappeared. A while later he came running to the depot with a box of candy he insisted was a gift from Reiny. Still laughing about it the next day, Reiny described how little Greg had walked in big as life, climbed up on a stool, and ordered a bottle of beer. Instead, Reiny sent him home with a box of Hershey bars.

⇒◆⇐

Employees and their families were provided free transportation on the Northern Pacific and half-fare on other railroads. We were, however, required to request a pass for each trip. Such a pass was issued to Marilyn and the kids, good for one round trip between Temvik and Linton. But because the conductor seldom collected the pass, they were able to make unlimited trips. Taking the train to Linton was convenient since they departed Temvik at 11:00 A.M. and returned at 3:30 P.M., allowing plenty of time to shop and still arrive home at a decent hour. And it was a pleasant ride through the countryside.

On one occasion, Marilyn took the train to Linton alone, but failed to show up at the depot for the 3:15 P.M. departure. When the train returned to Temvik, the conductor was very apologetic as he explained how the engineer had blown the whistle for several minutes before finally leaving without her. The kids and I picked her up after work.

Tommy Tschider was conductor on the Local. He was just over five-feet tall, and he was long past retirement age. Tommy was extremely meticulous about everything he did and was always immaculately dressed. Both summer and winter he wore a white shirt, bow tie, striped overalls, and a suit coat. And he was never without his little English cap.

Tommy was an excellent conductor and a good person as well. He made a big hit with our children by handing them sacks of candy on his weekly trips through Temvik. Unfortunately, Tommy's railroad career was nearing a climactic end.

Railroad officials in Jamestown had long been after conductor Tschider for violating "Rule G" — use of alcohol while on duty. It was well known that he carried liquor in the caboose, but in spite of several surprise searches, none of the officials had been able to find it. I never learned how they finally discovered his hiding place; it seems likely that someone tipped them off. In any case, a railroad detective found his cache cleverly hidden beneath the coal in a coal pail.

Tommy was removed from service and offered the opportunity to retire, an approach designed to spare an employee the ordeal of a full-blown railroad investigation, the outcome of which was predetermined. Everyone missed Tommy, especially our kids.

⇒◆⇐

Our first winter living in the Temvik depot was a disaster. Most living quarters were cold and drafty, but we weren't at all prepared for what happened one weekend in November. The depot abutted a high embankment adjacent to the track. The empty space below the main floor faced west, and it offered little protection from the elements. The living quarters also faced west, with the kitchen and dining area at the north end. A bitter cold front had moved in on a Friday afternoon with little warning. It was accompanied by high winds and rapidly falling temperatures.

As the wind grew stronger, the linoleum in the kitchen and dining room began to rise and fall, like there was a giant bellows beneath the floor. In addition to that, the curtains fluttered like flags in a wind. By nightfall the temperature had fallen below zero with little letup in the wind. We were very fortunate to have had an ample supply of lignite coal on hand.

There were stoves in the dining room, bedroom area, office, and waiting room. I had to use extreme caution stoking them with coal due to the tremendous draft caused by the high winds. Even with four stoves it was difficult keeping the place warm. We moved pieces of furniture to strategic locations on the floor to hold the linoleum down and then turned to an even more urgent task, that of stuffing rags into the cracks around the doors and windows. There was no rest for me that night; I was kept busy hauling coal and making certain the stoves didn't overheat. Just three years earlier, while on the extra board at Pettibone, I had loaded the waiting room stove with coal one evening and forgotten to close the draft. When I returned from the café an hour later, the stove was red hot. The paint on the walls and ceiling had turned into little dark curls. Another ten or fifteen minutes and I would have been too late.

By Sunday afternoon the wind had abated enough for me to nail a layer of roofing paper along the lower half of the outside wall, providing some relief from that brutal north wind. I couldn't believe the difference it made.

The next summer, a Bridge and Building crew renovated the living quarters; they lowered the twelve-foot ceilings and installed new windows and doors. The most appreciated improvement, however, was replacing the coal stoves with oil-burning space heaters. From then on we lived in what we thought of as the "lap of luxury." I was reminded of what the agent at Esmond once told me about his living quarters on the second floor. He recounted, in very poetic language, how he had nearly killed himself each winter hauling forty tons of coal up the stairs and twenty tons of ashes down.

In December of 1956, just before the holidays, the Superintendent's office notified me by telegram I had been bumped by a fellow employee. It was devastating news. We had finally moved to a town we really liked, and now this. There was nothing to be done; we simply had to make the best of it and prepare for the inevitable. Thank God we were young enough to withstand this very unpleasant upheaval in our lives.

———⇒◈⇐———

On to Dodge

THE ONLY DECENT PLACE at which I could exercise my bumping rights was the agency at Dodge. I called the agent, Bob Jesswein, and told him I was considering bumping him and would be driving up the next weekend to look over the living quarters. He was furious and refused to even discuss it; he responded as though the bumping was my fault.

When I arrived in Dodge on that bitter cold Saturday morning in December, Bob was gone, the shades were drawn tight, and all the doors locked. Angered by his unreasonable attitude, I borrowed a hammer from the hardware store, removed a window, and took a look around. The living rooms were even nicer than those in Temvik, so we made the decision right then to move to Dodge. We didn't have much time to think about it; the living quarters in Temvik had to be vacated by January 3rd.

The weather remained bitter cold over the holidays, well below zero. In addition to the cold we had to battle both snow and wind during loading. Even though our furniture was old and worn, we worried about damage during the move. All major pieces of furniture had to be blocked and braced against the walls of the boxcar, then nailed down with metal straps. Blankets and mattresses were used for padding.

In spite of the fact train crews were ordered to use extreme caution while switching carloads of furniture, they paid scant attention to "deadhead" loads — the term given freight transported free of charge. The greatest danger was in switching, and there was going to be plenty of that before all our earthly possessions made it through the division point at Mandan. A careless brakeman could cause the engine to hit a boxcar too hard, causing enormous damage. With no insurance, there was little we could do but hope for the best.

It was a sad day when we left Temvik; many lasting friendships had been made during the years we lived there. I sold our cow, chicken house, barn, and a few personal items to local people. Everyone in town gathered to extend their best wishes and to present us with a going-away gift. It was a touching gesture we have never forgotten.

Some months after we got settled in Dodge, Bob Jesswien called and apologized for treating me so shabbily over the bumping; he was genuinely sorry, and we became reasonably good friends. Like me, he later became a postmaster, but he was killed shortly afterward in a tragic automobile accident. It was somewhat ironic that it was he who nominated me to be vice president of the North Dakota Association of Postmasters and then worked hard to see that I was elected. He continually expressed regret for the way he had treated me.

The name "Dodge" conjures up visions of the old west, and there were many similarities to its namesake of an earlier era, Dodge City, Kansas. There must have been a town constable, but if so, he made himself extremely scarce. The two bars never seemed to close. In fact, much of the time they were open every day of the week. One Sunday afternoon a brawl started out in front of the saloon a block from the depot. Five or six men stumbled out the door, hollering and yelling, pointing at each other, and threatening all sorts of violence. Just when we expected fists to start flying, they all made up and staggered back indoors. It was somewhat of a disappointment to the spectators.

Halliday was another wild town on the Mandan North Branch. I had worked there on two separate occasions while on the extra board. On Saturday night, Main Street became a beehive of activity; there were people everywhere, many of them local cowboys out celebrating. There were four bars in town, all filled to capacity. By midnight, at least four or five fights had broken out, and there was no admission charge. The only thing missing were the six-guns.

The Fort Berthold Indian Reservation was just a few miles north of town, which led to an occasional confrontation between whites and Indians. But, for the most part, everyone got along well together. In the early '50s, when I was doing relief work at Halliday, Indians still suffered the ignominy of being denied the right to buy liquor. Of course there were always those willing to buy it for them, for a price. One blatant example of this practice was a local horse buyer. He bought wine in case lots, which he swapped for horses. This was an illogical transaction, so far as the Indians were concerned, but was a common practice back then. I learned through bitter experience there was a downside to the "wine-for-horses" business.

The local horse buyer generally shipped one or two carloads every Saturday morning. Before loading, however, a state inspector was required to check the brands. If he found just one altered or incorrect brand, the entire shipment had to be aborted. It was not at all uncommon for the inspector to find one or more that had been stolen. It was especially irritating to me when that happened, since I didn't get paid unless the shipment went forward. My entire weekend would be ruined, with nothing to show for it. The horse buyer was out even more. He was mandated by law to locate the owners of any horses that had been stolen, and he had to continue feeding them until he had done so — not to mention the loss of any wine he had traded for them.

The bartender at the Malloy Bar in downtown Halliday told me an interesting story about Al Boelter, the depot agent I was filling in for. The Malloy Theater was located on the main floor, just above the Malloy Bar. Back then, liquor could be sold Monday through Saturday only. One Sunday evening, shortly after the movie had begun, Mr. Malloy was quite startled when Al came rushing up to the ticket window with a Western Union telegram. He was surprised when he read the following words: "Would you please go down stairs and get me a pint of whiskey?"

A bone-chilling incident happened in Halliday that I shall never forget. Most stations I worked at while on the extra board had plenty of office space, and that's where I slept at night. Halliday, however, was different. The office was so small I was forced to set up my cot in the waiting room. I didn't mind, except there was little privacy and no lights. And, unfortunately, there wasn't a lock on the entrance door. That didn't particularly worry me, since outlaws and burglars seldom bothered depots.

It seemed like I had just fallen asleep, a little after midnight, when the door burst open and in marched five young Indians, perhaps in their late teens or early twenties. The waiting room was in almost complete darkness; the only light came from the moon shining through the windows. All five began jumping around, dancing and hollering, celebrating some unknown occasion. They didn't appear threatening in any way; they were just having a good time. I don't think they noticed me right away, since I was in a corner of the room and had remained perfectly still.

My billfold was under my pillow and my clothing tucked beneath the cot. I thought the best strategy was to remain quiet as possible and pretend to be sleeping. The critical point came when one of them began shaking me, but I refused to budge. I could visualize them chasing me around the waiting room in my underwear.

What ultimately saved me from some unknown fate was the fact one of them was apparently in the army and had to meet the passenger train in Mandan, nearly one hundred miles distant. No 26 departed at 3:10 A.M., so I reasoned they'd be leaving soon if they wanted to make it in time. They tipped over a waiting room bench but did no significant damage. When I got up in the morning my socks were missing. I'm sure they took them as a practical joke, something I might have done. My worst fears had been unfounded.

Until Garrison Dam was completed there were but two ways to cross the Missouri from Washburn within a reasonable driving distance. The safest and surest route was over the Bismarck-Mandan Memorial Bridge. But to save time and expense, while on the extra board, I sometimes took the Stanton Ferry, which cut nearly sixty miles from my journey. Taking that route was a calculated risk, however, due to the unreliability of the ferry captain. If he took a notion to go on a party, he might not show up for hours, or even days. When that happened, which wasn't often, it would result in a lot of wasted time on the road. I soon learned not to wait too long. Over the years, there had been a ferry operating on and off at Washburn, but not during the time I lived there.

The fee charged for crossing the Missouri on the Stanton ferry was $2.00. The captain told me of an incident when a carload of people from Fort Berthold tried to leave without paying. They failed to notice he hadn't quite docked yet and roared off into the river. Fortunately, no one drowned.

The ferry was old and rickety, with barely room for one car. It was powered by a six-cylinder Chevrolet engine, which missed a few beats now and then. The engine died completely one day, causing us to drift nearly two miles down stream before power was restored. The current was extremely swift and dangerous prior to completion of the dam.

In winter, after the ice froze to a depth of twelve inches or more, everyone crossed to the other side over a staked-out track. Crossing in winter was infinitely faster than in summer, and it was free. The Washburn Ferry, which had operated intermittently, and the one at Stanton were expensive to use and time-consuming.

Due to the river's bad temperament and strong current, the main channel often shifted during the night, resulting in many sandbars being washed away while others were created. This constant shifting raised havoc with the ferry business. In winter, from the force of fast-moving water around sandbars, the ice was often cut away, leaving dangerous areas of open water. For that reason, it was absolutely vital to flag the point of crossing each day. Not to do so was an invitation to disaster.

One cold winter night in early December of 1949, a wedding dance was being held in the small town of Hensler, just across the river from Washburn. Despite sub-zero temperatures and drifting snow, Ross Fahlgren and two others decided to cross the frozen Missouri and take in the dance. Ross drove alone while the other two followed in a pickup truck. All three left between 10:30 and 11:00 P.M. Just before midnight, the two men in the pickup returned with faces white as chalk. They were entirely incoherent, both trying to talk at once. If ever I saw the look of fear on a man's face, it was on that night. They described how they had been following Ross when half way across the river he had simply driven off into open water and disappeared.

Those first to arrive on the scene discovered Ross had accidentally taken the wrong trail, one which had been abandoned two days earlier. An additional six feet and the men in the pickup would have suffered a similar fate. Steam rising from the open water in the bone-chilling night air blended almost unnoticed with the swirling snow. By the time I arrived, there was little evidence of this tragic accident, except for a few tiny bubbles rising to the surface.

Some time the next morning, a Saturday, the McLean County Engineer determined the car lay about thirty feet below the surface. After working for nearly two hours, a grappling hook was secured to the car's bumper, and a giant bulldozer was unloaded near the river's edge. But minutes later, it too went to the bottom after breaking through the ice less than twenty feet from shore.

Miraculously, the bulldozer had landed atop a sandbar just four feet below the surface. The motor continued running, with just an exhaust pipe above water. It would be spring, however, before it could be rescued. Even after the completion of the dam, the Missouri continued to be dangerous and unpredictable.

Sunday morning dawned extremely cold, but the sun was out and the wind had died down. A large crowd stood in silence near the open water where the life of Ross Fahlgren had ended so tragically. A long rope had been attached to the grappling hook, and as many as one hundred sightseers were enlisted to help pull the water-filled car to the surface. Surprisingly, it seemed to take such little effort. It's doubtful Ross suffered but momentarily in the frigid waters. There was no evidence he had made any effort to escape. Since Washburn was established back in 1882, there have been many stories of men disappearing while crossing the ice, some with teams and wagons.

⟹◆⟸

Working for the State Fur Co.

THINGS WEREN'T GOING WELL ON THE RAILROAD. The number of stations being closed was a big concern to the younger employees on our division. Most anxious were those with families, like myself. The trucking industry was making significant inroads into the railroad's business. Shortly after arriving in Dodge I began reading the "help-wanted" section of the *Bismarck Tribune*.

An advertisement for an assistant manager at the State Fur Company in Bismarck sounded appealing; it was an old established company in the business of selling fur coats, jackets, stoles, and other fashionable wearing apparel. They also cleaned and stored furs and did repair and remodeling. I applied for the job in early spring of 1958 and was hired shortly thereafter. The railroad granted me a leave-of-absence during which time I retained my seniority, with the right to return to work if I wished.

Working for the State Fur Co. was a totally new experience for me; I had never worked in sales. It was a good job, but I discovered early on that it might not last. Ben Buman, the owner, had reached retirement age and was already considering selling the business when I was hired. Had I known that at the outset I would have looked for something more permanent. Ben was a good employer, patient and understanding, and he made every effort to ease the transition to my new job. One disagreeable aspect was the requirement that I travel western North Dakota during the prime selling season, from October through January.

I only worked for Ben a year, but in that short time I learned a great deal about furs. It was my responsibility to open the store each morning, unlock the vault, and remove the display racks holding the most expensive furs. There were coats valued from $100 all the way to $10,000. The most expensive ones usually remained in the vault and were shown by appointment only. A year after I had left his employ, Ben was robbed by a group of con artists that had managed to get away with furs valued at over $ 5,000.00. Two women had somehow talked their way into using the vault to change clothes and then walked out with several pieces of valuable merchandise hidden beneath their coats.

On one occasion, I delivered a beautiful mink coat valued at over $8,000 to the owner of a large department store. When I walked into her office and handed her the box, she removed the coat, looked at it briefly, then threw it over the back of a chair like it was something she did every day. With a cigarette dangling from her lips, she wrote a check for the full amount.

One day Ben asked me to deliver a mink jacket to a lady living just a few blocks from the store. I recall thinking it was strange she hadn't come by to try it on. It was early afternoon in late August, and the temperature was in the high 80s when I arrived at her door. It was dark inside her apartment, so it took awhile for my eyes to adjust. When they finally did, I was shocked to see a nearly naked, middle-aged woman standing before me. I stood in stunned silence until she finally said, "Well, haven't you ever seen a woman dressed like this before?" I threw the jacket on a chair and literally ran out the door without a word. Back at the store everyone laughed. One of the furriers had had a similar experience a year earlier with the same woman. Ben thought it was quite amusing, explaining that she was likely an exhibitionist.

Marilyn and the kids remained at Dodge, and I drove home weekends. Later, I made a down payment on a house and we moved to Bismarck. I found living in a larger city to be expensive. After making the mortgage payment, health insurance premium, and the usual household bills, there was very little money left. I had often heard the term "living from hand-to-mouth" but had never been in that predicament myself, until then.

⋙─◆─⋘

Back to the Railroad and Memories of Windsor

AS THE END OF MY LEAVE-OF-ABSENCE DREW NEAR, I was faced with a major decision: either stay with Ben, or return to the railroad. It wasn't easy, but after careful consideration I decided it would be in my best interest, and that of my family, to return to my former job on the railroad. An important part of that decision was the fact I needed just three more years to qualify for a railroad pension.

The thought of being posted once again to the extra board and being away from home was not a pleasant prospect. It was anyone's guess how long it would take before I would be the successful bidder on a permanent position, but I didn't mind. My love of railroading hadn't diminished, and I decided to take my chances.

I wasn't alone; most railroad employees were dealing with some level of uncertainty. In spite of my concern, working for the Northern Pacific was still the most exciting job I'd ever had, and I felt it was worth the risk. My first day back was like coming home after a long absence. The only other time I'd experienced such a feeling was the day I'd returned to Elmwood Farm after my discharge from the Navy.

Little had changed on the railroad, except that business wasn't quite as good as it had been. I had to brush up on my telegraphy and study for a rules test I had to take within two weeks. A rules examination covered all regulations governing the movement of trains and was required every two years, or immediately after a lengthy absence.

Returning to the extra board was like a new beginning. It brought back memories of the day I had been assigned temporary second trick operator at Windsor, my first job lasting longer than two weeks. Windsor was the second station west of Jamestown, and during the winter months, December through March, helper engines were required for westbound freight trains leaving Jamestown Yard. The old steamers lacked traction in winter and needed the assistance of a pusher engine to help their train up the long hill west of town. Back then, diesel engines weren't yet available for use in freight service.

The station at Windsor remained open twenty-four hours a day, seven days a week to accommodate the helper engines, which came only as far as the Windsor Depot. They required written train-orders from the dispatcher before they could return to Jamestown.

The scariest night of my then young career had come during a blinding snowstorm, when three eastbound trains and one westbound were marooned in the small town of Windsor at the same time. In addition, a helper engine was on the elevator track. Two freights, one behind the other, occupied the main line, and one each on the two sidings. The crews milled around inside the office making a mess of the varnished floors. They were all tired, wondering when their train would be allowed to leave; most of the crews lived in Jamestown, just fifteen miles east, and they were anxious to get home. Due to the storm, all trains were ordered held at the terminals until the weather moderated.

The air inside the depot was thick with tobacco smoke accompanied by a high density of railroad profanity. I had five conductors to contend with, all vying for a chance to talk on the one direct line to the dispatcher. Each was eager to explain why his train should be the first to leave. My desk was covered with train-orders.

Snowed in on the eastbound siding was a freight train that included seven carloads of cattle – immediately ahead of the caboose. The yardmaster wanted that train in Jamestown as soon as possible to protect the cattle from freezing. After a long delay, the dispatcher finally cleared them to leave. The conductor alerted his crew, and they hurriedly donned their heavy coats, lit their lanterns, and made their way through a hurricane force wind to their train. We peered into the night from the depot as their engine charged back and forth, struggling to break free from a siding covered with drifts.

Just after the engineer whistled to leave town, disaster struck. Unknown to them, a knuckle had snapped, causing the train to break in two. Those on the engine didn't learn until after they had arrived in Jamestown that half their train was still in Windsor, including the seven cars of livestock.

Since visibility was down to zero, hand signals could not be seen for more than a few feet. The dispatcher gave orders for the crew of the helper engine to try and save the seven cars of stranded cattle. The engineer, one with many years experience, backed into the siding and jerked the frozen cars loose, one at a time, then took them safely into Jamestown Yard. He and his crew were hailed as heroes.

The rescue effort had been extremely dangerous and was in gross violation of the "Book of Rules," especially since signals from a brakeman's lantern were nearly impossible to see during this worst blizzard in years.

It had been a long, difficult day, one bedeviled by sub-zero cold, high winds and snowdrifts hard as stone. When the last train left that evening, and my shift was about to end, I sat in the operator's chair exhausted. The third trick man came on duty at midnight, but by then the worst was over. The only train scheduled was a snowplow leaving Jamestown to clear the tracks west to Bismarck.

The rotary plow opened the line, but the drifting had continued. So the next morning the superintendent ordered the main line to be cleared again. The drifts were hard, but not real high, resulting in a decision to use the "Russell Plow," one designed for speed. We had little notice it was coming and hadn't had time to prepare. When the plow hit the drifts in front of the depot, flying chunks of snow broke nearly every pane of glass facing the track. Thankfully, the storm windows bore the brunt of the assault.

It was midday before the weather moderated, and the agent asked me to tear the tattered roofing paper from alongside the depot and dispose of it. It felt good to get some fresh air. I gathered up as much paper as I could carry and stuffed it inside the potbellied stove in the waiting room. That's when the fire from hell nearly burned the depot down. The smoke was ghastly, it smelled like pure tar, and the stove began to quiver and shake. Then it started to jump up and down like it was doing a dance. It looked to me like it was going to explode any second, so I, along with everyone else inside, ran for the hills. There was no way I dared shut the stove down, it would definitely have blown sky high. Fortunate for me, as soon as it had burned down a little, I was able to douse the flames with a pail of water. That was the last time I ever put roofing paper inside a stove.

The one café in Windsor served meals inside an old, dilapidated hotel building, one that hadn't seen an overnight guest in decades. Mrs. Backman, the owner and cook, had a unique method of arriving at one's bill. Her dinners were served family-style with but one entrée. Too bad if the menu didn't suit you – it was eat what she had or starve. All customers were seated together at a long, communal table. During the meal, Mrs. Backman sat perched on a stool behind us making notes, busily preparing each check according to how much food one consumed. No one escaped paying for second helpings or an additional cup of coffee.

⟹•◆•⟸

On to Pettibone

LATER THAT SUMMER I WAS SENT TO THE SMALL TOWN OF PETTIBONE to relieve the agent, Art Cooper, who was seriously ill. Art had never attended any of our union meetings, or any other railroad functions, so I had never met him. He had a slim build, was about sixty years old, and of medium height. His tousled white hair and bushy eyebrows accented his long, craggy face, giving him a fierce, intimidating look. The Coopers remained in the depot living quarters throughout his illness, and Mrs. Cooper continued to live there for some time after his death.

Art was a member of an ancient organization called the "Order of Rosicrucian." It was a semi-secret society that believed its practitioners were endowed with certain mystical powers. Art was a member in good standing and firmly believed in his ability to alter the well being of any person. He practiced those beliefs on himself, hoping to regain his health, which, by the time I had arrived, was rapidly deteriorating. One of his first acts after becoming seriously ill was to go on a vegetarian diet.

Several years earlier, when Art was still well, a young man living on a farm south of town suffered from a rare form of mental illness. The boy's father had taken him everywhere in search of a cure without success. After discussing his condition with friends, Art Cooper was mentioned as a person rumored to have certain supernatural powers, and therefore might be worth consulting.

Desperate to help their son, the parents invited Art to their farmhouse. He arrived the next Saturday morning with all his mystical apparatus, the most important piece of which, was a crystal ball at the center of a rectangular piece of black cloth on the kitchen table. The patient was about twenty years of age, and he was solidly built. After he was brought into the room and seated, Art placed his hands over the crystal ball and began to chant, making all sorts of unintelligible sounds that gravitated up and down his larynx with varying degrees of intensity. Without warning, the young man suddenly lunged at Art, grabbing him in a stranglehold about the neck. It was only through the quick intervention of the parents that Art was saved from certain death by strangulation. After that horrible encounter, Art narrated how he'd rushed home for a shot of nerve tonic.

Months later, after he had begun his vegetarian diet, Art passed away. It was a sad time for his wife and family — and for me as well, since I was living in the office, able to hear everything that transpired. I finally moved to the waiting room for a little privacy.

———◈———

Pete Sorenson was Section Foreman at Pettibone, and he spent a lot of his spare time in the depot telling me stories about his early days on the railroad. One story that stands out was an experience he'd had while inspecting the rails along the Mandan South Branch where much of the track parallels the Missouri River. Pete was going along at a good clip in his "track-car" when he noticed a fish pole sticking in the riverbank. Being an old fisherman, his curiosity was immediately aroused. He came to a stop and made his way down the steep embankment. There wasn't a person in sight.

The temptation facing him was too great — Pete grabbed the pole and was busy reeling in the line when someone from above called out in a loud voice, "Are you catching anything, Pete?" Looking up in surprise, Pete recognized none other than his boss, the Division Roadmaster. He tried his best to explain but the roadmaster suggested his story sounded a little far-fetched. Pete also told me that trainmen regularly hunted pheasants and other wild game from their caboose. I took that story with a grain of salt until one day during hunting season I heard gunfire a half-mile outside town, just before the local arrived.

There were a number of freight and passenger trains traveling the main line every day, therefore the first order of business each morning was a general call from the dispatcher's office with a "train lineup." The lineup listed all trains expected to be moving over our end of the division within the next four hours. It was the dispatcher's best estimate of leaving times for freight trains and passenger trains. It was essential that this information be made available to all railroad personnel, providing them with a general idea as to when a train could reasonably be expected; and it was especially important to section men working on or near the track. There have been many instances of employees losing their lives for failing to observe a lineup. During the middle '40s, after a prolonged blizzard, several section men were killed in a deep snow-cut near Wing, North Dakota, after being surprised by a train.

Every depot on the main line had two phones, one a direct line to the dispatcher, over which train movements were authorized, and the remaining line was to be used strictly for company business.

Leroy Martin, alias "Donald Duck," was a brakeman on the Local the day I got a surprise call from the conductor. I was filling in for the agent at Tappen when a call came from Medina, the next station east, and it wasn't exactly about company business. An elaborate prank was being hatched in order to teach Leroy a lesson in responsibility, and they needed my cooperation. It seems that Leroy was more than a trifle lazy, perfectly content to stand around making small talk, while his fellow employees did all the work.

The Local ran between Jamestown and Mandan, traveling west one day, and east the next. They delivered freight and did any necessary switching along the way. It was the busiest train on the track. On this particular day, they were headed west, and had about twenty minutes switching to do on the elevator track in Tappen. While the rest of the crew did the work, Leroy, as usual, sat inside the depot telling tall tales.

When they had finished switching, the engine pulled back onto the main line, three blocks west of the depot, and the brakeman coupled up the train. That's when the engineer whistled two short blasts, an indication they were leaving town. When Leroy heard that, he bolted out the door like a young racehorse leaving the starting gate. He literally flew down the track in a futile effort to catch up, waving and hollering for them to stop. Of course, they had no intention of stopping. Leroy returned to the depot exhausted. He couldn't believe they'd left him behind and spent the next half-hour lamenting the fact he might be in serious trouble. I let him stew awhile before telling him there was a way he might be able to catch up to his train. A westbound freight leaving Jamestown could be given a message to pick him up at Tappen and drop him off at Steele, two stations west. Meanwhile, the Local would wait for him on a siding.

An hour later, as part of the plan, the freight stopped, picked up Leroy, and dropped him off at Steele. When he climbed into the caboose, the conductor exploded, predicting dire consequences for his lack of attention to duty.

On their return trip the next day, the conductor called and asked me to address the following message to Leroy: "I want an immediate explanation why you were absent from your assigned train when it departed Tappen at 11:10 A.M. Monday, September 25th." I added the signature of the superintendent, sealed it in a company envelope, and handed it to Leroy when the Local arrived at Tappen. Leroy read the message and went into shock. He spent the remainder of the trip composing a reply, naturally with a lot of help. Finally, as they neared Jamestown he was told the truth. I never saw Leroy on the Local again. He worked on the branch lines thereafter, where a brakeman's life was more serene.

⇒►⇐

Chasely and the Snowstorm of 1951

THERE WAS A BIG SNOWSTORM IN THE LATE SPRING OF 1951. I was working at Chaseley, but had been at home in Washburn for the weekend when it began snowing. It didn't end until all the roads were completely blocked. Desperate to get to my job Monday morning, I hired a local pilot to fly me. When we landed in a farmer's yard at the edge of town, half the townspeople came running out to see who it was.

Most of the snow melted during that next week, filling the ditches and sloughs with water and inundating many roads. Friday afternoon I sent Marilyn a telegram telling her I'd be taking the train to Turtle Lake Saturday morning and asking her to meet me. Turtle Lake was the terminal station on the Turtle Lake Branch.

We left Chaseley about 10:30 A.M. Saturday morning. Everything went smoothly until we reached Hurdsfield, eight miles west. That's where the big party began. The train crew sent me up town for groceries while they completed their work. The shopping list included a dozen bottles of malt and a quart of 190-proof alcohol. Topping off malt with a shot of 190-proof alcohol resulted in one of the most powerful drinks known.

The Local on this branch was a "mixed train," consisting of an engine, baggage car, a passenger coach and however many loads and empties were destined for stations along the way. I didn't want to be seen drinking in the coach, so I rode in the baggage car. By the time we reached Denhoff, I had noticed a definite increase in speed. The telephone poles were literally whizzing by the window.

There was a speed limit of thirty-five miles per hour on this branch, but just a mile out of McClusky, it felt like we were going wide open. I didn't get too excited until the furniture began slithering back and forth across the steel decking. When the baggage-man slid the door open and threatened to jump, I began paying attention. The baggage car was swaying so violently by this time, we had to hold on for dear life.

When our speed reached what I considered a critical point, I braced myself for a quick look out the door and saw Turtle Lake just around the bend. Thank God the train began to slow. I will never forget the look of relief on the baggage-man's face. He had been absolutely terrified, and I was a little scared myself.

—⇒◦⇐—

Chapter X

Driscoll Bound

ORTUNATELY, AFTER JUST A FEW WEEKS on the extra board, I was the successful bidder on the Agent/ Telegrapher position at Driscoll. It was a good location, right off Highway 10, and only thirty-five miles from Bismarck. There was a good school, and it was on the main line of the Northern Pacific. What more could one ask for. I was enthusiastic about the prospect of a simpler life, one where I could spend more time with my family.

Marilyn and the kids, however, were not exactly thrilled about leaving our new home. They had become accustomed to life in Bismarck and were understandably upset. I knew first-hand that changing schools could be difficult, but going from large to small was significantly less upsetting than the other way around. At least I thought so.

Greg was fortunate to have completed first grade in Bismarck and appeared to be off to a good start on his academic career. His report cards indicated above average grades, and he was rewarded at home with high praise. However, at the end of the third period, his card bore an obvious forgery. A grade of "C" had been changed to an "A." Greg's expertise as a forger left a lot to be desired. I congratulated him on a good report card, but pointed out the one irregularity. BANG! He slammed his small fist on the table declaring, "That's it, I'm not going back!"

The next spring, we bought Greg his first bicycle. He learned to ride in record time, and we hardly saw him after that. I awakened about 6:30 one morning to find him missing from his bedroom. He loved his bike so much, he had left home at daybreak to go riding and has been addicted to anything on wheels ever since.

There was only one vacant house for rent in Driscoll. It was small, but seemed adequate until something better came along. As it turned out, we lived there more than twenty years. In spite of its many shortcomings, it holds innumerable happy memories for our family, and it brings forth a feeling of great nostalgia when we recall our days there.

My salary on the railroad was considered a little above average, but with the kids growing up so rapidly, expenses were mounting. Stephanie and Susan were about to become teenagers, with Greg right behind. Judy wasn't in school yet, and George had yet to make an appearance. I began working at various jobs after hours to supplement our income. While we didn't have any great material wealth, we were a happy family. It was during those years, while our children were growing up, that we would later remember as the happiest days of our lives. Today, whenever our family gets together, most of the stories we tell revolve around those early years in Driscoll.

Marilyn was three months pregnant with George the spring of 1960, and we began discussing ways to break the news to the rest of the children. To achieve that end, we decided to play a little game one evening at the dinner table. I explained that someone was coming to live with us, and they were to guess who it might be. They guessed and guessed, naming everyone they could think of, including some that were no longer among the living. Finally, Stephanie's face lit up like a Christmas tree, she exclaimed, "Mama's going to have a baby!" They were all happy and excited over the prospect of a new brother or sister.

George was born on October 8th, and he immediately inherited several doting mothers and an admiring big brother for a roommate. The girls took turns carrying him around, feeding him, and otherwise spoiling him. We all enjoyed this late addition to our family. It seemed like he was never a baby. Before we knew it he was walking around.

⋙⋗◆⋖⋘

Our daughter, Judy, was an exceptional child. When she was only four years old, she complained one day of not feeling well, though there were no obvious signs of illness. She lay on her bed while Marilyn ran to the store for some medication. When she returned five minutes later, little Judy was nowhere to be found, but taped to the door of the refrigerator was a note scrawled in large letters: "I at rckees hus. Judy." Marilyn quickly deciphered the message, determining Judy was at our neighbor's visiting their little boy, Ricky. We were shocked to learn little Judy could almost read and write.

Everyone contributed to the spoiling of George, but we all liked him so much no one seemed to notice, or care. One Saturday, while we were entering the old F. W. Woolworth Store in downtown Bismarck, he ran off. We had no idea where he had gone until we heard some loud howling down the street, in front of the Patterson Hotel. A woman held him by the hand, trying to quiet him down. With tears streaming down his cheeks, he had told her, "My name is George W. Cunningham the second, I'm three years old, and I'm from Driscoll, North Dakota." He was mighty glad to see us and never strayed from our side again.

There was only one occasion when he overstepped his bounds. It happened in the Lucas Department Store when he kicked his mother in the leg. She took him in the restroom and gave him a good paddling. It was to be the first and last time he was ever severely disciplined.

A year later, after he had turned four, Marilyn went to work, and I was left the job of babysitting. From that point on, until he started school, George and our dog, Wilbur, spent a lot of time with me at the depot. I set up a cot in the office where they both took naps each afternoon. George rode his tricycle around the waiting room during inclement weather and out on the platform when it was nice. He was good about staying indoors when trains were due, but I had to keep a watchful eye out. He enjoyed life in the depot, there was always something exciting happening. George recalls his railroad days with a great deal of fondness.

An experience that very nearly ended in tragedy happened in July of 1964. Don Fisher had driven back to North Dakota from Denver in a new Ford pickup to visit his parents north of Driscoll. The Fisher family milked a lot of cows and shipped most of their cream by rail. The morning after his arrival home, Don came to town in his new pickup with a ten-gallon can of cream. It was strictly against regulations to drive onto the platform, due to the close proximity of passing trains. But despite my best efforts to see that this regulation was observed, it was seldom taken seriously, and almost impossible to enforce.

It was nearing 9:30 A.M. on that fateful summer day when Don drove up and carelessly backed a rear wheel off the edge of the platform. The truck's back-end landed with a bang, just inches from the inside rail. I became alarmed since the westbound "hotshot" No. 601, was due momentarily going "hell-bent for election."

Don didn't appear to be at all concerned, but when he tried to drive away, the pickup refused to budge. I glanced east just as an automatic signal dropped, indicating 601 had just passed Steele, only eight miles away. My heart skipped a beat. Tiny beads of sweat began to trickle down my ribs. If 601 came by with Don's pickup halfway off the platform, there'd be parts flying every direction. It would not only mean the end of Don's pickup, but the front of the depot would likely be destroyed as well. In addition to that, and even more dangerous, it could cause a serious derailment. The situation was critical to say the least and I was absolutely terrified.

I ran inside the depot and dropped the semaphore to the most restrictive position. That meant 601 would have to stop, but try telling that to a half-mile long freight train traveling sixty-five miles per hour. I grabbed an emergency signaling device called a "fusee," lit it, and ran toward the train desperately signaling them to stop. The engineer should have acknowledged with two short blasts of his whistle, but he just kept coming.

After I had ran about one hundred yards I chanced to look back toward the depot. To my surprise, a farmer had backed up and was preparing to pull Don's pickup off the platform. By now, 601 was only two miles away and coming fast. There was no way they'd be able to stop in time so, hoping for a miracle, I dropped the fusee, ran back to the office, and quickly returned the semaphore to the proceed position. The pickup was jerked free just seconds before 601 thundered past the depot at full throttle.

It was pure happenstance that a man with a chain in his truck had come by in the nick of time, saving us all from certain hell and damnation.

When I finally sat down, my legs were like rubber. My entire body shook and it was an hour or more before my breathing returned to normal. I never learned the name of the engineer on 601 that day, or if he ever saw my signal. The incident was too unnerving for me to make any inquiries.

⟫⟪

The saga of the wayward horse began on a warm night in early August. A westbound freight train had been directed by the dispatcher to take siding at Burleigh, about twelve miles east of Bismarck. It might be interesting to note that this siding was originally know as "Seventeenth Siding," then "Blaine," then "Clark's Farm," and finally Menoken. While Menoken still exists as a village, the name of the siding was changed to "Burleigh" by the railroad, back in 1891, in recognition of Dr. Walter Burleigh, Indian Agent and Dakota Territory delegate to Congress.

Half way into the siding, a horse, which had apparently escaped from a nearby pasture, ran directly into the path of the engine and was killed. The next morning, the section crew dragged the dead horse from the side of the track to a water-filled pothole alongside the pasture fence.

A few days later, another westbound freight entered the same siding, which is intersected midway by a road. When a train is expected to block a crossing longer than fifteen minutes, the train crew must "cut the crossing" in order to provide motorists access to the other side, and that's what happened on this night.

In the darkness, a railroad lantern is difficult to see, so the brakeman lit a fusee to signal the engineer. Later, when their train had been coupled together and they were ready to leave, the brakeman simply threw the burning fusee toward the pothole of water. As he began walking toward the train there was a tremendous explosion. Fearing for his life, the terrified brakeman ran the remaining distance to the engine at breakneck speed.

Several days passed before an investigation into the matter disclosed that the burning fusee had landed directly on top of the bloated remains of the dead horse and then had quickly burned through the hide igniting the methane gas inside. That was good news to the brakeman, who had worried all the way to Mandan that some evil terrorist was trying to blow up the train.

⇒◆⇐

One unpleasant aspect of a telegrapher's life was the constant battle against mice. Most depots were old, without basements, and had foundations made of heavy wood timbers. The nearness of grain elevators only exacerbated the problem. Poison was the preferred method of control, but it sometimes caused other problems, like mice crawling into some inaccessible place to die. When that happened, the smell would soon become intolerable, and one would have to keep searching until the remains were found. When I worked at Pettibone, a mouse suffered rigor mortis behind the built-in office safe, and it took the better part of two weeks to locate his corpse.

A friend of mine, working at the small town of Goodrich, was sleeping in the office when he became nauseated by the smell of a dead mouse. The sickening odor always seemed greatest at night. It was several weeks later, as he was packing up to leave, that he discovered a mouse had somehow been crushed between the folding joints of his cot, right below where his head lay.

Mel Diers, the railroad signal-maintainer, usually left his track-car running while he came in to check on trains. Mel hadn't been inside the depot more than a minute one morning when we heard the engine on his track-car begin to accelerate. We both ran to the window just in time to see George at the controls, moving slowly down the track. Fortunately, Mel was able to catch him, narrowly averting yet another disaster.

George and Wilbur took care of the office in the afternoon while I went for my coffee break. If the phone rang or a customer came by, George would leave Wilbur in charge and come running. No one got in the office when Wilbur was on guard. On one occasion, however, he wouldn't let the trainmaster in. He didn't say he couldn't come in, he just stood in front of the door snarling. The trainmaster definitely didn't like that. Funny, Wilbur had never pulled that stunt on anyone before. I didn't appreciate him taking such a personal dislike to one of my bosses.

Driscoll had almost graduated from the days of outdoor toilets. But when we were returning to the depot one afternoon, George said he needed to go, badly. Luckily, just behind the café was an old two-seater. As soon as I had him in position, he took one look down the hole, then exclaimed, "Dad, don't let me fall down there, or it'll be the end of George!"

One afternoon two intoxicated bums were in town celebrating Memorial Day by knocking on doors, asking for money. I had heard what they were doing, so when they reached our neighborhood I pulled the shades and cautioned the kids to remain perfectly quiet. Instead of listening to that advice, George thought I meant for him to be on the welcoming committee. The minute they knocked on our door, he pulled back the shade and hollered, "Here they are, here they are!"

———≫◆≪———

Paul Paslay was an elderly bachelor living alone on his ranch north of town. He was the Driscoll historian and acknowledged expert on Indian lore. He was often asked to speak about local skirmishes that had occurred between the cavalry and Indians.

He boarded the train for Bismarck at least once a week, usually arriving at the depot well before departure time. He enjoyed standing at the ticket window telling anyone willing to listen about his early days on the prairie. George and I never tired of hearing about General Sibley's battle against the Sioux at Cottonwood Lake, just north of town.

Some years earlier, Paul had been the victim of a near fatal accident with a runaway team of horses that had resulted in the loss of his left ear. George was fascinated by the hole where the ear had once been and always managed to sit perched on the counter just inside the ticket window in an effort to get a closer look. When he could stand the suspense no longer, he brazenly put his eye right up to Paul's head. I couldn't believe he had done that and jerked him away; Paul never said a word; he acted as though it hadn't happened.

During the years I lived in Driscoll, I had made several visits to the Paslay ranch. Like most bachelors, Paul had his share of idiosyncrasies. Except for one or two years, he had spent his entire life on the family homestead. His sister, Bernice, had the distinction of being the first white child born in their township.

The Paslay house was much like a museum. Paul had saved many artifacts, some dating back to the time he was a child, and he kept them prominently displayed. A portrait of his father hung from a giant nail on the living room wall and bore an uncanny resemblance to Jesse James.

Paul pictured himself as a latter-day frontiersman and often dressed the part. One of his more famous trophies, one he had mounted himself, was the head of a buck deer, which hung next to the picture of his father. His ability as a taxidermist was brought into question, however, when one was confronted with the only deer head in history to have a broad smile on its face and light bulbs for eyes.

Don Fisher's family had lived a few miles north of the Paslay Ranch. The Fisher boys had worked for Paul since they were quite young, and they had become good friends. Long after the family had moved away, the boys continued to stop by to visit Paul whenever they were in the vicinity.

Paul called me aside one day to tell me a story about one of those visits. It was apparent that whatever he was about to divulge was to be something quite dramatic, since he lowered his voice and spoke in a most confidential manner. It seems Tom Fisher and his girl friend had brought along two target pistols one afternoon and had asked if they might go out behind the barn for a little target practice. Paul was not only happy to oblige; he offered to get his six-shooter and join them.

After they'd each fired off several rounds, the girl friend became highly agitated by Tom's critical comments regarding her marksmanship. Finally, in total exasperation, she turned to him and shouted, "Tom, if you don't keep your damn mouth shut, I'm gonna shoot your balls off!" Paul was mortified. He had never heard such scandalous talk coming from a woman. Tom didn't pay any attention, but Paul quickly holstered his gun and made an immediate beeline for the house, just in case he might become a target of her bad temper.

⇒•⇐

One of Paul's neighbors, Adam Wilkins, was a nondescript, middle-aged man that, like Paul, lived the life of a bachelor. Adam was not socially active and suffered from paranoia, perhaps a result of living such a secluded life. He raised livestock, but had gotten himself into serious trouble with the Humane Society over his failure to care for them properly. Adam had a "survival of the fittest" philosophy and fed his animals accordingly, forcing them to forage about the pasture for the bulk of their food. It was his thinking that his pigs could survive living off the undigested grain in fresh cow manure. The story going around in town was that his grown hogs resembled dogs. They had developed skinny, elongated bodies with long legs. They could run like deer, jump a four-foot fence with ease, and would attack anything that looked edible, including sheep.

Adam was convinced his neighbors were stealing his mail and was often seen hiding near his rural mailbox inside an old car body, trying to catch the guilty person. Paul stopped to visit with him one day and was immediately accused of being a thief.

Unfortunately, Adam wasn't blessed with good looks, nor did he bother to dress in a way that might attract the opposite sex. Furthermore, he hadn't the faintest idea how to ask a girl out on a date. That's when he confided in Andy Dobert, his neighbor to the east. Andy was often consulted on matters Adam deemed beyond his own ability to deal with. Having raised several daughters, one still at home, Andy felt well qualified to offer advice on the subject of dating. "Take the bull by the horns," Andy said. "March right up to the front door and ask the girl out to a movie." The very next night there came a knock at Andy's door.

There stood Adam, big as life, all dressed up in a new pair of bib over-hauls asking to see his daughter. Andy couldn't believe his eyes. After some hesitation he had no choice but to call her. She turned Adam down flat, and Andy decided to quit offering advice to the lovelorn.

⤐◆⤐

There were two "Hazels" in Driscoll. To keep them straight, we called one "Big Hazel" and the other "Little Hazel." Big Hazel was un-married and lived alone in a renovated boxcar a block from the depot. She was employed as a postal contractor, transporting mail between trains and the post office.

Regardless of the hour, I had to be at the depot to meet No. 4, com-monly known as the "milk train." But Big Hazel could go home if they hadn't yet arrived by 9 P.M. No. 4 was seldom on time in winter, espe-cially during the Christmas holiday season, so we'd wait in my office on those long, cold evenings and play rummy.

As the years passed, Big Hazel would sometimes become preoccu-pied and forget all about the trains, especially No. 3, which arrived with most of our daily mail around10:30 A.M. When that happened, I'd in-vite everyone in the depot to observe her front door. Exactly one sec-ond after No. 3 sounded its whistle east of town she'd come blasting out her door like a NASA rocket on its way into space. Her screen door would still be banging by the time she reached the tracks, a half-block away. Despite the fact she was in her sixties, Hazel could outrun most people half her age. It wasn't uncommon for me to hold the train until she arrived with the mail, all out of breath. Once, when the crossing was blocked, she actually crawled beneath the train with her sack of mail.

Big Hazel was an ardent animal lover. Whenever a stray dog was abandoned on the streets of Driscoll she'd come to the rescue, taking it under her wing until a suitable home could be found. Her two-wheel cart, used for transporting mail, was a familiar sight along Main Street. Inside her cart one day on the way to the depot was a bedraggled little female dog. Following behind was every mongrel in town, all of them yipping and yapping, each one trying desperately to get at the little fe-male. Big Hazel managed to beat them off with a sack of mail until she reached the safety the depot. She kept the poor little stray inside until those horrible beasts had left the area.

While waiting for a train one afternoon, Big Hazel decided to teach George the ABCs', and was doing fine until midway through it became necessary for her to prompt him. When she pronounced the letter "P," George immediately accused her of saying a bad word. Hazel doubled over in fits of laughter and kept on laughing for days.

Throughout the '50s and well into the '60s there were still a number of people that took the train on a regular basis. No. 3 left for Bismarck at 10:40 A.M. and returned at 4:30 P.M. One of my customers, Haral Christianson, wasn't exactly a frequent passenger, but he did take the train once or twice a month. He told me of an incident that happened on one of his trips when a young woman, just across the aisle, was having a difficult time trying to breast-feed her obstinate child. When the conductor stopped for her ticket, Haral overheard the mother say, "Now, Lester, if you don't eat your dinner like a good little boy, I'm going to let this nice conductor have it!"

Oscar Olson farmed several miles north of town. Oscar was a good person and a real gentleman, but, unfortunately, not cut out to be a farmer. He had a difficult time supporting his family on the few acres he owned.

When Oscar needed assistance, which was often, he called upon his neighbor, Oliver Knudson. Oliver got a call one afternoon that Oscar urgently needed help with haying, but when he arrived with his tractor, Oscar still hadn't shown up. He finally came an hour later. Dragging behind his team and hayrack was a quarter-mile of woven-wire fence that had somehow got snagged beneath his wagon. Oscar, not unlike the legendary baseball player, Satchel Paige, never looked back "in case someone was gaining on him."

In early November of that fall, the weather had turned cold and Oscar still hadn't filled his barn with hay, so once again he called for help.

Oliver brought along his farmhand tractor, which would make easy work of filling the haymow. He planned to show Oscar how to operate it, then leave for town. The haymow door was narrow, just wide enough to accommodate an average load, if one used a little care.

With Oliver observing nearby, Oscar made his first stab at the barn. He had an extra large load causing the tractor to lumber crazily over the frozen ground. Moving right along, just inches from the open doorway, a front tire suddenly hit a frozen cow pie. The entire load lurched sideways and missed the door, resulting in a horrendous crash. Boards and debris flew everywhere. When the dust settled, Oscar discovered he had just made the haymow door six feet wider than before.

During the bitter cold months of winter, Mrs. Olson kept the cream in the living room to protect it from freezing. Her teenage daughters were accustomed to endless telephone conversations. One evening after a call had been mysteriously interrupted, one of the girls explained that she had forgotten the cover was off the cream can, and had accidentally dropped the phone inside.

The big prisoner escape was one of the more bizarre stories involving the Olson family. It happened on a cold night in late October and was widely reported in the media. Oscar was proud of the part he had played and became a big celebrity in Driscoll.

A light snow was falling the night two dangerous prisoners were being transported to Bismarck. Somehow, they had managed to escape at a gas station in the small town of Sterling, twenty-five miles short of their destination. One of the prisoners was captured immediately, but the second man got away.

Shortly after 11:00 P.M. that night there came a knock at Oscar's door. A stranger, nearly frozen, said his car had quit and asked if someone could take him to town. Oscar offered to let the man spend the night on his couch and to take him wherever he wanted to go the next day. There had been bulletins all evening, both on radio and television, regarding the escape of two criminals, but the Olson family was completely oblivious of such news, and had no idea one of the wanted men was in their living room at that very moment.

After breakfast the following morning, Oscar and his wife gathered up the stranger and left for town. A mile down the road the man offered

Oscar an additional $20 if he would take him to Bismarck. Oscar agreed, but said he would have to stop for gas. The station attendant recognized Oscar's passenger from the description given and called the sheriff. Upon reaching the outskirts of Bismarck, they were forced to stop at a roadblock. After being surrounded by police, the escaped prisoner gave up peacefully. Oscar and his wife, however, were in a state of shock, completely unaware they had been harboring a dangerous criminal. Oscar was interviewed on television and by members of the press. He basked in the warmth of notoriety from one end of the state to the other.

———⋙◆⋘———

The family automobile sounded like it was going through a change of life, so Oscar decided to take it in for an overhaul. That meant they'd be driving the old truck for a while. Days later he received a call the work was finished, and that the engine "purred like a kitten." Oscar drove the car home happy as a lark, and since they hadn't been anywhere for over a week, he decided to celebrate by taking the family on a trip to town.

Just as they were about to leave, Oscar suddenly remembered the car was low on gas. He ran quickly to a back shed and returned with five gallons, poured it in, and they were off. Two miles short of the Driscoll turnoff, however, the car began trailing clouds of thick yellow smoke, and the engine was making terrible noises. Oscar couldn't believe it. The car had run so well up until then.

When they finally reached the outskirts of town, after a mile of jerking and chugging, the engine went into cardiac arrest and died, abruptly ending their big trip. The next day, Oscar discovered that in his haste to get started, he had mistakenly poured five gallons of fly spray into the tank instead of gasoline.

———⋙◆⋘———

There were two brothers, George and Olaf, that farmed together north of town. After Olaf passed away, George became the sole owner of the farm. Though George was well past middle age, he had never married, and he had often told me how he desperately wished he could find a wife. That wish was to be fulfilled sooner than expected and would haunt him for the rest of his life.

George and I were members of the Driscoll Men's Club and had served on many committees together. Since he had always lived a somewhat sheltered life, he was more than a little naïve when it came to dealing with "city slickers." For example, one night at a Men's Club meeting, a member asked George if he'd be interested in purchasing a dance ticket at half-price. George loved dancing and was certainly interested in such a bargain. After he got home, however, he discovered the ticket was for a dance that had been held the previous week. Drat!

In the late spring of 1983, after a brief courtship, George got married. No one knows how he managed to keep his love affair secret. None of his friends had been told, so when the news was made public, it naturally came as quite a shock.

It was a tempestuous relationship from the beginning. George admitted the two of them had been fighting since shortly after the ceremony. Within weeks of their honeymoon, he came to town one afternoon with his right eye completely closed and a knot on his forehead the size of a small orange. He was in a terrible state, and I asked if he'd been in an accident.

Almost in tears he said, "My brother Olaf went all through World War II without so much as a scratch. I stay on the farm taking care of the home front and almost get killed by a can of beer." Explaining further, he moaned, "That crazy wife of mine went berserk and threw a full can of beer across the room. It hit me right between the eyes, and I thought I'd been killed." George survived, but the marriage continued to falter.

A month later, Driscoll was in the midst of its 100th anniversary celebration, and George and I had been assigned to the sanitation committee. On the morning of the second day, while taking a load of refuse to the dump-ground, his wife met us on her way into town. She flagged us down and demanded to know where I was taking George. As she drove off she hollered out her window, "Leave that no-good bastard out there with the rest of the garbage!" George sat stone-faced, not uttering a word.

They were divorced a few months later, but not before his wife had appropriated most of his money. The farm had to be sold as part of the settlement, and she managed to get a generous share of the proceeds. It was a tremendous loss for George and he was devastated.

After his auction he moved to Bismarck where he re-married a few years later to a nice lady. He lived out his life broke, but in relative peace.

⊰⋄⊱

Prior to our anniversary celebration, several committees had been named to plan special events. Since the Men's Club was expected to be one of the principal supporters, we decided to raise some much-needed cash by holding a raffle for a second-hand automobile. I was named as a "committee-of-one" to look into the matter. The person I decided to contact was Mac McKinney, a large, well-known car-dealer in Bismarck. During our meeting, Mac told me he would sooner give us a donation of $500. I was delighted with this proposal and assured him our club would be also, and they were.

To put this story in better perspective, I must explain that Mac McKinney was a close political ally of Herman Linsen, a local bar-owner and member of our club. This fact had not been seriously considered by the membership. In fact, I don't think anyone from our club had given it a second thought. Herman had been a member in name only, mostly due to a long-time feud between him and other club members. It had started two years earlier after a Valentine party for our wives, a party that had included a social hour followed by a dinner and dance. Since the refreshments would constitute the single largest expense, the club had decided to solicit bids.

We received three bids, all from members of the club, including one from Herman. When the bids were opened, however, Herman's was the highest, and therefore rejected. That's when he got mad and threatened to take legal action against us, his reasoning being that since he was the only bidder with a bar in Driscoll, he should have received special consideration. Perhaps he had a point. Despite his objection, we voted to buy the refreshments from the low bidder.

So when Herman found out about the $500, he immediately called Mac and squelched the whole deal. I received a letter from McKinney shortly afterward, explaining how his company was over budget on advertising, and that he was therefore rescinding his earlier offer of the $500. It was a bitter disappointment for our club.

One of our members had been buying cars from Mac for years. He drove to Bismarck early the next morning and told McKinney he had bought his last car from him, that he was disappointed with Mac's decision, and that the rest of the members felt the same way.

Mike Lund, McKinney's sales manager, was a former Driscoll resident, and had many friends and customers in our area. He called me the next morning expressing his regret over what had happened, explaining there had been a misunderstanding, and that he would be down the next day with the money. Mike was well liked and known to be a man of his word. He delivered the check the next day as promised. But the feud between the club and Herman continued.

One fortunate aspect of this whole episode was the fact that I managed to remain on good terms with Herman. I was careful to keep it that way too, since I knew first hand that he had powerful friends in high places and was an extremely vindictive man. Once he'd been crossed he never forgot it, and would go to great lengths to make life miserable for his enemies. It simply didn't make sense to alienate him.

A giant parade was planned for the first day of our centennial. There were entries from all over the state, and we were expecting large numbers of people. Herman and his son, Fred, had set up a beer garden next to his bar. They had erected a large tent and hired extra help for the occasion. When the big day came, Herman discovered that the parade was being routed in such a way as to completely by-pass his bar and beer garden. He was outraged, and he accused the committee of a conspiracy against him. While he may have had some justification for his suspicions, there was little he could do about it and the route of the parade remained unchanged.

Vic Stoller joined our club later that fall. Vic lived in Bismarck and had recently been hired by the State Health Department as an inspector. Since Driscoll was on his itinerary, those members on the outs with Herman immediately conspired with him to issue a deficiency report for Herman's bar. Vic made a serious mistake when he went along with their plan, since he was still on probation. When Herman received a copy of the report he called Bismarck, and the unwitting Vic Stoller was terminated the next day.

There are many interesting tales regarding Herman Linsen. Some are true, some half true, and the balance pure fiction. Herman's wife, Mary, came from a small North Dakota town, but her parents were born in Germany. As the story goes, her father arranged for Herman to come to this country for the express purpose of marrying his daughter. In those days, it was common for marriages to be arranged in this way. Such a union was based, in large part, upon one's station in life. In the old country, it was difficult, if not impossible, to marry above one's place in the social order.

Herman hadn't yet become a citizen when WW II broke out, and he was rumored to have in his possession a powerful shortwave radio. In any case, he was one of the first to be interned at Fort Lincoln as a security risk. After Mary's parents appealed to Senator Langer for help, Herman was released to Langer's personal custody, and he became the Senator's chauffeur, personal bodyguard, and fixer of problems.

One of Langer's campaign strategies was for Herman to travel from town to town where he'd mingle with the local people, telling them the Senator was due any minute. As soon as a small crowd had gathered, Langer would drive up, shake hands with everyone, say a few words, and then follow Herman to the next stop on their itinerary. They never passed a church service without stopping, especially if it was a funeral. They'd march in unabashed to a front pew, from where the senator could look around and be recognized. This style of campaigning paid off handsomely.

Whenever a federal position was to be filled, it was Herman's job to contact the interested parties. Then, after consulting with the Senator, a decision would be made as to which applicant was most deserving — usually based on one's contributive ability. Over the years, Herman became very skillful at this type of work, and he came to know a number of powerful politicians. While most of them pretended to be his friend, they both feared and distrusted him.

One of Herman's good friends and political allies was a prominent North Dakota politician, Ben Miller. Both Ben and Herman were widely known for their thick German accents. Although Ben's wasn't quite as pronounced as Herman's, it nevertheless caused him to make an occasional embarrassing "faux pas." During a campaign for reelection, Ben had once declared, "I don't chust represent the people in Perly County, or chust the people in Pismarck, I represent effree Nordakotan as-a-whole."

Both Ben and Herman were experts at predicting elections. Herman had the uncanny ability to correctly read the pulse of the voters, and could not only predict the winner of an election, but often by what margin. He never expressed any political convictions of his own, but he did spend a lot of time visiting with people from all over the state during an election year. You might say he was the first nonpartisan pollster.

Ben was often invited to appear on local television the evening of an election to give his assessment of the early returns. In more recent times, however, he came into serious conflict with the major networks. While in the studio of one station projecting a local candidate for congress as the likely winner, a national network on another channel had already declared that candidate as losing. Modern technology had passed Ben by.

After Langer's death, Herman continued to be active in the political arena. When I wrote Senator Burdick about a summer post office job for my daughter, Stephanie, he referred me to Herman. Herman told me those jobs had already been filled, but that she could work in Burdick's Washington office if she wished. Stephanie was only seventeen, and I didn't think she was quite ready for Washington, D.C., so I declined on her behalf.

Herman called again the next day and inquired if she would be interested in a job in the tourist town of Medora. I assured him she'd be delighted. He arranged for her to be interviewed by Mac McKinney, who happened to be a good friend of Harold Schafer, wealthy Medora promoter and owner of the Gold Seal Company. After the interview, McKinney sent her to see Erma Wolters, Schafer's secretary in Bismarck. The following Monday we took Stephanie out to Medora where she spent a delightful and rewarding summer. The year was 1967.

Marilyn and I were in Herman Linsen's bar one Saturday evening with another couple waiting for him to take our order. Herman was not a handsome man, yet there were a number of women who found him appealing. He was about five-foot, nine-inches tall with a stocky build and a large, bulbous nose. He often intimidated people with his tough-guy manner. With his hair parted down the middle and an apron on, he resembled a bartender from an old western movie.

When he finally came to take our order, he asked the woman sitting opposite Marilyn and me how her love life was. She said to him, "Herman, you must have something the girls like!" And then, while he held onto his pencil and paper, she reached over and unzipped his pants.

In all the years I had known Herman, it was the first time I'd ever witnessed the slightest hint of embarrassment. His face turned beet-red, and he doubled over like he'd been shot in the stomach with a double-barreled shotgun, after which he ran for the back room like a wounded doe.

Herman and my good friend, Bud Pfeifer, were involved in several business ventures. Herman generally came out ahead on these deals, but there was one exception. And that was when he and Bud decided to go into the sheep business. They each bought a like number and planned to share the profits. Bud, of course, had them pastured on his farm just a few miles from town, and was responsible for their feeding and care.

One afternoon I received an urgent telephone call from Herman. He wanted me to go out to the farm immediately and count the sheep. When I asked the reason, he replied, "I have to find out how many sheep are left. Every damn time one dies, Bud says it was one of mine."

Because Bud was my good friend I didn't want to get involved, but I did finally agree to drive him around while he counted. We drove to the sheep pasture and Herman began counting. He soon found out what I already knew — it's not easy counting several hundred sheep in an open pasture. After several tries he complained that each time he got started counting, the sheep would move, causing him to get all mixed up. After a futile half-hour, Herman threw his tally sheet out the window and we returned to town. On the way home he lamented, "We have to sell the sheep before all mine die."

———————

Bud was continually hiring people that were down and out, but more often than not, they were just plain worthless. Most suffered from one or more self-inflicted disabilities: laziness, alcoholism, being fugitives from justice, and others. Nearly anyone wanting work got hired, because Bud didn't have the heart to refuse. The only one that got turned down, that I'm aware of, was a retarded man with one arm. Bud's generous nature cost him dearly over the years.

The only hired man lasting any length of time was Jack Johnson. Jack was a dark, swarthy man with little ambition. He was, however, a reasonable improvement over most of the men Bud had hired in the past. Because of his dark skin, local punsters nicknamed him "Blackjack." He took up with a local woman named Minnie and, after the wedding, moved into a tiny house at the end of Main Street.

In addition to working for Bud, Blackjack had several sidelines, one of which was repairing cars. He had Ben Ellison's old Dodge sedan in his garage and had just finished overhauling the engine and replacing the transmission. He also engaged in miscellaneous odd jobs, including carpentry work. He was just a little good at everything, but not real good at anything. His first credible carpentry job was a small shed with two windows, both of which he had installed inside out.

Blackjack and Minnie visited Herman's bar nearly every evening, usually staying until closing time. Minnie was a very enterprising woman. She took great pride in her ability to keep the more affluent customers entertained in titillating conversation while Blackjack remained in the background. Though he kept his distance, he was always included in the food and beverages that became an adjunct to Minnie's pursuits.

One evening, after consuming several drinks, Blackjack became tired and decided it was time to go home. But Minnie was having such a delightful time with a local rancher she refused to go. After she promised faithfully to leave within the hour, Blackjack walked home alone. He didn't own a car.

As one hour grew into two and she hadn't returned, Blackjack became suspicious and went looking for her. The bar had already closed and she was nowhere to be found. Desperate to find her he ran home and backed Ben Ellison's Dodge out of the garage.

After searching the streets and alleys he came upon the rancher's truck parked in an isolated area near the west edge of town. Blackjack ran to the truck where, sure enough, he found them. He banged on the door with his fist, yelling for Minnie to get out. When she refused, he picked up a rock and smashed out the side window.

In less time than it took the last shard of glass to hit the floor, the truck spun around in a cloud of dust and roared off down the street without the benefit of lights. The race was on. Minnie and her friend hit the railroad tracks wide open. Blackjack was in close pursuit, nearly airborne as he flew over the crossing in Ben's old Dodge. At that point, nothing mattered to him, other than getting Minnie by the neck and strangling her. He didn't care about Ben's car, his safety, or anything else.

Just across the track the road veered eastward then turned abruptly north. Blackjack negotiated the first curve with relative ease. But seconds later, after jamming the accelerator to the floor on the second curve, he lost control. There was a squealing of tires and a thunderous crash as the old Dodge impacted the high side of the ditch and rolled over. Once the dust had settled, Blackjack crawled from the wreckage with little more than a bruised rib cage, but Ben's old car didn't fare so well; it was reduced to a mangled pile of junk.

The next day was Sunday, and we were on our way to church when we saw smoke rising from the front yard of Blackjack's house. Nailed to a post was a lighted kerosene lantern. Just below the lantern we could make out a crudely painted sign, in large black letters, that read: "WIFE FOR SALE."

A small pile of smoldering ashes was all that remained of Minnie's limited wardrobe. Three or four pair of partially burned shoes lay scattered nearby. One apparent incongruity as we drove by was several pair of undergarments hanging from a clothesline, obviously overlooked by Blackjack.

I learned later that while Blackjack was trying to regain his senses following the crash, the rancher had dumped Minnie off at her sister's, just a block away. It didn't take Blackjack long to guess where she was. He hammered mercilessly at the front door proclaiming to the whole town what he planned to do to if she didn't come out at once.

In the meantime, a Burleigh County deputy sheriff had arrived on the scene with an awesome-looking club in his hand. His presence had an immediate calming effect on Blackjack. All the threats he had made earlier were immediately forgotten.

In the aftermath, Ben lost his car, the rancher was sued for divorce, and Minnie was divested of a closet full of clothing. Blackjack and Minnie reconciled a few weeks later, however, and over the next few years they became the parents of several children. After Bud moved to town, Blackjack and Minnie took up residence on the farm. Peace reigned for several months, right up until the day the eggs and chickens began to disappear.

Prior to Blackjack and Minnie's move to the farm, Bud had been the owner of a sizable flock of chickens that provided an ample supply of eggs for his family. Not only were there no longer any eggs, the chicken population began dropping drastically. Blackjack insisted a wild animal was getting them. Bud, however, was skeptical; he suspected Minnie was collecting the eggs early in the morning before his arrival and that she might also be butchering the chickens. Rather than have a confrontation, Bud decided to buy his eggs in town.

A few weeks later I was helping repair a well out at the farm when I removed the cover to the well pit. I was amazed at what I saw; it was half-full of chicken feathers. I called to Bud: "I think I've found where the wild animal lives!" He was angered by Blackjack's blatant lying, but refused to confront him.

There was always some big project going on at the farm, usually under the supervision of Blackjack. One such undertaking took place in late fall and involved pouring a concrete floor inside a hog barn. Bud didn't own a mixer, so he sent Blackjack to borrow one from a neighbor. After the floor was poured, a covering of straw was applied to help protect the concrete from freezing. When Blackjack inspected the building later that evening he was horrified to find several hogs wallowing around in the cement. In his haste to retire for the evening he had forgotten to close the door.

In addition to that, when the neighbor came to retrieve his mixer a month later, he discovered Blackjack had left one batch inside, ruining the mixer. Hired men were hard to find, but Blackjack cost more than he was worth.

Bud was a unique person. For many years he had earned a good living in road construction, and he was good at it. Farming was in his blood, however, and was therefore destined to be his vocation in life, regardless of the obstacles.

Each summer and fall, Bud put up huge quantities of hay, most of which was baled and sold to a cattle dealer. I sometimes helped on weekends and holidays. We had worked steadily in unrelenting heat for two weekends and had accumulated several hundred bales which we stacked six high in a long, neat row. Late Saturday afternoon, when we were nearly finished for the day, I noticed a thin plume of smoke rising from one end of the stack. It didn't look serious, but when we pulled the bales apart in an effort to locate the source, flames erupted everywhere. Before we knew it the entire stack was on fire. There was little we could do but drag the machinery to safety.

Blackjack was the only one who smoked, so Bud and I suspected he had dropped a lighted cigarette inside a bale. Bud had been raised in the world of hard knocks, so he accepted this as just one more bump along the way. He had the unique ability to look to the future, and not dwell on what happened today or yesterday.

During the winter months, when there was little else to do, Bud bought stacks of hay from local farmers. We'd bale it up, load it on his truck, and deliver it to a Bismarck sales barn. One Saturday in January the temperature had been dropping all afternoon, reaching several degrees below zero. The days were short, and it was already quite dark by the time we'd finished baling. On our way home over a snowy country trail, miles from nowhere, the engine suddenly quit. Bud checked under the hood of the old Studebaker truck and determined the fuel pump had malfunctioned — not a drop of gas was getting to the carburetor. He'd tried everything without success, and it was getting colder and darker by the minute.

Blackjack and I had given up and were resigned to returning home on foot when Bud came up with a plan. He drained gas from the tank and then sat on the fender feeding it into the carburetor, a little at a time, while Blackjack drove. It took us two hours to drive the six miles home, but we made it, fortunate not to have frozen to death.

———⪢◆⪡———

In earlier days, when Bud's parents were still on the farm, life was hard. Bud's father, Billy, often spent the afternoon and evening in town, sometimes not returning until the wee hours of the morning. In addition to being a heavy drinker, he was short-tempered — a bad combination. When he arrived home, regardless of the hour, it wasn't uncommon for him to order the entire family downstairs with their band instruments to join in as he played the fiddle. Bud was the only one unable to play an instrument, so he had to do a jig.

Billy Pfeifer was a notorious non-conformist: he didn't care a hoot what other people thought, or what they did; he had his own way of doing things. One year he decided that buying a truck made more sense, and was a better investment, than purchasing a tractor. He used the truck for everything, including pulling the plow.

Bill was a harsh disciplinarian, and his word was final. Despite his diminutive stature, there was no disputing who was boss on the farm.

Most every farm kept a number of cats around to keep the mice under control, and the Pfeifer farm was no exception. Late one Saturday afternoon, Billy drove into the yard after spending most of the day in town. He was in a bad mood, worse than usual, and decided to take it out on their big yellow tomcat. There was something about that cat he didn't like, and he'd probably been contemplating some sort of revenge all the way home.

The minute the car came to a stop Billy hollered at Bud, "Find that damn yellow tomcat and bring him here. I'm gonna to shoot that worthless son-of-a-bitch." Bud was just twelve years old and dared not question a direct order from his dad. By the time he rounded up the cat, Billy was marching out of the house with his 12 gauge. "Tie a piece of twine around his neck and hang him from that nail above the barn door," Billy ordered. Bud did as he was told. BOOM! went the gun. Despite the fact he was only a few yards away, Billy missed the cat with all but a couple of pellets. He did manage to sever the twine, however, and when that tomcat hit the ground, all four feet were in super road speed. It was so scared that when it came upon a pile of hay nearby, it dug its way underneath with all the speed and ferocity it could muster.

"Bud, run get some matches," Billy hollered, "I'm gonna light that hay afire." As flames shot into the air, the terrified cat leaped out with its tail in flames and began clawing its way up the side of the barn. "Bud!" Billy screamed, "Get that damn cat before he gets in the haymow!" Bud made a lucky flying grab and threw the cat a safe distance from the barn. That big yellow tomcat was never seen again.

⋙◈⋘

Mike Werner had never married. He lived with his mother in a big old house at the edge of town. It was the only remaining building of a once thriving farm. Mrs. Werner was a nice old lady in her early eighties. It was a pity she'd been putting up with her shiftless son for almost sixty-five years. Mike spent most of his days in the Driscoll Bar fantasizing about what he was going to do when he got rich.

When he retired at age sixty-two, there was a noticeable improvement in his standard of living. That fact could be measured by the increased amount of time he spent in the bar. Back when Mike was still trying to earn a living farming, I once heard his mother comment, "Mike is down combining in the bar again." In addition to his Social Security, he earned a few extra dollars working part-time for Bud, generally doing fieldwork with a tractor.

Mike could not be relied upon to think for himself or even make minor decisions. Shortly after he had retired, Bud sent him to mow a field of alfalfa east of town. He took a wrong turn and had already cut twenty-five acres belonging to a neighbor by the time Bud got there.

When the mower somehow got out of time, Mike took a sledgehammer and hit the cast-iron gearbox a good crack, breaking it into several pieces. It was easy to see why Bud never hired him, except under the most desperate circumstances.

A week after his Social Security check arrived, Mike was usually broke. Then he'd start charging and borrowing wherever he could, mostly from Bud. On one occasion, he claimed he had a tumor in his chest, and desperately needed $20 to go see a doctor. No one believed him, of course, but when he became increasingly insistent, Bud decided there might be some truth to it after all and finally consented to lending him the $20. Instead of leaving, Mike hollered for the bartender, "Drinks for the house!" Drat!

The next day he was out in the field trying to work off his loan. When it was nearly dark he parked his tractor to ride home with Bud inside his heated cab. It had been a long, cold day, and they decided to make a pit stop at the bar on their way home. It was bumpy driving over the field, and Bud accidentally expelled a little gas. Mike said, "If you can do it, so can I." But it sounded to Bud like something quite serious had just happened. After smelling up the inside of the cab, Bud ordered him to ride outside the rest of the way. When they finally reached town, Bud suggested he go home and clean up. "I'm OK," Mike said, "it's all dried up." But when he bellied up to the bar, the rest of the customers stampeded to the far end.

Due to his generous nature, Bud was often taken advantage of by so-called needy people. For example, a local citizen desperately needed $600 to buy equipment for a septic tank pumping business. After coming on hands and knees pleading for a loan, Bud lent him the money. Not only was he not repaid, the guy refused to pump his sewer.

Some time later, the same man invited Bud to his house on urgent business. Bud was all excited, he was certain it was to repay the $600 loan, or at least part of it. He rushed to the man's home, but instead of a payment, the guy had the unmitigated gall to ask for an additional $5,000 to pay off the overdue mortgage on his house.

—=>•◦⊂=—

During harvest one summer, Mr. Olausen came to the depot and asked if I'd be interested in shocking a field of barley for $50, a substantial amount. I told him I would think it over and let him know. $50 was a big temptation since we were planning a vacation before school started, and it would provide us with extra money to spend. It would mean a lot of evening work if I worked alone, but if I could get the kids to help, we could finish the job in no time.

We talked about it at the supper table that evening and everyone was in favor, promising faithfully to help. In the back of my mind I knew I'd made a big mistake. It was terribly hot the day we arrived at the field. One by one the kids retreated to the car, leaving me to work alone. Judy gave up within the first hour, but that was understandable, she was only four. Susan and Greg each went for half a day, and Stephanie lasted a day and a half. Which was pretty good.

It didn't take long to figure out why he'd offered me $50. There were so many bundles, and they were so heavy and tangled, I didn't think I'd ever get done. I still hadn't learned to think things through. What a relief when the last shock was finished.

Mr. Olausen paid me a few days later with six small cream checks, and the rest in nickels, dimes and quarters. There was money for everyone.

⇒◇⇐

The position of city marshal evoked little interest, so when Mike's name appeared on the ballot, he was elected. Soon afterward, my neighbor across the street discovered his dog foaming at the mouth. He tied it to a tree and called Mike. They decided over the phone that the dog should be put away immediately in case it had rabies. Mike said he'd be right over. He arrived a few minutes later wearing his badge and had a revolver hanging from his gun belt. "Where's the dog?" Mike demanded in his best marshal's voice. The owner pointed to the tree. "Everyone step back, this is dangerous business," Mike warned. Several shots rang out in rapid succession: BANG! BANG-BANG! BANG-BANG-BANG!

When the smoke cleared, the dog was still very much alive. All Mike had managed to do was scare him a little. After looking around in disbelief, everyone began laughing. Mike got mad and went home, and a farmer had to be called to finish the job.

⇒◇⇐

Four-year old Erick Meland, son of the local grocer, came into the post office one afternoon and asked permission to bring my dog, Wilbur, a bone from his dad's store. I told him it was a great idea. Wilbur spent his days with me at the post office sleeping. So chewing on a bone outdoors would give him something to do. A short time later, little Erick came racing back inside all excited. "Your dog got mad at me." he said. "He growled when I tried to get the bone back!" I then explained how dangerous it is to go near a dog while he's eating. That didn't placate Erick at all, and he stomped out the door in a huff.

Ten minutes later he came in wearing a cowboy hat and carrying a small cap gun in his hand. "Is your dog in here?" he demanded.

—————≡◇≡—————

Everyone in town knew Wilbur by name. Like most dogs, he was very protective of our property, except he somehow seemed to know that the post office was different. At home, though, he created quite a stir anytime a stranger came by. He particularly disliked the garbage and meter man. Art Barnes picked up the garbage every Monday, and Wilbur would stand guard nearby waiting for him.

In an effort to get on good terms, Art brought along a big bone one day. "Nice Wilbur, here's a big juicy bone for you," Art coaxed. Wilbur took the bone, carried it a safe distance, then came running back barking worse than before. Art became so enraged he chased him around the yard for ten minutes shouting, "You ungrateful bastard, I'm gonna get you if it's the last thing I ever do." Nothing changed, however, except Art finally learned to ignore him.

Wilbur had other enemies as well, cats in particular. Our neighbor to the south had several cats, including a big, ornery tomcat that harbored a distinct dislike for dogs.

All the while that big tomcat strutted about the yard, Wilbur obediently stayed behind the fence separating our two properties, hoping for some unexpected opportunity to vent his inborn anger against this feline miscreant. The day finally came when he could stand it no longer. In a moment of supreme frustration, he jumped the fence and went in for the kill. That's when he got the surprise of his life. As soon as he got close, the tomcat jumped up and landed squarely upon his back. They made six or seven speedy laps around the yard with Wilbur yelping all the way, more out of fright than from pain. He was completely cured of chasing cats right then and there.

Another time while he was inside the post office, Wilbur thought he could hear a strange dog just outside. So he stood by the door wagging his tail, whimpering for me to let him out. His plan, I'm sure, was to completely destroy this impudent intruder. To his surprise, however, instead of some mangy little mongrel, there stood a huge, ugly-looking German Shepherd. Wilbur took one look, then almost knocked me down in his rush to get back inside. He may have been a little stupid, but he wasn't suicidal.

When my youngest son, George, was still home, I often had difficulty getting him up in the morning. To save me a trip upstairs, I'd call on Wilbur. I swear that dog knew exactly what I wanted, and he loved doing it. He'd race up the stairs all excited, and in no time I could hear George pleading, "Quit it, Wilbur! Stop it, Wilbur! Wilburr!" It wouldn't be long and they'd come bounding down together. George and Wilbur were best friends; they really loved each other.

When we show our family films, Wilbur is one of the stars, and George has memorized his every nuance. He lived to be seventeen years old; that's 119 in man-years. Near the end of his life he had lost his hearing and was nearly blind. It was a sad day when we decided it was best to have him put to sleep. I buried him out by the garden and wrote George while he was away at college. It took a long time for him to get over it; perhaps he never did.

⟹⬦⟸

Bud's next-door neighbors were the parents of two good-sized daughters. They were big and they were strong. Every year on Halloween, they delighted in dragging his tools and machinery from his shop to the middle of Main Street. He decided to hide inside one Halloween night and give them a little surprise.

He didn't have long to wait. The two girls, along with their friends, crept inside the darkened shop looking for moveable objects. Bud waited in the shadows until they started on the more valuable items, like tools and his supply of tires. The only light came from the moon shining through the doorway. The older and huskier of the girls lifted one end of a workbench, then called softly to Bud's shadow, "Hurry up and grab the other end." When there was no response, she strained her eyes for a better look. When she finally recognized Bud, her scream could be heard all over town, "Ohhhh, my gawwwd!" She dropped the bench and stampeded out the door, running toward home howling like a banshee.

Years earlier, Bud had purchased the then defunct John's Hotel in Driscoll, which included a near-by ten-acre tract of land. The land was to be used for pasturing sheep, but there was no available water. When he ran a garden hose from his house to the ten acres, only two blocks away, his next door neighbor objected. He not only objected — he'd get up in the middle of the night and chop the hose in half.

Until a well could be dug, Bud removed the spare tire from his car and hauled water in the trunk. He ran into trouble later that fall, though, after he forgot to empty one load and it froze, causing his car to resemble a rocket on the way to the moon.

Bud was often forced to improvise. He could fix almost anything and was a genius at finding ways to accomplish a nearly impossible task. I tried everything to get my car started one sub-zero cold morning and was ready to give up when Bud placed a pan of hot coals beneath the oil pan. He had the car going in ten minutes. This was before anyone had heard of head-bolt heaters. The day the motor blew up on his school bus, he towed it into his shop, overhauled the engine, and had it running in time to make the route early the next morning — an incredible feat.

Shortly after his wife had passed away, Herman closed his bar. Almost immediately, a new one opened across the street, which was a significant improvement. In most small towns, a bar provides much of the local entertainment, and that was the case in Driscoll. The new business was packed every Saturday with people from the surrounding area. That's where they gathered to discuss local affairs in a friendly and relaxed atmosphere.

It was on just such a Saturday that Bud's wife had promised to prepare barbecued ribs, his favorite meal. Bud was looking forward to a pleasant dinner that evening and asked his friends to remind him to leave for home no later than 5:00 P.M. Everyone was having such a good time, before we knew it the clock read ten o'clock, and Bud still hadn't left. The next day I inquired if his wife had forgiven him for being late. He replied regretfully, almost in tears, "When I got home, my barbecued ribs were hanging all over the lilac bushes."

———≫◦⊂———

Our children were growing up rapidly and doing well in school. The teaching staff wasn't always the best, but most of the students received a reasonably good education. A large percentage, in fact, went on to higher institutions of learning. Some, however, weren't exactly college material.

For example, the civics teacher had instructed the senior class to turn their examination papers over once they had completed the test and then leave the room. One of her students, usually the last to finish, surprised her by being first to turn his paper over, long before the others. After glancing through his answers, her face turned white, then purple, and then red. First answer: "I don't know." Second answer: "Who the hell cares." Third answer: "Who gives a shit."

Mrs. Zieman taught a history class in an auxiliary classroom adjacent to the main building. She was not the most beautiful of God's creatures and was cursed with a screechy voice that sounded much like that of a cat when its tale gets stepped on. She was well past retirement age, adding to her inability to maintain discipline.

Shortly before class time she'd station herself behind the door to wait for the last of her students. Once the bell sounded, however, she'd immediately close the door, then jot down the names of any tardy scholars. On one occasion, Beverly Miller came charging through the doorway at the very last moment, without noticing Mrs. Zieman still behind the door. After a brief look around, she shouted, "Where is the old hag?" The door slammed shut with such a bang that poor Beverly was nearly frightened out of her wits.

———≫◦⊂———

Driscoll Bound

When our children were small, we spent many holidays with our parents in Washburn. What fun it was to arrive Friday evening and stay until Sunday afternoon. Marilyn's mother, Grace Wahl, was an excellent cook, and we always looked forward to her delicious meals. In addition, there were always plenty of sandwiches and cookies for the journey home.

Grace had nerves of steel, but my father-in-law, Hank, would head for his barbershop when he could no longer tolerate the noise level. I went along one Sunday afternoon to help him treat the family dog. Topper was an ornery little Scotch terrier who'd been suffering from an acute case of constipation. Hank carried a large bottle of castor oil in his pocket, and he intended to remedy the situation. When we reached the barbershop he instructed me to hold Topper's mouth open while he administered the medication. Well, I had a sneaking suspicion Topper wasn't going to take to the castor oil treatment one little bit, and I therefore insisted Hank do the holding, while I did the pouring.

Hank was a husky man with giant hands and fingers. He grabbed a reluctant Topper and forced his mouth open while I began to pour. That's when old Topper went berserk and began biting and chomping on Hank's big fingers with the ferocity of a starving mountain lion. Hank screamed in pain, "You son-of-a-bitch!" Before I knew what happened, Hank had grabbed old Topper and sent him sailing out the front door. I was thankful it wasn't my fingers that were all chewed up.

During prohibition, Hank decided he'd make some homemade wine. When it was ready, he picked Grace's freshly painted kitchen to do the bottling. Grace came home unexpectedly that very afternoon, surprised to find her kitchen occupied and the door closed. What she saw when she peered inside caused her to feel faint, there stood Hank and a friend, both covered from head to toe with the remnants of their product. Everything was purple. Their bodies were purple, the walls and furniture were purple. The entire kitchen was purple. With wine dripping from his face, Hank explained that for some unknown reason, the bottles began exploding and never quit until the last one blew up.

Hank was always referred to as "Grandpa Hank" by our children, and eventually by all of us. In addition to giant arms and hands, he had big feet, which caused him no end of pain and discomfort. For that reason he wore canvas shoes, even in winter. No one dared to even breathe near those tender feet, especially the kids.

We had given our son, Greg, a cork gun for Christmas. He was having a good time shooting at various targets while Hank and I read the Sunday paper. I paid no attention until, for some diabolical reason, he poked a cork deep inside the barrel, held the gun above Hank's big toe, and pulled the trigger. "Jesus Christ!"Hank bellowed. The papers flew in the air as Hank's big arm shot out in a sweeping grab. Luckily, Greg was well out of reach by then, and stayed that way for the remainder of the day. Hank limped about the house for the next hour muttering irreverent platitudes under his breath.

Two years after the gun incident, I ordered Greg a guitar for Christmas. I thought it would be better to give him something less violent than a gun. When it came in the mail a few weeks later, I took it to the depot and carefully read the instructions. With great difficulty, I managed to learn the basic chords to one song, and practiced diligently the two weeks prior to Christmas. Greg wondered what was in that odd-shaped box, and was really excited when he saw it. A few minutes later, I shocked everyone when I played and sang my rendition of the only song I knew, "Down in the Valley." Greg loved the guitar and almost wore it out the first year. Two years later, I bought him an electric model, which he kept throughout his high school days. He took three or four lessons, but for the most part learned to play on his own.

Our daughter, Judy, was an enterprising young girl. It was on the evening of her seventh birthday that her classmates began knocking at our door. They were all dressed up and each carried a gift. Judy, however, had failed to inform the rest of us that she was giving herself a birthday party. Fortunately, we were able to get into the store for some ice cream. It turned out to be a great party, and she received many nice gifts.

When she found a dime under her pillow after losing a tooth, and later discovered we hadn't yet thrown the tooth away, she promptly sold it to George for a nickel. When the "tooth fairy" failed to leave him a dime, as Judy had predicted, he was furious, and reported the failed transaction to me. What was I to do but leave another dime that night.

On his eighth birthday, George pleaded with me to buy him an air rifle. His pleadings were accompanied by endless promises to be careful. Against my better judgment, I finally gave in and bought him the gun. I made it clear that any infraction of gun safety would bring an instant end to his days as a great hunter. He assured me over and over that I had no reason to worry. Ten minutes after he left with the gun I received a call from a lady down the street accusing George of shooting her daughter in the hind-end. He claimed it was an accident. Nevertheless, it brought an end to the gun business. I was reminded of a time many years earlier, when I'd made a similar mistake, and had to pay the price.

Bud Pfeifer's son, Kenny, and George were the same age and the best of friends. Bud had a great deal of confidence in his children and gave them wide latitude. Kenny had a paper route when he was but nine years old and, incredibly, had been driving vehicles from the age of seven. So when Sunday came around, no one was surprised to see him delivering papers in Bud's Volkswagen. One Sunday, near the Fourth of July, Kenny and George were out on the route when Bud received an urgent telephone call that his car was on fire. We discovered that George had been throwing firecrackers out the window when his lighted punk had accidentally ignited their entire cache of fireworks. The car had been abandoned amidst a barrage of explosions. Thick white smoke poured out from the windows, but no one was hurt, and the car wasn't badly damaged.

The city of Steele was ten miles east of Driscoll; we shopped there occasionally for items we couldn't get at home. Ray "The Chief" Blotsky owned a large garage on the highway leading into town, and I patronized him whenever my car needed servicing. Ray was a very accommodating businessman who treated his customers fairly and expected no less from them.

Gottfried Hammond, a local restaurant owner, was widely known as the stingiest man in town. One day when he brought his car in for an oil change he handed Ray six quarts of Montgomery Ward oil. "I like to use my own oil." Gottfried said with a sly grin on his face.

Ray changed the oil without comment, charging a small fee for labor. The very next day he drove to the store and purchased a package of hamburger. He then went directly to the café where he called for Gottfried. Ray pushed the package across the counter and, with a broad smile on his face said, "I want a hamburger steak, but I like it made with my own hamburger." Gottfried hesitated a second, then grabbed the package, fixed the steak, and never said a word. Nor did he ever furnish his own oil again.

Ray bought a second-hand cash register from a company in Bismarck. It worked really well for two weeks, but then one day it quit, and he had to call for a repairman. Two hours later, the salesman he'd bought the machine from came walking in. After carefully removing a chewed-up one-dollar bill, the machine was back in working order, all in less than ten minutes. Since the machine wasn't guaranteed, Ray asked what he owed.

"$25 for the trip and $25 for removing the dollar bill," the salesman said. Ray was angry over the $25 for removing the dollar bill and said so. "That's a reasonable fee, since you couldn't repair it yourself," the salesman assured him.

About a month later a miracle happened. The same salesman walked in saying he had a flat tire just down the road. Ray fixed the tire in no time, then presented a bill for $50. The salesman was furious. "Well," Ray said, "Since you couldn't repair the tire yourself, $50 seems like a reasonable fee."

I'm not certain of Ray's tribal affiliation, but he enjoyed being addressed as "The Chief." On special occasions he wore his headdress, and could dance as well as any Indian around. He once received an invitation, including free airline tickets, to attend the wedding of a wealthy tribal member's daughter. The highlight of the wedding, and a big surprise to Ray, was when Johnny Cash walked up front and sang.

—⟫◦⟪—

"Gordy" Flemming worked for many years as school janitor and all around fix-it man. After retirement, he went into the small engine repair business. He ordered business cards printed, which he handed out lavishly to friends and acquaintances. Just below his name was a picture of an engine, followed by the words "prompt, courteous service." Everyone acquainted with Gordy immediately crossed out the word "prompt." He was many things, but prompt definitely wasn't one of them.

He came rushing into the post office one day all upset, complaining there had been a robbery at his shop. Someone had stolen a lawnmower belonging to "Ray the barber." He was beside himself, wondering how he was going to break the bad news to Ray. Two days later I went for a haircut and told Ray what had happened. "There was no robbery." Ray said, "He had my lawnmower for almost two years and I finally got mad and went to get it. He wasn't home, so I threw it in the car and left."

Gordy's new riding lawn mower was his pride and joy. He kept it in tip-top condition and always parked it near the house where he could keep an eye on it. Gordy's son, Milford, was a sophomore in high school. Two or three times a week Milford would wait patiently beside the garage for his friend to drive up, then take Gordy's gallon-jug of gas and pour it into his friend's car.

Tired of furnishing gas for their little pleasure trips, Gordy decided to play a trick on them. He filled the jug with colored water, then waited for Milford's friend to drive up. He turned deathly pale, however, when he glanced out the window a few minutes later and saw Milford pouring the contents of the jug into the tank of his new mower.

Gordy was the proud owner of a small pickup, which also served as the family car. Art Barnes called one day to say he needed a pull because his car wouldn't start. Gordy, always eager to help out, drove right over. As they gained momentum the car started, and Art gave an urgent signal to stop. That's when the horrendous crash occurred. Art had forgotten to tell Gordy he had no brakes.

During the energy crisis of the 1980s, Gordy decided to seek his fortune in the coal-hauling business. He bought an old, worn-out two-ton truck with a steel box and hoist. The truck appeared to run well enough, but it was swaybacked. Some super-heavy object had apparently been dropped inside the box, severely buckling the frame. So it was a strange sight the day Gordy and his wife pulled up to the post office on their way to the coal mine, some seventy-five miles distant. Barely five feet tall, Gordy had to prop himself up on a pillow to see over the steering wheel.

He kept revving up the engine to alert everyone nearby that it was he, Gordy Flemming, at the controls. Each time he depressed the clutch to engage the transmission, his head would disappear. That was a signal he was about to leave. They both finally waved good-bye amid a noisy grating of gears, and chugged off down the road. Alas, we didn't see either of them for three days. No one heard about the big breakdown until much later. Gordy didn't like to talk about it except to say that it had happened miles from nowhere. He sold the truck and never mentioned the coal-hauling business again.

—≥•◦•≤—

Calvin Billingsly and his younger brother, Art, had grown up on a farm near Driscoll, but had attended school in the small neighboring town of Sterling, about five miles from their farm. Calvin was often at odds with his teacher, whom he described as being "three ax-handles wide." When he was made to stay an hour after school one afternoon for disobedience, Art waited for him outside. After the two of them reached the outer limits of the school grounds, Art turned and hollered as loud as he could, "Goodnight lard-ass!" They both stayed after school for the remainder of the week.

Calvin and Art were out hunting gophers one summer afternoon when Art began complaining that his 22 rifle shells were no good. Several had misfired and he kept turning them inside the rifle's chamber, trying to decide if it was the shells, or a faulty firing pin. Finally, BANG! "Ouch!" Calvin hollered.

"What's the matter with you?" Art asked.

"You damn fool, you just shot me in the leg," Calvin moaned.

He carried the lead from that bullet in his leg until the day he died. He showed it to me once, a big white lump just below his knee.

⇒·◦·⇐

Mrs. Herman walked into Norm's General Store one afternoon with her spoiled rotten seven-year- old son. After withstanding a great deal of whining, she bought him a sack of candy. Still not satisfied, he ran behind the counter and grabbed a big chocolate bar. When he was ordered to put it back, he took a huge bite, right through the wrapper.

When a group of local schoolgirls had gathered for a picnic, their teacher bought each a candy bar, asking them to save the wrapper on which a valuable coupon had been printed. When she asked for the wrappers, however, one girl had eaten hers, explaining there had been so much chocolate sticking to it, she couldn't lick it all off.

⇒·◦·⇐

One Sunday afternoon in late September, we arrived home to a huge commotion on Main Street. Several neighbors were gathered near the post office talking excitedly. They hastily related how John and Hazel Trautman, a retired farm couple living on a farmstead south of town, had both been shot. There was no word on their condition, or who was responsible. Police and ambulances had been speeding through town, and roadblocks had been set up.

Later that evening, as additional information became available, we learned that a neighbor boy had shot the Trautmans with a small-caliber revolver earlier that afternoon. Both victims had been rushed to the hospital in serious, but stable condition. John had been shot twice, but managed to identify the shooter, and sheriff's deputies had the young man cornered in a field near his home.

After his parents had left for the day, the boy had made his way across a pasture to the Trautman farm with a loaded gun he had taken from his father's bedroom. When he arrived at the farmhouse and knocked on the door, he told Mrs. Trautman he needed a can of gas. The boy was well known to her, and while he was acting somewhat strange, she had no reason to suspect anything unusual.

John donned a jacket and began walking toward the gas barrel when the boy suddenly pulled the gun from his pocket and fired. John felt a twinge of pain but kept on walking. Mrs. Trautman, when she realized what was happening, screamed to her husband, "John, he's shooting at you!" The boy fired again hitting John a second time, then turned quickly and fired point-blank at Hazel, hitting her in the abdomen. She sank to the floor of the porch, while John, not quite fully aware of what was happening, moved quickly toward the boy. John was tall and lanky, in excellent physical condition for a man his age. Despite the fact he had been wounded twice, he managed to lash out with one arm, knocking the gun to the ground. The young man stood dumbfounded, not knowing what to do, then he panicked and ran across the yard toward home.

Sometime later, sheriff's deputies spotted him hiding in a nearby field. When they moved toward him, he raised his hands and gave up peacefully.

After a short hospitalization, John recovered fully from his wounds and lived into his nineties. Hazel, however, was plagued with health problems thereafter and passed away not many years later.

The boy responsible for this bizarre incident was only fifteen years of age at the time. He came from a good family and had never been in trouble before. He spent the next six years in the reformatory and was never seen in Driscoll again. When asked by the authorities why he did it, he said, "I just wanted to see what it would be like to kill someone."

John and Hazel had a pretty fifteen-year-old daughter who was the boy's classmate in school. She wasn't home at the time of the shooting, but it was generally believed that she may have been the real target and would most certainly have been killed as well, had the boy's plan succeeded.

Soon afterward, a tourist from Canada stopped at the Driscoll Café for lunch. He was heard to comment, "I'll bet there's not much excitement in this town." Had he been in Driscoll the day of the shooting, he may have thought differently.

━━◆━━

Charlie Beck advertised himself as a house painter; his specialty was farm buildings, and he had just finished a job for a local rancher.

Any repeat business, however, was mostly nonexistent. The principal drawback to hiring Charlie was the fact that by the time he finished a job, everything in sight had been freshly painted. That included cars, trucks, tractors, grass and even farm animals. His high-pressure sprayer was fast, according to Charlie, and he couldn't make any money if he had to worry about every little bit of paint that went astray.

Little more than five-feet tall, Charlie was often seen strutting about town like a little peacock, dressed in his paint-spattered coveralls. I often thought he must be related to Mike Werner, since most of his painting was done in the bar. Despite being a small person, Charlie was an incredible loudmouth, given to making all sorts of derisive remarks about the people around him. He seemed not to worry about any consequences.

Pete Thompson, on the other hand, was a mild-mannered rancher living just outside town. Pete was a tall, broad-shouldered gentleman who enjoyed life and never spoke a bad word about anyone. You might say he was the exact opposite of Charlie.

One afternoon, Pete and Charlie happened to sit next to each other in the Driscoll Bar. Pete said little, but Charlie, as usual, talked incessantly. After listening to several sarcastic remarks, Pete became angry and admonished Charlie to curb his tongue. That advice had no discernible affect until Pete suddenly jumped from his stool, tore off his jacket, and slammed it down against the concrete floor. As the air filled with dust, I ran for cover, with the expectation that a certain little sawed-off runt of a painter was about to get killed. But when the dust settled, Charlie was no where to be found. He had vanished out the back door with such speed no one saw him leave. Pete stood in the middle of the floor alone, with a bewildered look on his face. It was one of those comical incidents one might witness on most any given day in the Driscoll Bar.

⇒•◇•⇐

Dave Olson had been doctoring his sick horse all spring and summer. Some strange ailment was preventing the unfortunate animal from standing. Every conceivable remedy had been tried without success. Dave and his son hauled water and feed every day, making sure their family pet was made as comfortable as possible.

One day there was a noticeable improvement, and they were filled with renewed hope. Then a few days later, almost like divine intervention, Earl Degnar heard about their sick horse. Earl was a self-proclaimed veterinarian. He knew everything there was to know about horses and had magnanimously offered the benefit of that extensive knowledge to the Olson family, free of charge. It took less than thirty seconds for his diagnosis. Earl knew exactly what the problem was and, almost miraculously, happened to have on hand the very pills needed to put the horse back on his feet.

That night the horse died. Earl's expert diagnosis, after reviewing the remains, was that the poor thing had died of a heart attack, no doubt about it.

———⊰◆⊱———

From the Railroad to the Postal Service at Driscoll

Changes were taking place on the railroad. The Northern Pacific and the Great Northern were preparing to merge, and there was talk of closing depots and abandoning branch lines. After working for twenty-one years, my job had become less secure than ever.

Shortly after our postmaster decided to retire, an examination was called by the Postal Service. I was named acting postmaster in 1968, and in 1970 I received the permanent appointment. It was wonderful not having to speculate about the future or having to worry about where I'd be the next week, or month. The pay wasn't too great, but the employee benefits made up for it, and I couldn't be bumped.

The Postal Service wasn't that much different from the railroad, so far as day-to-day routine was concerned. There were many similarities such as hours of service, preparing requisitions, office accountability, and public relations. Both sick leave and vacation time were earned and credited each pay period and could be taken in increments of as little as two hours. On the railroad, sick leave was mostly nonexistent, unless you were dying. And taking a day off, regardless of the reason, was next to impossible. Of course, much of that has changed in recent years.

Our grandchildren, Jackie and Jenny Edwards, were frequent visitors in our home. Sometimes I'd sneak them into the post office and let them work at my desk using all those important looking rubber stamps. One day I made the mistake of leaving them alone a few minutes while I went for coffee. They were four and five years old at the time. The next day, all my box-holder customers brought tiny slips of paper to the window, wondering what they meant, and where they had come from. The girls had scribbled what they called letters, stamping them "unclaimed," or "unknown" and then distributed them, one to every box. I had a hard time explaining how that had happened.

My son, Greg, an engineer for the Burlington Northern Santa Fe, was living in Jamestown early on in his career. Due to my past employment with the railroad, we had much in common, which made my visits more meaningful. One Saturday morning his westbound freight took siding at Driscoll, and he invited me to ride with him all the way to Mandan in the cab of a big new diesel engine. What a thrill it was.

As a special gift, the president of Burlington Northern gave each employee four tickets for a ride on an old steam-powered passenger train. Greg shared his tickets with Marilyn and me, and we had a remarkable ride from Mandan to Jamestown. It was an incredible trip, one we shall never forget. We traveled at record speeds, with the steam engine's shrill whistle blowing for every town and crossing. Automobiles raced along the highway beside us, recording our nostalgic journey back in time. There were crowds of people watching from every byway.

While visiting Greg in Jamestown one Sunday, I wasn't sure if I could still find the old railroad roundhouse, and a little skeptical when my young grandson, Robert Jr., insisted he could show me how to get there. Robert was only four years old, but he insisted he had been to the roundhouse before and knew exactly where it was. After a few blocks he pointed and said, "Turn here and go two blocks that way." Further down the street he ordered me to make yet another turn. I said nothing but regarded him with some skepticism. Sensing my lack of confidence he looked up and said, "What's the matter, Grandpa, don't you think I know where I'm going?" I soon learned that little Robert was a master at directions, on our way back home he pointed south and matter-of-factly announced, "Only three blocks down that way is the ice cream store!"

———◈———

When my grandson, Tracey Kalainov, was five years old, I decided to impress upon him how important it was to support his church, so I handed him a quarter for the Sunday collection. When the basket was passed, however, I couldn't help but notice the quarter hadn't left his hand. After Mass, I asked for an explanation. "Well," he said, "just when the man came to me, I remembered something I wanted to buy." A pretty good answer on the spur of the moment.

Tracey's sister, Lindsay, was attending preschool when I inquired about her ability to get along with the other children and whether or not she liked them. Everything was fine; she liked her classmates and her teacher. Then I asked if she had ever been disciplined her for misbehaving. "No!" was her emphatic reply. I spelled the word "s-l-a-p" and asked if she had ever done that. She pondered my question for a minute, then asked, "Grandpa, does that spell pinch?"

———◈———

Grace Lutheran Church stood just across the street from our house. Pastor Jim was a big man, weighing 300 pounds or more, and he drove an old pickup truck. He had a full beard and a deep voice — an awesome combination for the younger members of his flock. One afternoon the ladies of the church were preparing to clean, but none had a key. They drove to the store and asked the manager if he knew someone able let them in. A small boy had just walked in and had overheard their conversation. He said, "God is down there right now." They were all a little startled, and one lady asked how he knew that. "Cause I just saw him drive up in his pickup," the young lad replied confidently.

One Sunday morning, while waiting for Pastor Jim to begin his sermon, an anxious mother tiptoed toward the back carrying her four-year-old daughter. Midway to the door the little girl asked in a loud, clear voice, "Mama, does God ever have to go poop?"

———⟫⚬⟪———

Albert Geist lived alone on his farm a few miles from town. His favorite pastime was having coffee at the café each morning with his friends. His great grandson, Jason, lived just down the street, and Albert often stopped to see him on his way home. Since Jason had recently enrolled in kindergarten, Albert inquired, jokingly, if he had learned to read yet. "Yes, I can read." Jason replied. Albert handed him a book and asked him to read something. "Well," Jason said, "I can read, but I don't read out loud."

———⟫⚬⟪———

Early one spring, my sister Genevieve, my mother, Marilyn, and I flew to Orlando, Florida, to visit Gen's son, a clinical psychologist. Paul and his wife had two youngsters, a boy and a girl. One might expect a man with his professional background to have well adjusted children. That definitely was not the case.

Immediately upon our arrival we rented a car and a three-bedroom furnished apartment, after which we went to visit my famous nephew and his family. I brought along two small presents for the kids, hoping to make a favorable impression. When the four-year-old boy, Brian, opened his gift, he immediately flung it against the wall as hard as he could, then in his shrill 5,000-decibel voice yelled, "I wanted Spider Man!"

I was aghast when my sister invited Brian to come spend the night with us. I felt that was a mistake, since he and my mother always seemed at odds with each other. When we were almost ready to leave for our apartment, Brian's little sister had some sort of fit. She had fled to the laundry room and began banging her head against the wall, apparently in retaliation for having had to remain home. Then, when we finally got in the car, Brian refused to fasten his seat belt. So we spent the next fifteen minutes squeezed into our compact rental car in unbearable heat, waiting for Paul to convince his son that the car would not move until he buckled up.

Nearly everything Brian did seemed to irritate my mother, but it wasn't until bedtime that things came to a head. Mom had just settled in for the night when Brian suddenly began whining. He had decided that her room was preferable to the one he was in, whereupon she reluctantly arose and moved her belongings to his bedroom, while he moved into hers. She had nearly dropped off to sleep a second time when Brian once again began to whine; this time it seems he had made a mistake and wanted his original room back. My mother painfully crawled from bed and moved back. Before closing her door, however, she cried out in anguish, "Will this hell ever end?"

Never at a loss for words, when Brian became angry with his mother during the Christmas holiday, he angrily said to her, "You're stupid, Dad's stupid, and Santa Claus is stupid too!"

After attending kindergarten, there was a noticeable increase in Brian's vocabulary. He had learned every swear word known to man, and was very fluent in their use. Like many children, he didn't particularly care for babysitters. His parents relied on an agency to provide professional sitters, seldom getting the same one twice. One evening, an Oriental lady had the misfortune to be called for duty. In spite of her difficulty understanding English, she was good with children and a capable sitter. When Brian's parents returned, however, she immediately asked them about a name Brian had called her. "He call me asshole," she said in broken English, "what that mean?"

Paul had infinite patience, which eventually paid off. As his children grew older, they not only discontinued their bad behavior — they became model young adults.

My sister, Genevieve, taught school for many years, including one year on the Indian Reservation at Fort Yates. While there, she became interested in Indian culture and tribal customs. When Brian was growing up, she had recorded a series of stories dedicated to him called *The Adventures of Running Bear.* They were very interesting and he liked them. It was sometime later that my mother bestowed upon Brian the Indian name, "Howling Wolf."

⇒◆⇐

Genevieve loved to entertain and was busy serving her guests one summer afternoon in July, when the warning sirens sounded, indicating a possible tornado. Marilyn's mother, Grandma Grace, became alarmed when she learned Genevieve didn't have a basement. "Please remain calm," Genevieve said, "My neighbor, Tom Baker, isn't home, but he has a basement and I have a key."

The sirens continued to wail as black, menacing clouds roiled overhead. With one eye toward the sky, everyone walked quickly to Tom's house, except for Grandma Grace. Despite her years, she ran and was anxiously waiting to get in by the time the rest had arrived. Genevieve unlocked the door and Grace went rushing in, only to be confronted by Tom sitting comfortably on his couch. Grace let out a scream, but everyone else began to laugh, including Tom. Fortunately, a tornado never materialized.

When Genevieve's daughter got married, all her neighbors were invited. In the confusion, no one remembered to take my mother to the church. It was just by accident that Tom Baker happened to see her standing outdoors alone, waiting patiently for a ride. If it hadn't been for him, she might have missed her granddaughter's wedding.

As Mom reached her nineties, her eyesight and hearing diminished rapidly, and we had to move her into an assisted-living facility. She was perfectly content to be there, no longer having to worry about cooking meals, making the bed, and the other daily chores that she felt obligated to do. After a nearly total loss of her eyesight, her greatest enjoyment came from listening to television talk shows. When it came to current events she couldn't be stumped. Her body was failing but her mind remained incredibly clear.

Mom looked forward to having her hair fixed each week, and with the help of a walker, was able to find her way along the corridors to the in-house salon. Occasionally, however, a problem would arise, or she'd get lost. Like on the day the fire alarm sounded, and everyone got

*My mother,
Myrtle Larson
Cunningham
She was my
inspiration for
writing this
book.*

jammed up in the hallway with their walkers, all trying to flee the building at the same time.

She preferred Friday for her hair appointments, always wanting to look her best for any company that might visit on the weekend. On entering the salon, it was the rule to remove one's glasses and leave them at the appointment desk, retrieving them on the way out. That is precisely what Mom did on the day of the big mix-up, except on her way out she had mistakenly picked up the wrong pair — those belonging to a lady from another room.

Being almost totally blind, Mom never noticed anything out of the ordinary. For her, wearing glasses was nothing more than a habit. The other lady, however, after donning my mother's glasses, returned to her room with great difficulty. All distraught, she immediately called her daughter, "You've got to get down here at once," she cried, "something horrible has happened!"

"What on earth is wrong, Mother?" the daughter asked.

"I've had a bad stroke!" the mother sobbed. "It must have happened while I was getting my hair fixed. I can't focus my eyes, and barely made it back to my room."

The daughter rushed right down and was preparing to call an ambulance when she noticed something different and asked, "Did you get new glasses, Mother?"

"No, I've had a stroke. I can't focus my eyes!"

"Well, the glasses you have on are certainly not yours," the daughter said.

It took two days to completely unravel the "wrong glasses" episode, and how it had happened. Of course, Mom was surprised to learn she had been the cause of her neighbor's terrifying experience.

My brother, Philip, was diagnosed with inoperable pancreatic cancer in 1997. The news was devastating for my mother; her own health was failing rapidly. Shortly afterward it became necessary to move her to a nursing home. She passed away ten days later on August 24, 1997. In the last six months of her life she had often expressed a desire to die, and after moving to the nursing home, she willed herself to do so. She was a remarkable woman in many ways.

My mother lived to be ninety-eight. Many years before she passed away, she had given away her meager belongings, leaving little behind to remind anyone of her many years of unrelenting toil on this earth. She never wished for, nor did she ever accumulate, any great wealth. She had, however, earned what was most important to her, the everlasting love, devotion and deep respect of her family.

What was most memorable was her endless struggle to sustain our family in difficult times, to counsel and lift our spirits in times of despair. Through hard work and enormous self-sacrifice she managed to hold us together, and she did so with great dignity and high integrity. Her endeavor toward this end continued until the day she died.

My brother, Philip, passed away April 16, 1998, eight months after Mom. A blessing she was spared the anguish of his death.

In this year of 2002, 107-year-old Grandma Grace is still going strong, despite suffering several broken bones, including a hip. At age ninety-eight she survived an operation for colon cancer. She is an alert conversationalist and still enjoys going out to dinner. "Amazing Grace" is an apt name given her by friends and relatives.

Henry (Hank) Wahl
on his way to the barbershop

Grace Wahl
"Amazing Grace" at age 107

Grandpa Hank Wahl, Marilyn's father, passed away in his sleep on August 12, 1965, at age seventy-two. My father, George Cunningham, died July 28, 1968, at age seventy-six. I was at his bedside when he passed away after suffering a heart attack.

Aunt Lenore died in her sleep April 3, 2000, at age one hundred. She lived a long, interesting life, doing what she loved most, teaching piano. Marilyn and I had just returned from a trip to California when I talked to her for the last time. She was so happy we were home, exclaiming how relieved she was that we were back in North Dakota. She passed away peacefully the next morning, like she had been waiting for our return before doing so.

For many years my sister, Genevieve, suffered from scleroderma, one of the most debilitating diseases in medical history. She did so silently, bravely, and with great courage. She earned the admiration of her doctors, her family, and all who knew her. She passed away June 30,

2000. She had provided for the donation of her body to the University of North Dakota Medical School in the hope that doing so might help medical science find a cure for this dreaded disease.

—————

Afterword

THERE ARE MANY STORIES that weren't included in this book. One that comes to mind was the surprise birth announcement of my grandson, Max Aguirre. If you recall some chapters ago, we had played a little game with our children regarding the expected increase to our family. A doctor had told our daughter, Stephanie, she would very likely never be able to have children. Then one day she called to say, "Someone is coming to live with us, can you guess who it is?" Max is now twelve years old. He plays the violin and the saxophone. He is a special person in our lives, as are all our children, grandchildren and great-grandchildren.

The things I have written here were meant to be light and amusing, I hope I didn't stray too far from my goal.

—————

Cast of Characters

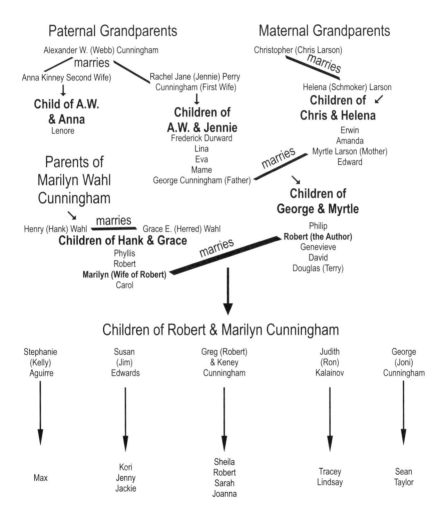

Paternal Grandparents

Alexander W. (Webb) Cunningham

marries

Anna Kinney Second Wife)

Rachel Jane (Jennie) Perry
Cunningham (First Wife)

**Child of A.W.
& Anna**
Lenore

**Children of
A.W. & Jennie**
Frederick Durward
Lina
Eva
Mame
George Cunningham (Father)

Parents of
Marilyn Wahl
Cunningham

Henry (Hank) Wahl ⎯⎯ marries ⎯⎯ Grace E. (Herred) Wahl

Children of Hank & Grace
Phyllis
Robert
Marilyn (Wife of Robert)
Carol

Maternal Grandparents

Christopher (Chris Larson)

marries

Helena (Schmoker) Larson

**Children of ✓
Chris & Helena**
Erwin
Amanda
Myrtle Larson (Mother)
Edward

marries

**Children of
George & Myrtle**
Philip
Robert (the Author)
Genevieve
David
Douglas (Terry)

marries

Children of Robert & Marilyn Cunningham

Stephanie (Kelly) Aguirre	Susan (Jim) Edwards	Greg (Robert) & Keney Cunningham	Judith (Ron) Kalainov	George (Joni) Cunningham
Max	Kori Jenny Jackie	Sheila Robert Sarah Joanna	Tracey Lindsay	Sean Taylor

Above — The Grandchildren of Robert & Marilyn Cunningham

———⟫•◇•⟪———

About the Author

ROBERT CUNNINGHAM IS A NATIVE NORTH DAKOTAN who spent the first years of his life in the village of Grand Rapids, southeast of Jamestown. When he was four years old, his family began moving to various small towns throughout the central part of the state.

Cunningham graduated from LaMoure High School in 1944 and enlisted in the U.S. Navy. After his honorable discharge, Robert moved with his family to Washburn where he met and married Marilyn Wahl. They moved to Minneapolis, Minnesota where he attended the Gale Institute. After graduation, he returned to North Dakota where he was employed by the Northern Pacific Railroad as an Agent/Telegrapher.

After twenty-one years with the railroad, he was appointed postmaster at Driscoll where he and his family continued to live. Subsequent to his retirement in 1991, he and his wife moved to Bismarck.

Robert has written several magazine articles and one unpublished book, *The Shrine Room.* He feels it is incumbent on everyone to do what they can to help preserve the history of North Dakota and to document the important role played in that history by the small towns across the state.

———⟫•◇•⟪———